Contents

719.094

1488065   TRINDER, B.   The making
                          of the
-0 APR 1987 609.41   industrial
                          landscape
              AS   7/83   12.95

9/12

THE MAKING
of the
INDUSTRIAL LANDSCAPE

By the same author

The Industrial Revolution in Shropshire
The Iron Bridge (*with Neil Cossons*)
The Most Extraordinary District in the World:
    Ironbridge and Coalbrookdale (*editor*)
Yeomen and Colliers in Telford (*with Jeff Cox*)
A Victorian MP and his Constituents
The Darbys of Coalbrookdale
Victorian Banbury

THE MAKING
of the
INDUSTRIAL LANDSCAPE
Barrie Trinder

J.M. Dent & Sons Ltd
London Melbourne Toronto

First published 1982
© Barrie Trinder 1982

Printed in Great Britain by
Richard Clay (The Chaucer Press) Ltd, Bungay, for
J.M. Dent & Sons Ltd
Aldine House, 33 Welbeck Street, London W1M 8LX

This book is phototypeset in 11/13 VIP Sabon by
D. P. Media Limited, Hitchin, Hertfordshire

British Library Cataloguing in Publication Data

Trinder, Barrie
    The making of the industrial landscape.
    1. Land use   2. Landscape—Great Britain
    3. Great Britain—Industries
    I. Title
    719'.0941   HD111

    ISBN 0-460-04427-3

Foreword

A wide-ranging study of this kind draws on many experiences and
discussions, and I am grateful to numerous students and colleagues
with whom I have had the pleasure of exploring industrial landscapes
and contemplating the problems which arise from them. I am indebted
to many scholars on whose work I have drawn. Particular debts are
acknowledged in the footnotes. I also wish to record my thanks to
numerous people who have helped in the provision of illustrations. In
particular Marilyn Soden, David de Haan and Alistair Penfold of the
Ironbridge Gorge Museum, Tony Carr of the Shropshire County
Library and Gaye Blake Roberts of the Wedgwood Museum have
cheerfully helped me to utilize the rich pictorial resources in their care.
Jeremy Lowe has kindly allowed me to use photographs and plans
from his study of South Wales. My greatest debt is to my wife who has
given much help with line drawings and has patiently encouraged the
whole project.

BST

Acknowledgments

The author and publishers would like to thank the following for permission to reproduce illustrations: Derbyshire County Library (Pl. 4); Ironbridge Gorge Museum (Pls 11, 22, 25); Ironbridge Gorge Museum: Elton Collection (Pls 6, 7, 9, 21, 23, 28, 29, 33, 34, 40, 41, 43, 47, 48); Ironbridge Gorge Museum: Bracegirdle Collection (Pl. 35); Aberdeen Art Gallery (Pl. 8); Josiah Wedgwood & Sons Ltd (Pls 10, 24, 50. Pl. 10 is from Josiah C. Wedgwood, *History of the Wedgwood Family*, 1908); A.M. Jenkinson (Pl. 15); Clwyd Record Office (Pls 19, 20); Neil Cossons (Pl. 26); J.B. Lowe (Pls 30, 52; Figs 8, 11); Cheltenham Library (Pl. 39); *Illustrated London News* (Pls 67, 68); Shropshire County Library Local Studies Section (Figs 2, 3, 4; 7 (*a*) and (*b*) redrawn from originals); C. Charlton, D. Hool and P. Strange, *Arkwright and the Mills at Cromford*, 1971 (Fig. 6); Edward Mogg, *London in Miniature* (Fig. 9, adapted).

Pls 1, 2, 3, 5, 12, 13, 14, 16, 17, 18, 27, 31, 32, 36, 37, 38, 42, 44, 45, 46, 49, 51, 53, 54, 55, 56, 57, 58, 59, 60, 61, 62, 63, 64, 65, 66, 69, 70, 71 were taken by the author.

List of Plates

List of Figures

1 Perspectives and Definitions

Mean houses, mills like prisons, streams flowing with noxious effluvia, chimneys, and all-enveloping, all-blackening smoke—industrial landscapes have traditionally been regarded with distaste and repugnance, even with shame. By contrast, tourists, artists and writers in the late eighteenth century marvelled at the discipline and order of Richard Arkwright's mills at Cromford or Josiah Wedgwood's pottery at Etruria, and were fascinated and awestruck by the terrifyingly dramatic sights of Coalbrookdale or Parys Mountain. It was in the 1830s and 1840s that industry came to be regarded with disgust, as something unworthy of the attention of cultivated people, as awareness spread of the squalor of working class districts in large industrial towns, and of the degrading conditions in which women and children were forced to work in mills and mines. An antiquarian, writing in 1912, dismissed Ironbridge as:

> an uninteresting and somewhat squalid town, situated on a
> steep declivity sloping down to the Severn, whose banks are
> here covered with slag and refuse.

Outrage is a legitimate reaction to squalor but disinterest is not. Anger that human beings should have lived in the formless, smoke-blanketed landscape of the Victorian Potteries should not obscure the reasons why it came into being, and the infinite variety of processes which created it. Nor should it impel anyone to assume without evidence that the creation of such an horrific landscape was a deeply deliberated act committed by unnamed exploiters, or that to live there was of necessity dehumanizing.

Attitudes towards industrial history have changed during the last quarter of a century. It is now relatively commonplace for a family excursion to have as its objective a ride on a train hauled by a steam locomotive, a visit to a blast furnace or a tour of a museum set up in the ruins of an old potbank. Water-pumping engines are maintained like

1

monuments in cathedrals. Lime kilns are preserved on bathing beaches. Water mills are lovingly restored to working order. A leading concern in the 'leisure industry' lures visitors to a tin streaming works in Cornwall and a paper mill in Somerset, as well as to a medieval castle in the Midlands and a waxworks in London.

Such developments reflect a growing awareness of the uniqueness of Britain's industrial history in the eighteenth and nineteenth centuries. While it is possible to admire castles, cathedrals and the birthplaces of poets in every European country, the monuments of the early stages of the Industrial Revolution in Britain are as unique as those of classical antiquity in Greece or those of the Renaissance in the cities of Northern Italy. Such monuments may not as yet have attained the status in official circles of medieval abbeys or prehistoric henge monuments, but the eagerness of individuals to restore machines and buildings, and the willingness of the public to pay to see them has, in this respect, been in advance of official and academic opinion.

There is often an air of unreality about industrial preservation, and sometimes an odour of sentimentality. The nailmaker, the potter, the miner, the miller's labourer and the locomotive fireman can suffer cruelly from 'the enormous condescension of posterity'. If question-quenching feelings of outrage need to be set aside when considering the industrial landscape, so too do those emotions which, rejecting the late twentieth century, see some kind of golden age in a period when steam not electricity was the predominant source of power, when all fibres were natural; when trades unions were weak and plastic uninvented. It is impossible to exaggerate the horrors of the worst environments created during the Industrial Revolution. The unpaved, undrained morass of the east end of Leeds through which A.B. Reach tramped in 1849, the sulphur-laden surroundings of the copper smelters in the Swansea Valley, the ill-built cottages scattered among the furnaces on the Black Country heaths, landscapes terrifying almost beyond late twentieth-century comprehension, are quite beyond re-creation. While it is possible to preserve the machines, the buildings and even the physical skills of the Industrial Revolution, its characteristic landscapes have changed beyond recall. They are, like great wars or cataclysmic political revolutions, aspects of the past for which one may be grateful as the sources of present-day comforts, but which one is thankful never to have experienced at first hand.

Industrial archaeologists in Britain have tended to concentrate their attention on the technological or architectural aspects of their subject, perhaps because they have been so concerned with the urgency of preservation. Yet there is a need to study the landscapes of industrial Britain if we are to gain a clearer understanding of the experiences of those who lived during the Industrial Revolution—and landscapes comprehend much more than machines and buildings. Many industrial monuments which are now preserved can only be understood if some effort is made to recreate the settings in which they once flourished. Fortunately an increasing degree of attention is being given to the landscapes of the Industrial Revolution. Urban historians have shown that the growth of cities in the eighteenth and nineteenth centuries was not a simple process of unimpeded expansion, but that it was shaped by a variety of factors connected with ownership, land use and communications. Others have attempted to analyse and classify various types of new settlement which came into existence during the Industrial Revolution. The importance of water power and the ingenious ways in which landscapes were changed so that it could be utilized have been demonstrated in numerous local studies. Transport historians have shown the impact on the landscape of those generations of railways which preceded the Liverpool and Manchester, the devastating effects of mid Victorian railway extensions on cities, and the efforts made to improve some utterly unpromising river navigations. Most regional and county-based accounts of landscape history now acknowledge the impact of industrial activities.

This book will survey the landscapes of England and Wales during the Industrial Revolution. Its approach is historical not geographical. The questions it seeks to answer concern phases of industrial development and the ways in which people reacted to them, not regions or particular industries. Its objects are to show how industrial activities, among many other factors, have shaped the landscape we see today and the way we perceive it, and to attempt to recreate in the imagination the landscapes of the Industrial Revolution—to re-activate the furnaces, the machines and the steam engines, to repopulate the back-to-back terraces, to set in motion once more the barges, the gin horses and the steam locomotives, to pour caustic solutions into streams and to fill the skies with acrid fumes. Only by such an exercise is it possible to appreciate the varieties and subtleties of past industrial landscapes, and to understand the remnants which we can see today.

The term 'industrial landscape' poses several problems of definition. It would not have been used in 1700. The word 'industry' in the sense of a branch of a particular trade or manufacture, or a systematic organization of labour, was known in the sixteenth and early seventeenth centuries, but the adjective 'industrial' did not come into general use until the end of the eighteenth century. It was only in the 1840s, when Thomas Carlyle wrote that 'the leaders of industry . . . are virtually the Captains of the World', that the word came to have its modern meaning. It is now customary to speak of the agricultural industry, the leisure industry and the communications industry, but in this book the word industrial will be taken as applying principally to what early eighteenth-century writers meant by 'mines and manufactures' and the systems of transport associated with them.

The period under review also requires definition. Industrial archaeologists in Britain have long debated in a somewhat sterile fashion whether their study is concerned with a range of human activities or a period of history. It would also be possible to discuss at length the nature of an industrial landscape. A case could be made for calling the flint mines at Grimes Graves in Suffolk, or the site of the 'axe factory' at Hyssington in Montgomeryshire, parts of industrial landscapes. Similarly, lead mines worked by the Romans, or streams which drove mills in the Middle Ages are components of landscapes which have been, in a sense, industrial, as are the present-day trading estates at Slough or Treforest, the oil refinery at Fawley or the Windscale nuclear power plant. This study is concerned with the landscapes of the Industrial Revolution, the momentous series of economic changes which took place in Britain in the eighteenth and nineteenth centuries, the 'take-off into self-sustained growth' which has been experienced by numerous other countries since that time.

The impact of industry upon the landscape is only one aspect of the history of the period but, as much as any other, it demonstrates the uniqueness of the British experience between 1750 and 1850. The growth of mines and manufactures at that time was not just an extension of what had gone on before. It was an activity on an altogether new scale which led to the growth of substantial manufacturing towns in Lancashire and the West Riding where there had been scattered weavers' cottages, and to the creation of a tortured landscape of blast furnaces, pit headstocks, canals and waste tips on the cottage-scattered heaths of the Black Country. It populated with miners and ironworkers the almost empty upper reaches of the South Wales valleys. It created landscapes of terrifying grandeur in West Cornwall, Anglesey, the Swansea Valley, in Snowdonia and the Ironbridge Gorge. The reactions of artists and writers to landscape are themselves evidence of the wider changes of consciousness during the period. This study is therefore concerned not merely with the mechanisms which changed the landscape, but with the ways in which such changes were interpreted.

It is impossible to isolate industrial factors from the complex history of the English landscape. The pattern of mines, factories, canals, railways and towns which grew up in the eighteenth and nineteenth centuries was shaped by boundaries defined during the Heptarchy, by the limits of medieval monastic estates, by the shapes of burghage plots laid out in new towns in the twelfth century, by tracts of common which had remained unenclosed because lordships of manors had been fragmented during the Wars of the Roses. In many areas mines and manufactures which once flourished have disappeared, leaving only fragmentary traces of their existence. Industry is only one theme among many in the complex history of the English landscape. It needs to be seen in the context of many centuries of man's activities, and its impact has to be sought in stretches of countryside which now appear entirely agricultural or ornamental.

It is difficult to separate the influence of industry upon the landscape from that of other factors, even in the eighteenth or nineteenth centuries. Mines and manufactories were but one part of civilization, and they influenced all aspects of the landscape directly or indirectly. The spectacular forest around Cragside Hall, Rothbury, the home of an industrialist, the sea front at Blackpool, the elegant spa buildings of Buxton or Cheltenham are all, in a sense, the products of industry, landscapes created by mines or manufactures. A farmstead, logically planned around a steam engine in the 1820s, with the fields about it drained by mass-produced clay pipes, manufactured in coal-fired kilns, with gates hung on wrought iron hinges, was essentially part of the same economy as a contemporary cotton mill or copper smelter. It could well have been capitalized with money accruing to the landowner from mineral royalties or urban house rents. It is not, however, the purpose of this book to consider in detail the development of the agricultural landscape in the eighteenth and nineteenth centuries, or the growth of towns dedicated to recreation. It is concerned principally with mines and manufactures and their immediate surroundings.

Certain factors shape industrial landscapes wherever they may be, and whatever activities may have taken place there. The geology of an area is one factor—its mineral resources, landforms and drainage patterns. The presence of coal, iron ore, non-ferrous metals or useful clays has obviously dominated the pattern of industry in many parts of Britain, as have the landforms in the regions concerned. The landscapes of the generally flat Warwickshire or Nottinghamshire coalfields are very different from those of the South Wales valleys. The availability of water power greatly influenced the pattern of industry before the mid nineteenth century, stimulating growth in areas where there were plentiful mill sites, and retarding it, or intensifying a search for alternative sources of power, where there were few.

Landownership also did much to shape industrial landscapes. In the Coalbrookdale coalfield in Shropshire, where most landholdings were of considerable size, the local economy was dominated by nine or ten large, all-embracing ironmaking concerns, operating within the estates they leased rather like colonial governments. In South Staffordshire, by contrast, landed property was very much divided and there were numerous small concerns in which two or three partners combined to mine coal, operate a blast furnace, work a forge or dig limestone. Great estates could stimulate industrial activity. They could also restrict it for aesthetic reasons. One of the agents on the Duke of Sutherland's Shropshire estate was told in 1834 that the company which worked the minerals on the estate would never be permitted to erect blast furnaces near Lilleshall Abbey. Industrial entrepreneurs were rarely all-powerful, and their influence was often pitifully small when contrasted with that of great landowners. The pattern of development of many industrial communities was shaped by property boundaries. One of the reasons why the cottages which housed the workers in the great Quarry Bank cotton mill at Styal are situated so far from the mill buildings was simply that the Greg family, who worked the mill, were unable to acquire land nearer at hand. The development of many urban industrial landscapes was similarly shaped by the policies of landowners. Appreciable differences can still be seen between parts of towns where numerous small owners in the eighteenth century were eager to maximize their profits quickly, and those where substantial landlords leased plots gradually with a concern for profits in the long term.

Transport systems form a vital element in most industrial landscapes. The need to bring raw materials in from a distance and to dispatch finished products to customers inevitably attracted manufacturers to navigable rivers, turnpike roads, canals, seaports and railways. The necessity to collect raw materials from a variety of local sources stimulated the growth of primitive railways, packhorse routes or tub-boat canals. Places where different systems intersected were by definition favourable locations for industrial development. At Etruria the turnpike road from Burslem to Newcastle crossed the Trent and Mersey Canal. At Hayle packhorse routes from the Cornish mines came to the coast. At Coalport the Shropshire Canal connected with the Severn Navigation. If transport facilities sometimes created favourable sites, where great riches were discovered, whether mineral deposits or sources of power, the resultant growth of industrial activity could stimulate the extension of a canal or a turnpike road, or the building of a branch railway.

The dominant element in any industrial landscape was the process itself—the mill filled with spinning machinery, the kilns, the furnaces, the pit headstocks. Most industries which had any impact on the landscape used power, so that waterwheels, leets and reservoirs, steam engines and chimneys, or horse gin houses, formed parts of the environments in which they flourished. Most manufacturing activities required storage and marshalling areas, so that warehouses and yards grew up around the structures concerned with the processes. Manufacturing activities are also shaped by chronology, by changing patterns of demand and by the development of new technologies. Some small concerns became large ones, and their establishments developed in a piecemeal fashion. Others, which began as major enterprises, faltered and their premises were subdivided and set to other uses.

Industrial enterprises could be self-stimulating. The establishment of a successful concern could demonstrate that a particular activity was successful in a certain area, it could create a skilled labour force which other employers could poach, it could make available products for finishing trades, it could create a demand for raw materials, servicing skills or transport facilities which others might move to fulfil. In some areas—in Birmingham, Sheffield, the Black Country—or among certain skilled trades in London, there grew up informal chains of production, groups of workshops carrying on different stages in the manufacture of certain items, which were totally interdependent. The secondary effects of successful industry on the landscape were also to be seen in the provision of social facilities—in the building of houses by speculators or the creation of company villages, in the erection of schools, churches and institutes, or the laying-out of walks or ornamental parks. Where manufacturing employment was available

7

predominantly for one sex, other enterprises might appear to redress the balance. Nailers' shops appeared amid the cotton workers' cottages in Belper because the mills provided work chiefly for women and children. Clothing factories were established in Crewe in the late nineteenth century because railway engineering was overwhelmingly a masculine occupation. Ultimately the establishment of a profitable industrial concern could set in motion the whole self-sustaining process of urbanization. Ironically, success tends to destroy the evidence in the landscape, and the impact of industry on the environment can often best be understood in those places where it was less than wholly successful.

Pollution was and is a feature of many industrial landscapes. From the mid eighteenth century smoke was an almost inevitable concomitant of mining and manufacturing. It is difficult to appreciate just how full of smoke a Victorian town or manufacturing district could be. A German traveller passing from Birmingham through the Black Country to Stafford in 1842 observed:

> I was delighted to have a clear view of the sky again. In Birmingham you can form no speculation on the weather. The rain is not felt till it has worked its way through the smoke, and the sun shows himself only as a yellow patch. Sunrise and sunset, stars and moonlight are things unknown. It is easy to understand why the English, having such towns, should be so passionately fond of rural life.

Such conditions were alarming, but the atmosphere appeared quite terrifying around ironworks, where the calcining of iron ore and the coking of coals released vast quantities of sulphur into the atmosphere, or in the vicinity of the copper smelting houses of Cornwall, the Swansea Valley, Anglesey or St Helens. On the slopes of the hills above some of the Swansea copper works, according to one visitor in 1815, there was:

> not a blade of grass, a green bush, nor any form of vegetation; volumes of smoke, thick and pestilential, are seen crawling up the sides of the hills, which are as bare as a turnpike road.

Water, too, could be polluted by the waste products of industry or the refuse of undrained, unplanned settlements. The Red River in Cornwall is still coloured as the result of long-abandoned mining activities. The Trent and Mersey Canal at the Harecastle Tunnel in North Staffordshire is stained by ochre from iron ore mines. The

Irwell at Manchester was reported to be destitute of fish in 1795, 'the water being poisoned by liquor flowing in from the dyehouses'.

Pollution was also caused by the deposit of solid waste upon the ground, creating in some cases man-made mountains. At Dowlais there was a great mountain of iron slag, so impressive that, had it been deliberately constructed as a monument to a medieval king or an eighteenth-century landowner, it would certainly have been preserved. The vast pyramids of china clay waste around St Austell are similarly monumental, as are the waste tips which surround the larger pits of the Northumberland–Durham coalfield at such places as Ashington. On a lesser scale, small heaps of coal measure clay, piles of iron slag or white barytes indicate the sites of many past enterprises.

Discarded products are also a feature of the industrial landscape. There are walls made of saggars or vitrified bricks from pottery kilns in the North Staffordshire Potteries or the Ironbridge Gorge. At Ironville rows of houses were constructed from blocks of iron slag. Larger blocks of slag have been employed in roadside walls at Ironbridge. The quay and harbour wall at Hayle are built of bricks made of copper slag from the smelters which formerly flourished there.

Subsidences are also legacies of industrial activity. The flashes of South Lancashire, caused by coal mining, or those in Cheshire, which are the result of brine pumping, are spectacular. Sinking, distorted buildings are still to be found in coal mining districts. Nowhere is the result of subsidence more impressive than in the Potteries, where the ground on which Wedgwood's Etruria works stood is now many feet below the Trent and Mersey Canal with which it was once level.

Quarries also survive in the landscape as permanent reminders of past industrial activities. Some, like the carboniferous limestone quarries of the Vale of Llangollen which supplied the Midlands ironworks, or the ball clay quarries of Devon, which supplied the North Staffordshire Potteries, were far removed from the manufactories they served. The traces of Victorian brick-clay and gravel pits are hidden in numerous suburban gardens. In the countryside the floors of larger quarries are often flooded, and many have become isolated retreats for badgers and orchids. Sometimes, like some of the North Wales slate quarries, they survive high on hillsides, landmarks for many miles around, hardly colonized at all by vegetation, like the temples of an ancient religion.

Much of the past industrial landscape was ephemeral: piles of raw materials waiting to be consumed, flimsy timber structures or loosely laid iron rails which were removed when the enterprise came to an end, finished products waiting to be taken away and sold, vehicles or vessels awaiting loading or unloading, gleaming machines which have been devoured by scrap merchants. What survives is usually very different from the landscape of the Industrial Revolution, whether it is a flourishing modern concern on an ancient site or a few piles of stones on a deserted moorland. What we see today, whether the small waste tip of a colliery of 1700, the massive engine house of a Victorian lead mine, a vast cotton mill now used as a mail order warehouse or a stagnant ditch which was once a busy canal, needs a massive effort of imagination if it is to be seen in its historical context. It needs to be explained as a feature of the total landscape, which industry, among many other factors, has shaped. It should also be understood as a human enterprise, a place where men and women once worked and gained their sustenance, where entrepreneurs fulfilled their ambitions, where products which brought benefits or dangers to mankind may have been manufactured, where pollution may have caused occupational diseases.

Industrial landscapes are not the result of impersonal forces like U-shaped valleys or limestone escarpments. They were created by men and, as far as the landscapes of the Industrial Revolution are concerned, usually by men who can be identified. One of the reasons why Britain was the first country to undergo an Industrial Revolution was probably the multiplicity of agencies of change, of social forces which gave rise to industrial enterprises.

One such agency may be defined as the seigniorial initiative. In its extreme forms in continental Europe this was often a royal initiative, as at the Fonderie Royale at Le Creusot, or the Saline de Chaux at Arc-et-Senan. Monumental buildings were planned in a style usually associated with palaces rather than manufactories. In Britain there were few such centralized initiatives, other than arsenals and naval dockyards, but something of the same spirit pervaded the enterprises of many great landed estates. In such contexts a manufactory was simply one means of utilizing the resources of an estate. It might be planned with an awareness of the consequences to the landscape, with a sense that the estate was likely to outlast the enterprise. The stimulus to such a development may have been simply a determination to exploit to the full the natural resources of an inheritance, which might thereby be passed to future generations at a greater value. It could also be a means of saving an estate from the debts of a previous generation.

10

At the other end of the social scale it is possible to observe an incentive to enterprise born of poverty rather than wealth. The squatter community eking out a sparse existence on a common was often driven by sheer lack of agricultural resources to take up 'industrial' occupations, to quarry stone, drive carts, make locks, produce shoes or carry coal. In an age when capital was difficult to raise such communities could prove decisive factors in the growth of industrial enterprises, even if they did not themselves generate large-scale concerns. They provided reservoirs of skills on which entrepreneurs in the district could draw—building workers, well sinkers, clockmakers or millwrights. By extracting minerals on a small scale they could establish the potential for larger enterprises. They could provide extra accommodation for incoming migrant workers at no cost to entrepreneurs. In such areas as the Potteries, the West Riding, the Forest of Dean, the Black Country, the Coalbrookdale coalfield and Snowdonia such communities, which might be compared with the peasant iron-working villages of Germany or Sweden, profoundly influenced the growth of industry and the making of the industrial landscape.

Between these two types of initiative came what was perhaps the most important in eighteenth-century Britain—the independent entrepreneur, the man with skills in manufacturing and selling who was able to raise sufficient capital from his own resources or by borrowing to build a textile mill, sink a mine or work a furnace. The great estates and the open common were both settings for industry. The ambition of aristocrats and the needs of squatters to gain a bare minimum of subsistence both helped to shape the industrial landscape. But, above all, such landscapes were the creation of entrepreneurs, men who did not necessarily foresee the consequences of their own actions, nor appreciate the scale of the economic and social changes of which they were part. It is easy to condemn them for the horrific environments which some of them created, or for the legacies of pollution which some of them bequeathed to subsequent generations. These changes were part of the price of the breakthrough from a way of life uneasily exposed to the dangers of bad harvests or plagues to one of relatively secure prosperity. The alternative to the grim canal-side mills of Lancashire, the bleak mining settlements of Cumbria and the poisoned atmosphere of the Tawe Valley was not a country which looked everywhere like the trim fields of the Vale of Taunton or the grain-laden acres of Thanet, but one where pressures of population would, in all likelihood, have led to disaster.

11

2 A Landscape of Busy-ness: England in the time of Daniel Defoe

England in 1700 had few landscapes which could have been described as industrial, and it is doubtful whether 'industry', defined as something significantly different from other economic activities, would have been a concept understood by people of the time. Mining and manufacturing were ways in which some people made their living, just as others earned their bread by farming, shopkeeping or seafaring. Some trades were concentrated in certain parts of the country, but those who worked at them often retained contacts with agriculture. There were fulling mills, paper mills and iron forges on the rivers and streams of most counties, but they were regarded simply as part of a local economy, not as something alien and different. Nevertheless, by the early years of the eighteenth century there were some developments which revealed the potential for growth in the mines and manufactures of Britain—omens, already affecting the landscape, of the changes in scale which were to come later in the century.

One of the most impressive features of the early eighteenth-century landscape was its bustling activity. The most modest natural resources were exploited in almost every part of the country. With the exception of coal, Britain possessed few mineral deposits which were of major significance in a European context, and some of these were still undiscovered in 1700. Yet wherever there were shallow seams of coal they were mined. Where there were suitable clays they were made into pots. Where there was limestone it was burned. Shallow, winding streams were made navigable and harbours created in the most unpromising creeks. Government intervention in manufacturing was limited, by continental standards; restrictions which had impeded the mining of copper and the making of paper were coming to an end by the early eighteenth century. In comparison with some continental states the government did little to improve communications. There were no canals linking the major river estuaries as there were in France, and the improvement of English roads was left to uncertain

12

local initiatives. Popular interest in trade and manufactures was considerable and William Wordsworth noted how, before about 1770, writers of travel books devoted most of their attention to towns, manufactures and mines. The popularity of the works of Daniel Defoe and his imitators indicates the extent to which the educated classes wished to learn of the characteristic products of Britain's various regions.

The system of distribution in England was as sophisticated as in any contemporary European country. Defoe, in his *Tour through England and Wales*, aimed to show:

> how this whole kingdom, as well the people as the land, and even the sea, in every part of it, are employ'd to furnish something, and I may add, the best of every thing, to supply the city of London with provisions; I mean by provisions, corn, flesh, fish, butter, cheese, salt, fewel, timber &c., and cloths also, with every thing necessary for building and furniture for their own use, or for trades.

Some distant parts of the country furnished only expensive luxuries, like the salmon sent by express horses from Carlisle, but Defoe correctly drew attention to an important feature of the economy of the time, that increasing numbers of products were being produced on a sufficient scale to be marketed nationally.

Stourbridge Fair, with its ephemeral landscape of tents, booths, carts and crowds, was one of the most typical spectacles of economic activity in this period. It took place early in September in a great field near Casterton, outside Cambridge, used from late September until August for the growing of grain. The field was bounded on one side by the Cambridge–Newmarket road and on the other by the River Cam, from which it was possible to gain access to the system of navigable rivers draining into the Wash. In one sense the fair was a relic of the economy of earlier centuries. In another, in that it displayed the products which were marketed nationally, it reflected the expanding manufacturing activities of the time. Defoe observed there the luxury tradesmen of London, the goldsmiths, hatters, pewterers and china-warehousemen. He saw clothiers from the West Riding, Lancashire and the West of England. He noticed vast quantities of hops from Surrey and Kent. There was much dealing in wool, in iron and brass goods from Birmingham, edge tools and knives from Sheffield, and glass and hosiery from the East Midlands. Wherries were brought on waggons from London to ply on the Cam, and hackney carriers came

13

to convey people to and from Cambridge. Within a week there were few traces left of the fair, other than piles of horse dung, reckoned to be as good as a summer's fallow for making the land fertile.

The inventories of market town mercers also provide some indication of products which were marketed nationally in the early eighteenth century. Many consumer goods were made by market town craftsmen and sold locally, but the mercers supplied most commodities which were brought in from elsewhere. The inventory of Benjamin Wright of Wellington in Shropshire, who died in 1700, shows that he had a stock of many kinds of cloth—serges, shalooms, linseys, kerseys, flannels, fustians, sagathy and various types of linen. He had a quantity of hosiery, woollen stockings, socks and caps, as well as haberdashery, tapes, threads and laces. He kept printed books, prayer books, primers and hornbooks, as well as quantities of white and brown paper. He stocked various imported spices, dried fruits and rice, kept tobacco, which he cut himself, and also provided hops for brewing.

Wright's inventory, like those of other English mercers of the period, reflects the prosperity and complexity of the cloth trade. Almost every region of England and Wales had a speciality, a fabric, usually woollen, which was spun, woven, finished and marketed nationally or exported. Textile manufacturing was centred upon towns like Exeter, Norwich, Manchester, Leeds, Colchester and Shrewsbury, but it was widely dispersed across the countryside. Most of the establishments in towns kept by clothiers, the middlemen around whom the trade revolved, were of relatively modest size. Moses Law, a clothier from Bridgnorth who died in 1712, left wool worth nearly £100, yarn worth a little more, over £400 worth of frieze (a coarse woollen cloth with a nap on one side) and about £100 worth of other cloth. He had a large house, though only a small proportion of it was given over to production, and owned eight looms, two quill wheels and two twisting wheels, a variety of combs and cards and a dyeing furnace. In all his possessions were worth nearly £2000. Most of the people he employed must have lived and worked elsewhere in the town or in the surrounding countryside. The towns were generally places where cloth was finished, collected and sometimes marketed. There were no buildings devoted to production on a massive scale, although clothiers like Law might have had a room where a few weavers or spinners worked. Since there were no great manufacturing establishments, there were no great surges of employees on to the streets at the end of a day's work, and even the most prosperous towns could appear sparsely inhabited. In Norwich, Defoe remarked that anyone who saw the city on a Sunday or public holiday would wonder where all the people could dwell, but that:

> the inhabitants being all busie at their manufactures, dwell in
> their garrets at their looms, and in their combing shops, so they
> call them, twisting-mills, and other work-houses; almost all the
> works they are employ'd in being done within doors.

The markets and the activities of carriers bringing in cloth from the countryside and dispatching it towards London were the features of the landscape of textile towns which most impressed visitors. In Colchester in 1728 a foreigner remarked on 'the great manufacture of Colchester baize so famous throughout Spain, Portugal and their American plantations', and noted that the cloth was taken to London in waggons carrying from eighty to ninety hundredweight, drawn by six horses. The same traveller noted that seven waggons in a week were sent from Frome to London, each loaded with a hundred and forty pieces of woollen cloth, each worth about £14, although this was not a regular occurrence. At Exeter Celia Fiennes met 'carryers entering into the town with loaded horses'. Defoe described the great cloth market held twice a week in Leeds in the wide street called Briggate. Early in the day two long rows of trestle tables were placed along the street, on which the clothiers from the surrounding countryside displayed their pieces of cloth. Trading commenced with the ringing of a bell at seven o'clock, and was concluded by nine o'clock, when the street would be cleared. A Portuguese visitor said of Leeds in 1728:

> It is surprising to a stranger, when he first comes to this town,
> to see a long street, full of shops or standings, piled up with
> pieces of cloth, for sale on a market day.

Such markets often had about them a sense of the theatrical or the ritualistic. In Shrewsbury the market for cheap Welsh cloth was held on Thursdays. Welshmen with country coats of blue cloth and striped linsey waistcoats would bring the cloth to the town on packhorses with halters of twisted straw, each horse laden with two pieces of cloth. They would trade in the Square with members of the Drapers' Company, who had an effective monopoly in the trade, until the market ended when the Drapers mounted a staircase to the upper room of the market hall. The cloth would be taken away in drays to warehouses, while the Welshmen spent the proceeds of their sales.

15

The size of the larger markets was impressive. In Manchester in 1698 Celia Fiennes noted:

> the Market place is large, it takes up two streets length when the Market is kept for their Linnen Cloth Cotten Tickings Incles, which is the manufacture of the town.

Many of the processes by which woven cloth was finished were carried on in towns. Celia Fiennes remarked that much of the low ground around Norwich was drained with trenches, whose water was used 'to white and bleach their woollen stuff, the manufacture of the place'. In Rochdale the River Roch and its tributaries were employed to drive fulling mills and their water was used in numerous dyehouses. At Exeter Celia Fiennes saw a fulling mill:

> they lay them (i.e. pieces of cloth) in urine, then they soape them and so put them into the fulling mills and soe worke them in the mills drye till they are thick enough, then they turne water into them and so scower them; the mill does draw out and gather in the serges, it's a pretty divertion to see it, a sort of huge notch'd timbers like giant teeth, one would think it should injure the serges but it does not.

When the cloth had been fulled it was dried on tenters or racks, which were characteristic features of the landscape around towns dependent on textiles. In Exeter the cloths were put:

> on racks which are as thick set one by another as will permit the dresser to pass between, and huge large fields (are) occup'd this way almost all round the town.

Another traveller observed in 1750 that outside the south gate of Exeter was:

> the great manufacture of narrow cloths and shalloons extending all down to the river, and the cloths when they are hung up make a beautiful appearance.

From the tenters the cloths went to be pressed. Papers were placed between each fold, and each piece put under a coal-heated hot press, then under a cold press. Some cloths were marketed in the white, but others were dyed. Steam from dyeing vats and the coloured effluvia flowing from them into rivers and streams were familiar sights in the textile towns.

The tenters, the dyehouses, the warehouses and the market places of the textile towns were the dominant features of the landscape of the textile industry in the early eighteenth century. The majority of the houses where yarn was spun and cloth was woven were scarcely distinguishable from any other dwellings. The kitchens of some traditional stone farmhouses in the Pennines were given over to weaving, and extensions were added to accommodate household activities. By the early eighteenth century the loomhouse of the Pennine region with its traditional 'weavers' windows' had already evolved, although the majority of surviving examples date from a later period.

There was a great contrast between the landscapes of those textile areas which lay in fertile agricultural regions, like Norfolk, Wiltshire or Devon, and those in the uplands. In the Pennines there seem to have been few restraints on the building of cottages, and the industry was able to grow in a way which was impossible in regions where the demands of agriculture and the powers of landlords were stronger. In the West Riding there was already a tendency in the early eighteenth century towards the growth of squares of cottages or 'folds', filling in the plots of land attached to single cottages. On many smallholdings in Lancashire weavers added loomhouses to their homes, clothiers built dyehouses and yarn chapmen might enclose new crofts on which yarn could lie to bleach. The most impressive description of the landscape of the upland textile regions comes from Defoe, who wrote of his descent from Blackstone Edge:

> the nearer we came to Hallifax, we found the houses thicker, and the villages greater in every bottom; and not only so, but the sides of the hills, which were very steep every way, were spread with houses, and that very thick; for the land being divided into small enclosures, that is to say, from two acres to six or seven acres each, seldom more; every three or four pieces of land had a house belonging to it . . . this division of land into small pieces and scattering of the dwellings was occasioned by, and done for the conveniences of the business which the people were generally employ'd in, and that . . . though we saw no people stirring without doors, yet they were all full within, for in short, this whole country, however mountainous . . . is yet infinitely full of people, those people all full of business; not a beggar, not an idle person to be seen, except here and there an alms-house. . . . This business is the clothing trade, for the convenience of which the houses are thus scattered and spread upon the sides of the hills.

Defoe noted that the availability of coals and running water made possible the manufacture of cloth, without which such a wild country

17

could not have maintained so large a population. He found the country:

> one continued village . . . hardly a house standing out of a speaking distance from another, and . . . the day clearing up, and the sun shining, we could see that almost at every house there was a tenter, and almost on every tenter a piece of cloth, or kersie, or shalloon . . . whenever we pass'd any house we found a little rill or gutter of running water . . . and at every considerable house was a manufactory or work-house, and as they could not do their business without water, the little streams were so parted and guided by gutters or pipes, and by turning and dividing the streams that none of those houses were without a river . . . as the dying-houses and places where they used this water emitted the water again, ting'd with the drugs of the dying fat, and with the oil, the soap, the tallow and other ingredients used by the clothiers in dressing and scouring &c. . . . the water so ting'd and so fatten'd enriches the lands they run through, that 'tis hardly to be imagined how fertile and rich the soil is made by it.

He observed that each clothier kept a horse to fetch wool from the market, take yarn to the spinners and cloth to the fulling mill and then to the market. Most of the weavers kept several cows and grew crops on three or four small fields adjoining their cottages. The majority of work was done in the home, but at the house of one master manufacturer:

> We saw a house full of lusty fellows, some at the dye-fat, some dressing the cloths, some in the loom, some one thing, some another, all hard at work and full employed upon the manufacture.

The Lancashire textile trade was similarly prosperous. Woollens, linens and silks were made in the county, but the most significant growth was in the manufacture of light wares, particularly fustians and calicoes. In 1718 the East India Company succeeded in persuading Parliament to prohibit the sale, use and ware of English calicoes, but such cloth could still be made and printed for export, and it became increasingly difficult to distinguish between calicoes and fustians. From the 1720s the printing side of the industry was increasingly concentrated in Lancashire. Between the first and fifth decades of the eighteenth century the consumption of raw cotton in England doubled. The success of the Lancashire industry arose from its long experience in linen manufacturing and the enterprise of the small yeoman class. By the middle of the century the principal entre-preneurs, the Manchester linen drapers, controlled the whole trade—the putting-out of cotton and linen yarn for spinning, winding, warp-ing, weaving and finishing. The rural textile workers remained a large and important body, but increasing numbers were living in the towns and becoming entirely dependent on the wages they received for working with textiles.[1]

The most significant individual developments in the textile trade took place outside the traditional clothmaking districts, however. In the 1740s John and Nathaniel Phillips established a manufactory at Upper Tean near Cheadle in Staffordshire, with a central loomhouse where swivel looms, copied from Dutch examples, were used to make tape. The new loomhouse abutted on to a timber-framed house of 1613. Much of the work was still put out to domestic workers, but the enterprise marked a significant development in scale and organization.

The textile industry was also well-established in Birmingham in the early eighteenth century, and it was there that John Wyatt and Lewis Paul began to spin cotton by rollers in the 1730s. A mill powered by two asses was set up in Upper Priory in 1741. After the partners went bankrupt the following year, Edward Cave established a water-powered mill in Northampton, but these ventures were ill-administered and soon came to nothing.[2]

Of much greater consequence was the application of water power to the spinning of silk thread. In the first decade of the eighteenth century Thomas Cotchett, a London silk reeler, set up a water-powered mill on the Derwent at Derby. The venture foundered, but the mill was subsequently leased to John and Thomas Lombe, who imported Italian technology, and about the end of the second decade of the century built a water-powered factory employing three hundred peo-ple. Defoe noted that it was 'a curiosity in trade worth observing'. In 1730 Gonzales was able to relate that it had five or six storeys, 26,586 wheels and made 97,746 movements producing 318,505,960 yards of thread in every twenty-four hours. Whether such figures were accurate or not is irrelevant. What is significant is that the mill was celebrated, and there was sufficient interest in it for such information to be worth publishing. Two similar mills were opened at Stockport before 1750, and the pattern of organization set in the silk trade was subsequently to influence developments in the cotton industry.

While most types of cloth were made in regions which specialized in certain fabrics, the cheapest forms of linen and some woollens were

19

made on a more localized basis. In upland and woodland areas, in particular, many cottages grew small plots of hemp or flax. The crops were retted, by soaking in small pits, and then dressed and spun before being taken to a local weaver to be woven into cloth for the growers' use.

Hosiery, like cloth, was marketed nationally, and it appears in most mercers' inventories of the early eighteenth century. Production was concentrated in such areas as the Kendal region, Dorset, the Richmond district in North Yorkshire and southern Northamptonshire. Thomas Pennant eloquently described stocking manufacture around Bala in North Wales:

> round the place women and children are in full employ knitting along the roads. . . . During the winter the females through love of society, often assemble at one another's houses to knit, sit around a fire and listen to some old tale, or to some ancient song or the sound of the harp. . . . Close to the south-east end of the town is a great artificial mound called Tommen y Bala, in the summer time usually covered in a picturesque manner with knitters of all ages.

By the middle of the eighteenth century many merchant hosiers in the East Midlands had established workshops next to their homes, where they would keep about a dozen knitting frames. The knitting frame was the invention of the Revd William Lee of Calverton near Nottingham in the sixteenth century, and it was due to him that the hosiery trade became established in the region. By the 1730s cotton was being woven on the machines as well as silk and worsted. The merchant hosiers of Leicester and Nottingham were providing employment for considerable numbers of domestic framework knitters, and were slowly establishing larger units of production.

Mercers sold paper, as well as fabrics, and the manufacture of this grew steadily in the eighteenth century. Paper was made from rags— the finest grades from linen rags—which were pounded in a vat. A mould, a tray with wires across the bottom, was dipped into the vat and held up to drain. The paper on the bottom was then placed on to a felt and a quire of 144 sheets and felts would be built up ready to go under a screw press. Once pressed the sheets of paper would be separated from the felts and laid on racks to dry. At a paper mill, water power was used to drive the machinery which pounded the rags into pulp, and a constant supply of pure water was essential for mixing with the rags.[3]

20

By 1700 there were about a hundred paper mills in England. Over half were in the South-East, clustered around London, and the rest were widely dispersed. Of the largest mills, with four or more vats, three were in Kent, one at Newbury, one near Hull, one near Manchester and another at Wolvercote outside Oxford. There were particular concentrations of mills on the Wye and the Colne in Buckinghamshire and Middlesex, on the Kennet in Berkshire, on the Wey in Surrey, the Culm in Devon and around Maidstone in Kent. Many papermakers took over mills which had been used for other purposes. In the early eighteenth century several fulling mills were so adapted in Kent, where the textile trade was contracting. The manufacture of paper at Sawston in Cambridgeshire, which is still an important papermaking centre, began in the 1660s, when Richard Allen took over a former fulling mill. Some paper mills shared water with mills used for other purposes. At Darley Abbey in Derbyshire in 1713 a paper mill, a corn mill, a hemp mill and a leather mill all used the same source of water. Few paper mills were more advantageously situated than that at Wookey Hole in Somerset, founded before 1610, which stood at the point where the River Axe emerged from the celebrated caverns. The water was pure, contained a quantity of lime beneficial for papermaking and could not be impounded by other millers.

Few travellers in the early eighteenth century who were not looking for ironworks would ever have seen a furnace or a forge. Dependent upon water power and upon the use of charcoal as a fuel, such works were situated in the remotest valleys.

Iron ore was smelted in a blast furnace, a substantial stone structure fed from above with raw materials and blown by water-powered bellows. A blast furnace operated throughout the winter months, for as long as water was available to power it, usually for between thirty and forty weeks. During that period iron ore, fuel and limestone, which served as a flux, would be fed into it continuously. Twice every twenty-four hours the molten iron would be let out into a bed of sand, the usual pattern of which was thought to resemble piglets feeding from a sow. The limestone, when melted, floated on top of the molten iron so lifting off some of the impurities. It was tapped from the furnace before the iron was let out, allowed to solidify and then thrown away. The slag, or cinder (or *scoria* as it was often called in the eighteenth century) is a hard, brittle, glass-like substance, with few uses other than as road metal.

The blast furnace needed a dependable source of water power.

21

Unlike a forge or a flour mill, it was not possible to stop the process for several hours or days if there was insufficient water to turn the wheel. If the bellows stopped working the contents of the furnace solidified, necessitating a long period of demolition and rebuilding. The arrangement of pools and leets providing water for a furnace was often, in consequence, highly sophisticated. Valleys were dammed to create pools, and elaborate systems of leets were dug to ensure constant supplies of water. Such pools and channels, together with overgrown accumulations of slag, are often the only remaining indications in the landscape of the existence of once-flourishing ironworks.

The pig iron produced at a blast furnace was a form of cast iron, an alloy of iron with a carbon content of about four per cent. Cast iron can be melted and poured into moulds to make elaborate shapes; it is strong in compression but weak in tension. Since the mid eighteenth century it has been employed for a widening range of purposes, but in 1700 its uses were limited. Some domestic pots and pans were cast in iron, and it was used for cannon, ornamental firebacks and grave slabs. The iron most in demand was wrought iron, a commercially pure form of the metal, strong in tension but weak in compression, which was employed in locks, nails, edge tools and chains. Pig iron was converted into wrought iron at a forge, where it was first melted in a charcoal-fired hearth called a chafery, in which the carbon was removed. After hammering it was reheated in another hearth, known as a finery, before being hammered again into rods, plates or whatever shapes were required. The finery bellows and the forge hammers were normally worked by waterwheels. Rods for nailers were usually made at a slitting mill, which was also water-powered.

Both blast furnaces and forges depended on charcoal, which was as much a factor in the location of an ironworks as the need for water power. Charcoal was made from coppiced trees—beech, ash, oak or hornbeam—deliberately grown for the purpose. The ironworks were no longer, as they may have been in earlier centuries, competitors with shipyards for full-grown timber trees. William Wordsworth described how, in the seventeenth century, the steeper and more stony enclosures of Lakeland farms were converted to closed woods for the supply of charcoal to furnaces. Wood was cut for charcoal after between ten and twenty years' growth, and was thus a crop of uncertain profitability. The *maintenance* of charcoal supplies posed few difficulties but, since it was difficult significantly to increase production, the iron industry's potential for growth was limited. The increased demand for iron in the early eighteenth century was met largely by imports from the American colonies and the Baltic.

Each ironworks stood within a hinterland from which it drew its supplies of charcoal. Such supplies were the subject of considerable competition. In most parts of Britain the iron trade was controlled by powerful partnerships, and works which did not belong to them had to search far afield for their charcoal. The need to obtain charcoal was one of the factors which led to the location of furnaces and forges in the remotest parts of the country. A furnace was built at Dolgun, a mile east of Dolgelly, in 1719, and there were several forges within reach of the upper limits of the Severn Navigation in Montgomeryshire.

The historic centre of the English iron trade in the sixteenth and seventeenth centuries was the Weald of Kent and Sussex, on the watershed between the rivers Ouse, Eden, Medway, Rother and Cuckmere. This was and is a well-forested region. It seemed to Defoe in about 1720 to be 'one inexhaustible store-house of timber, never to be destroy'd, but by a general conflagration'. Large areas were laid out for the cultivation of coppice wood although there were complaints, corrected by Defoe, that the demands of the ironworks were responsible for the destruction of timber trees. Iron ore was mined in bell pits sunk in such strata as the Wadhurst clays and the Middle Hastings sands. They were rarely more than twenty feet deep, and usually filled with water when they were abandoned. The waste from these pits was often sold as marl, and areas of abandoned workings were frequently covered with woodland.[4]

The landscape of the Wealden ironworking districts could appear impressive and distinctive in the early eighteenth century. Turning north from Battle, Defoe passed through:

> the deep, dirty, but rich part of these two counties (i.e. Kent and Sussex) . . . the great foundaries or ironworks . . . in this county . . . are carry'd on at such a prodiguous expense of wood.

Between Guildford and Godstone he noticed that the country was:

> exceedingly grown with timber, has abundance of waste and wild grounds, and forests, and woods, with many large ironworks at which they cast great quantities of iron caldrons, chimney-backs, furnaces, retorts, boiling pots, and all such necessary things of iron; besides iron cannon, bomb-shells, stink-pots, hand-grenadoes, and cannon balls, &c. in an infinite quantity.

23

The Wealden iron industry was in decline by the early eighteenth century, however. About 1720 there were around thirty ironworks still operating in Sussex, Surrey and Kent, whereas at the Restoration there had been in the region of eighty. Ore was neither rich in iron nor easy to obtain. Charcoal was costly, and becoming more expensive as the cultivation of hops and the consequent demand for poles created competition for wood supplies, and charcoal itself was in demand for use in oasthouses. Wages were high in the South-East, and supplies of water were uncertain in the summer months. Many of the Wealden ironworks had complex water supply systems, based on reservoirs created by building dams or 'bays' across the valleys of streams. Such pools often silted up, necessitating either an expensive programme of dredging or the heightening of the 'bay', usually achieved by the dumping of slag, as at Warren Furnace on the River Eden. Blast furnaces were usually built near to their supplies of ore, on small streams, where the pools systems required constant maintenance. Forges were more commonly on the larger rivers. The Wealden iron-works concentrated increasingly on specialized cast iron products in the early eighteenth century, particularly on armaments. Most of the cannon foundries had casting pits, deep holes in which the moulds for cannon could be placed in a vertical position, several of which have been excavated in recent years, and boring mills, evidence of which is sometimes provided by masses of borings rusted in the furnace leets. The industry made heavy demands upon the inadequate roads of the region. One Sussex ironmaster wrote in 1743:

> have gotten 20 9-pounders to Lewes . . . these 20 have torn the roads so that nothing can follow them and the country curse us heartily.

The landscape of the ironworking region of Kent, Sussex and Surrey was changing steadily in the early eighteenth century. At some furnace and forge sites the leets and waterwheels were put to other purposes. At Barden near Tonbridge and at Beech near Battle flour mills were built on the sites of furnaces. At Maresfield and at Brede the water supplies were used to work gunpowder mills, and a silk mill was driven by the leets which once powered the ironworks at Thursley. The silted beds of ironworks' pools, which were universally called 'hammer ponds' in the Weald, whether they drove hammers or not, provided excellent land for growing hops, and many were drained and used in this way. Other pools, like those at Gravetye, Eridge and Hamsell were used ornamentally, in park landscapes.

24

The Wealden iron industry had already declined substantially by 1700 and it continued to diminish in size. Its influence on the landscape had been substantial, even in an area so heavily wooded. Its pools, even when drained, continued to affect land use. The waterpower facilities it had created were often put to other purposes. The influence of the industry can be seen on modern maps in such placenames as Barden Furnace Farm, near Tunbridge Wells, Furnace Mill at Lamberhurst, Forge Farm and Furnace Farm south of Goudhurst on the edge of Bedgebury Forest, Huggetts Furnace south of Crowborough, Furnacefield Wood south of Ticehurst, and the Iron River between Uckfield and Lewes. There are grave slabs which were cast at Wealden furnaces at Rotherfield, Wadhurst, Hartfield and Uckfield.

Another important ironworking area was in South Yorkshire and the East Midlands. In 1717 there were four blast furnaces and eight forges in Yorkshire, four furnaces and four forges in Derbyshire and a furnace and five forges in Nottinghamshire. The significance of the region lay more in the uses to which iron was put than in the quantities produced. The most important activity was the manufacture of tools and cutlery around Sheffield, and many of the smiths used iron which was imported from the Baltic. Defoe found the town of Sheffield:

> very populous and large, the streets narrow, and the houses dark and black, occasioned by the continued smoke of the forges, which are always at work: here they make all sorts of cutlery-ware, but especially that of edge-tools, knives, razors, axes &c., and nails; and here the only mill of the sort which was in use in England for some time was set, viz. for turning their grindstones, though now 'tis grown more common.

The Sheffield trades were well-established long before 1700 but were steadily increasing in prosperity. There was specialization within the various villages: Norton was known for its scythes and sickles while Shiregreen manufactured table forks. The region had many advantages as an ironmaking centre. There was iron ore and charcoal for blast furnaces, and ample supplies of coal for the smiths' hearths. Swedish and Russian ore could easily be imported via the tributaries of the Humber. The local millstone grit was, as its name implies, an ideal material for grindstones, and the district's many streams provided power for hammers, bellows and grindstones. In 1672 there were 596 smithies in the region, and by the middle of the eighteenth century some 133 water-powered grinding wheels.

Many of the metalworkers were rural craftsmen, living in the large parishes on the edge of the Pennines to the west of Sheffield. A typical metalworker's house in Ecclesfield consisted of a three-celled dwelling with a farm building on one side of a yard between the house and the street, and a row of file-shops with eight anvils and four hearths on the other side. The buildings stood in a croft of about two acres. The occupants probably enjoyed rights of common pasture, and the use of strips in open arable fields. The agriculture of the region was predominantly prosperous, probably more so than in the textile areas around Halifax. Farming was not just a sideline, but one of two principal sources from which the metalworkers made their livings. The landscape consisted of clusters of such establishments, set in folds, with smoke pouring from the various hearths, and a constant passage of materials to and from the hammer- and grinding-shops which were grouped along the stream banks, all set within a context of arable fields and common pasture.[5] The hand forges, tilt-shop and grinding-shops at the Abbeydale Industrial Hamlet give a vivid impression of certain aspects of the landscape of the area in the eighteenth century.

Some of the Sheffield trades used steel rather than wrought iron. At the beginning of the eighteenth century steel was usually made in a furnace in which wrought iron bars were packed with charcoal in closed clay vessels, normally called coffins, and slowly heated for as long as a week. The bars would be covered in blisters when removed, and this type of steel was usually called blister steel. Several furnaces of this kind were built in the North-East in the early eighteenth century, one of which survives at Derwentcote near Rowlands Gill in Co. Durham. About 1740 Benjamin Huntsman of Sheffield discovered that the quality of steel could be greatly improved by breaking blister bars into small lengths and melting them in crucibles of refractory clay. The crucible-shop became a characteristic feature of the landscape of the Sheffield region, and an example can still be seen at Abbeydale.

A third ironworking region extended through the West Midlands and the Welsh Borderland, along the banks of the Severn, the Wye and their tributaries, and was linked by overland transport and coastal shipping to other works in Cheshire, Lancashire and the Lake District. The region was dominated by powerful partnerships like those of the Foley and Knight families, who controlled widely dispersed works of all sorts. Iron at various stages of manufacture was constantly exchanged between different works, usually being carried on barges on the Severn. Forgemasters often mixed pig iron from various sources in order to make wrought iron with particular qualities, and forge accounts show that large quantities of iron must constantly have been travelling through the region. At Wolverley Forge in the Stour Valley the sources of pig iron in 1732–3 included Charlcott and Willey in Shropshire, Flaxley in the Forest of Dean and Philadelphia and Principio (Maryland) in the American colonies. Three years later the nearby Mitton Forge was employing iron from Scotland, Newent in the Forest of Dean, Charlcott and Willey, and Principio and Baltimore in Maryland. The hub of the iron trade was the river port of Bewdley, through which pig iron from South Wales and the Forest of Dean passed upstream from Borderland forges, and where wrought iron rods were landed for distribution to the smiths of North Worcester-shire and South Staffordshire.[6]

The blast furnaces in the region were clustered around the coal measure rocks from which they drew their iron ore. There were several in South Wales, at Neath, Caerphilly and Kidwelly, and perhaps as many as ten in the Wye Valley and the Forest of Dean. Three were to be found on the slopes of the Clee Hills in South Shropshire, and four in the vicinity of Coalbrookdale in the east of that county. There were three in Cheshire, three in North Staffordshire and two in the North Wales coalfield.[7]

One of the region's most remarkable sites is at Bringewood on the Shropshire–Herefordshire border, deep in the Downton Gorge on the River Teme. A blast furnace was established here by 1600, and con-tinued to produce iron for about two hundred years. By 1700 there was a forge at Bringewood, and in 1741–2 a tinplate mill was built there. The district is well-wooded and doubtless most of the charcoal was obtained locally, as was the limestone. Pit coals for the tinworks were brought from the Severn Gorge some twenty miles away. Most of the iron ore was carried from mines on the summit of Titterstone Clee Hill, about ten miles away, but some came from Shirlett Common near Much Wenlock, and some from Southall Bank in the Coalbrook-dale coalfield some twenty-five miles distant. Pig iron for the forge came from Charlcott Furnace on the opposite side of the Clee Hills, Hales Furnace in Staffordshire and Bristol, the latter probably being American iron, while some use was made of 'Sussex castings', possibly scrap from one of the Wealden ironworks. There are few significant structures left at Bringewood, apart from two waterwheel houses, but the swift currents of the Teme, the complex system of leets and the very

27

remoteness of the site—its insulation from the surrounding country-side by thick woodland and the steep sides of the Downton Gorge—convey a vivid impression of the landscape of the iron industry before the Industrial Revolution.

The best-preserved structure in the region is the blast furnace at Charlcott in the parish of Aston Botterell in Shropshire, which stands on the Cleobury Brook, a tributary of the River Rea. It probably dates from the early years of the eighteenth century, and is of local red sandstone, built into sloping ground running down to the stream. There are large piles of slag in the vicinity and the nearby farm is called Cinderhill Farm. Adjacent to the furnace was a paper mill which shared the power of the stream.[8]

There were dense concentrations of ironworks along several rivers in the region. In the valley of the Angidy Brook, which flows into the Wye at Tintern, there are three ponds and the remnants of forges, wire mills and a furnace, together with numerous ironworkers' cottages. The valley of the Stour for many miles from its confluence with the Severn was lined with forges and slitting mills, among them those at Mitton, Wolverley, Hyde, Cookley, Whittington and Cradley. Mills working in the early eighteenth century to the east of Birmingham, on the Tame and its tributaries, included a blade mill at Holbrook, a forge and rod mill at West Bromwich, a slitting mill at Bustleholme and forges at Rushall and Wednesbury. On the River Rea, which flows southwards from the Clee Hills to join the Teme at Newnham Bridge in Worcestershire, there was the blast furnace at Charlcott and forges at Norton, Hardwick, Prescott and Cleobury Mortimer. In the valley of the Worfe and its tributaries there were two forges at Lizard, a blast furnace at Kemberton and a slitting mill at Ryton. The River Tern rises in the Staffordshire hills east of Market Drayton and then flows across the North Shropshire plain to join the Severn at Atcham, downstream from Shrewsbury. On this river and its tributaries, the Roden and Meese, there were forges at Winnington, Moreton Corbet, Sambrook, Caynton, Wytheford and Upton Magna, as well as a major works, known as the Tern Works, at Atcham. The latter was begun in 1710 alongside a corn mill which was probably the parish mill mentioned in Domesday Book. By 1717 its output of finished wrought iron was three hundred tons a year, one of the largest in Britain. Its equipment included a slitting mill, a hoop mill, a wire mill and a mill for rolling brass plates, as well as a steel furnace. One of its proprietors claimed that it was 'the first Joint Work of this kind in England, and for its

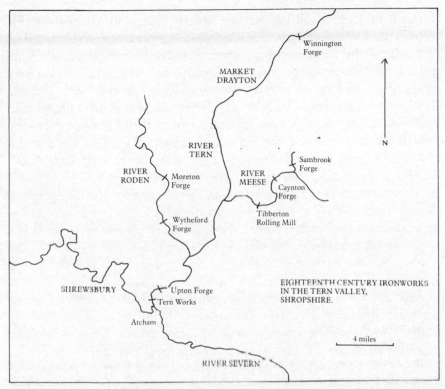

Figure 1 Eighteenth-century ironworks in the Tern Valley, Shropshire

goodness of building Europe Can't produce the like'. The works was erected on the property of the Hill family who, by the 1730s, were complaining of the noise made by the forge hammer at night. The forge closed in the 1750s and there are now few traces of it apart from small quantities of slag. The leets and dams have been incorporated into the ornamental features of a park created in the late eighteenth century around the new mansion of Attingham Park. At this and numerous other sites in the region the landscape is now entirely rural, but in the early eighteenth century it would have been shrouded in smoke from forge chimneys, and would have echoed to the thud of hammers, the swish of water over waterwheels and the gasping of bellows.

The most significant development in ironmaking in the early eighteenth century made little immediate impact upon the landscape, although it set the pattern for all future ironworks. In 1708 a Quaker ironfounder from Bristol, Abraham Darby, leased a derelict blast

29

furnace at Coalbrookdale in the Severn Gorge in Shropshire. He rebuilt the furnace and, early in the following year, began to smelt iron ore using as his fuel not the traditional charcoal, but coke made from pit coal. While the use of coal for this purpose had been discussed for a century, it had never previously been so employed with success. Darby's process spread only slowly. There were technical drawbacks to it which cannot now fully be understood. It did not produce iron which could readily be forged into wrought iron, but since it did produce a good foundry metal and since Darby was primarily concerned with making castings, it served his purposes.[9]

Three factors at Coalbrookdale set the pattern for the landscape of future ironworks. The use of coke in the furnace led to the coking of many piles of coal in the vicinity. The success of the foundry created an array of pattern-shops, moulding-shops and warehouses in the area. Finally, in the early 1720s the casting of iron cylinders for steam engines began at Coalbrookdale. In 1742 one such engine was used to recirculate water between the lower and upper pools of the ironworks, thus avoiding the need to cease operation in the summer months. Large pools and steam engines were thereafter to be found at most of the ironworks established in the mid eighteenth century.

The wrought iron rods produced by forges and slitting mills were of little use to householders. Some iron was distributed to blacksmiths, who fashioned it into useful objects, and some found its way to the few nailers who were to be found in most market towns. The principal destination for the iron made in the West Midlands–Borderland region was the hardware district to the north and west of Birmingham. Here, in parishes like West Bromwich, Kingswinford, Sedgley, Tipton and Halesowen, there was much woodland and heathland, large areas of common which were mostly enclosed by encroachment during the seventeenth and eighteenth centuries. The existence of such commons is revealed by many place-names: Blackheath, Wall Heath, Cradley Heath, Fallings Heath, Rounds Green, Greets Green and Tansey Green. Pastoral farming was combined with the manufacture of hardwares. The rich coals of the district lay so shallowly that it was often impossible for the lords of the manors to exercise their traditional controls over mineral rights. The capital needed to work as a smith was small. A plot of an acre or so might be encroached from the common, or rented, and a small cottage and a workshop with hearth, bellows and a water trough erected upon it. Coal might be dug up on the spot, or acquired from nearby shallow workings. Iron rods were

obtained from middlemen, who often purchased the finished products. The trades were specialized to a considerable degree. On the
coal measures there was a concentration of nailers, the poorest of the
trades, while the towns and villages on the edge of the coalfield were
concerned with more elaborate items, saddlers' ironmongery at Walsall, locks at Wolverhampton, scythes at Bellbroughton and a whole
range of valuable small metal products at Birmingham. The landscape
was dominated by the open commons, on which innumerable
encroachments had been made by squatters whose cottages, with their
attendant smoking workshops, covered large areas. Cows were still
pastured within the folds and small patches of barley, wheat and flax
were cultivated.

Foreign visitors marvelled at the cheapness of British coal and its
widespread availability. A traveller in South Wales in 1728 observed
that coal was so cheap that there were fires in the meanest cottages. In
the 1740s a Swede found that the fog caused by the use of coal fires in
London made him ill, and noted that coal was only carried by land to a
distance of about fourteen miles from the capital, beyond which it was
usual to use wood or whatever other fuel was available locally. Coal
was so cheap in the mining regions of Shropshire that domestic fuel
was virtually never recorded on probate inventories, but in such towns
as Bishop's Castle, remote from any mines, not only coal but also furze
and firewood were regularly listed and accorded high values.

Coal was being mined in all the principal British coalfields by the
beginning of the eighteenth century: in South Wales, the West Riding,
Flintshire and Denbighshire, around Bristol, in Nottinghamshire and
Derbyshire, North and South Staffordshire, Shropshire, Warwickshire, Lancashire and the Forest of Dean. It was also mined for local
use from many small outcrops in remote areas. By far the largest and
most flourishing coalfield was that of Northumberland and Co.
Durham, which supplied the whole of the east coast, London and
much of the south coast and gave employment in the coasting trade to
numerous mariners from such ports as Yarmouth.

The road from Durham to Newcastle, said Daniel Defoe, 'gives a
view of the inexhausted store of coal and coal pits, from whence not
London only but all the south part of England is continually supplied'.
The pits of the coalfield were the deepest in Britain, the seams the most
productive then being exploited and the surface installations the most
impressive. The coalfield's transport facilities are strong evidence of its
prosperity. The North-East was one of the two birthplaces of the

English railway, and by the early eighteenth century it had by far the largest network of wooden railways (although they were usually called waggonways) in the world, some of the lines extending five miles or more from the coast or the banks of the rivers Tyne or Wear to the collieries. At the riverside or on the coast coal was loaded from the waggons on to boats by means of staithes, high wooden piles on to which the railways ran, and through which spouts guided the coal released from doors in the wagon bottoms into the holds of waiting ships. Sometimes staithes were roofed, so that coal awaiting transit could be protected from the elements. On the Tyne and Wear much of the coal was loaded into keels, double-ended lighters, oval in shape, between twenty and thirty feet long and with a capacity of twenty-one tons of coal. The keels were rowed downstream and the keelmen would then heave their cargo into the hold of a waiting sea-going vessel. The staithes dominated the riverside landscape. Two adjoining staithes at the confluence of the Tyne and the Derwent built before 1721 were respectively 390 and 360 yards long, with berths for twenty-six and twenty-four keels.

Early eighteenth-century railways in the North-East included massive embankments, spindly wooden bridges across ravines and some stone bridges. Among the latter was the Tanfield or Causey Arch, built by the stonemason Ralph Wood in 1727 at a cost of over two thousand pounds. The bridge spans one hundred and five feet, and the semi-elliptical arch rises about thirty-five feet from its base to its keystone. For about thirty years it had the longest single span of any bridge in Britain, and became a celebrated object, perhaps one of the first industrial monuments to attract the attention of travellers. In 1739 it was reported as 'Tanfield Bridge, Gentleman come to see on purpose, who say it is the largest they ever saw, and must be a very great Expence to the owners'. A traveller noted in 1732:

> It is ye highest Arch I ever saw, perhaps has not its Equal; it has not been built many years, 'tis a little Stream yt flows under It; ye occasion of making it so high was, yt ye Coal-Carts might go on plain ground.

The other birthplace of the railway was the much smaller Coalbrookdale coalfield in East Shropshire which stretched some ten miles north to south across the Severn from Lilleshall to Broseley. Already prosperous, due to the easy carriage of coal afforded by the Severn, during the seventeenth century a network of railways grew up, few of them more than a mile long, which took the produce of the mines to the riverside. The routes were shorter, the gauges narrower and the waggons smaller than on the railways in the North-East, but the Shropshire lines were called railways not waggonways, trains of several coupled waggons ran on them, and by the middle of the eighteenth century they included some self-acting inclined planes descending the steep slopes of the Severn Gorge.[10]

As in the North-East, many coal-using industries sprang up in the Coalbrookdale coalfield. The pattern of landholding in the Severn Gorge and the unsuitability of the steep slopes for agricultural uses encouraged the growth of a population of cottager-miners, potters, tobacco-pipe makers, bargemen and others, not unlike the weavers of the West Riding or the hardware manufacturers of Sheffield or the Black Country. Many of these people lived in cottages surrounded by small crofts. Their houses were often enlarged by the addition of extra

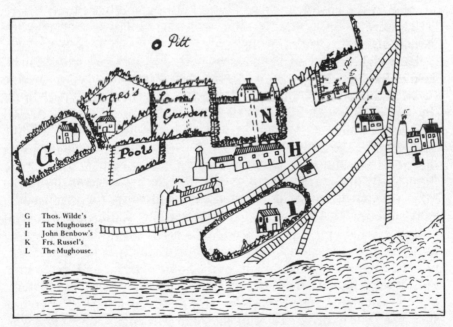

G   Thos. Wilde's
H   The Mughouses
I   John Benbow's
K   Frs. Russel's
L   The Mughouse.

Figure 2 Squatter-type settlement in the Severn Gorge, Shropshire, in the early eighteenth century: the landscape at The Calcutts, Broseley, *c.* 1730. There are several cottages in folds, some of which have been extended. Some of the properties have pottery kilns and were called 'mughouses'. The railway sidings were the terminus of a line about a mile long which brought coal from Broseley to the banks of the Severn; 122 waggons were held in the sidings in 1748. (*Redrawn from the Broseley Estate Book*)

33

rooms to make up short terraces, or new cottages were erected in the corners of the crofts, either to accommodate children or, through rents, to bring in additional income. This pattern of building is reflected in numerous wills of the early eighteenth century. A collier who died in 1712 owned a house near the riverside in Madeley which he had bought from the lord of the manor. He had divided it into three, and he and his wife occupied two rooms and a brewhouse at the east end, where a loft and the adjacent garden were occupied by a son. The middle two rooms with an outbuilding and part of the garden were occupied by another son, while three rooms at the west end formed the home of a daughter and her husband. A miner who died in 1761 had built a new house in the garden of his cottage, and given his eldest son the choice of the two dwellings.[11] Similar patterns of settlement could be found in the Forest of Dean, where numerous straggling squatter communities grew up near to the coal workings.

The most significant change to the landscape of the coalfields in the early eighteenth century was the appearance of the steam engine designed by Thomas Newcomen. The first such engine to work successfully was erected at Conygre near Dudley in 1712 and used to pump out water from coal workings. The Newcomen engine was a remarkably mature design, the first self-acting machine, apart from the clock, and demanding no parts which were not within the capacity of contemporary craftsmen. As remarkable as the maturity of the machine itself was the speed at which the invention was taken up. Between 1712 and 1733 about a hundred such engines were erected, the majority of them being employed to pump out water from mines.[12]

A Newcomen engine dominated any landscape, for it normally stood in an engine house up to forty feet tall. Within the house a massive iron or brass cylinder stood on a brick-encased boiler. Inside the cylinder was a piston, linked by a chain to a bulky oak beam, which pivoted on one of the outer walls of the house. The far end, extending outside the building, was connected with the pump rods in the shaft of a pit, to which it gave a reciprocal motion. It was not possible to use such an engine to drive a rotating machine. The engine's heat loss was very great, and the boiler consumed vast quantities of fuel, yet for many purposes—the pumping of water from coal mines where the cost of slack for the boilers was insignificant, from the richest lead, tin or copper mines, or for the supply of large cities—the Newcomen engine was an eminently practicable commercial proposition.

The Newcomen engine appeared in most of the English coalfields in

34

the first half of the eighteenth century. An engine had been built in the North-East by 1715, at Tanfield Lea in Co. Durham, and before 1720 there were engines in the Shropshire and Warwickshire coalfields. In 1700 Sir Roger Newdigate, oppressed with debts and ambitious to build a new country house in Middlesex, became a venturer in coal mines on a large scale, sinking new pits at Griff near Coventry, drained by waterwheels, a windmill and horse gins. After his death in 1709 his pits were leased by Richard Parrott and George Sparrow, who in 1714 erected 'an engine to draw water by the impellant force of Fire'.[13] The importance of the Newcomen engine was recognized by a French visitor to Britain in 1747 who wrote:

> England has more than any other country of those machines so useful to the state, which readily multiply men by lessening their work; and by means of which one man can execute what would take up to thirty without such assistance. . . . Thus in the coal pits at Newcastle a single person can, by means of an engine, equally surprising and simple, raise 500 tons of water to the height of a hundred and eighty feet. The drawing of this water facilitates the digging of the coal out of the pit, which coal is the greatest advantage to the nation, by abundant supplying the deficiency of wood for firing.

Industries grew up on most of the major coalfields using the cheap fuel and sometimes other raw materials from the coal measure rocks. On Tyneside and in Nottinghamshire, South Yorkshire and the Stourbridge area there were glassworks, dependent on the refractory clays found in the coal measures. The traditional 'English' glass cone, usually about fifty feet in diameter at its base and up to eighty feet high, evolved during the first half of the eighteenth century. The restored cone at Catcliffe near Sheffield dates from 1740. In Bristol in 1730 there were fifteen glasshouses meeting the demands of the wine trade and the Hot Wells at Clifton. In Cheshire there were salt boilers using coal from Staffordshire, but increasingly from Lancashire, to evaporate brine. A salt works might consist of a pump operated by a horse gin, a small furnace in which the brine would be boiled in an iron pan over a coal-fired grate, with a shelter to cover the filled baskets of salt and the barrels of blood purchased from butchers, used to speed up the process of evaporation. One of the chief concentrations of saltmakers was on the Tyne, and Defoe saw the clouds of smoke above the saltworks of South Shields as he approached Durham City some fourteen miles away.

35

Pottery was manufactured in many parts of Britain, wherever there were suitable clays and coal was sufficiently cheap. There were potters in Derbyshire, where the village of Ticknall gave its name to Tickney ware, a form of earthenware listed in many Midlands probate inventories. In the Severn Gorge there was a cluster of 'mughouses' producing coarse earthenware, and in the West of England there were potters at Calstock and Bovey Tracey. At Prescot in Lancashire there were 'two or three houses for coarse earthenware' and numerous 'mughouses' were to be found in the St Helens area.

The greatest concentration of potters, however, was in North Staffordshire. A traveller approaching the area from the north in 1750 wrote:

> We came to Madeley Hill, where we first met the vein of that clay for which this country is so famous, and is us'd in making the common earthenware, bricks, tyles and pipes for conveying water. . . . They bake 'em in kilns built in the shape of a cone which makes a very pretty appearance, there being great numbers of them in all the country beyond Newcastle.

The potters were already importing raw materials from a distance. White clay, first brought to the Midlands for making tobacco pipes, was being used in stoneware. Flints from Kent and Sussex were used from the 1720s, when Thomas Benson discovered how to grind them in water. Mills for grinding such materials became established in many tributary valleys of the Trent. North Staffordshire was an area of slackly controlled, irregular settlement: a map of the mid eighteenth century shows the hilltop village of Burslem with a host of small farmsteads around a green; there are bottle ovens in many of the crofts, and opposite the public house in the centre of the village a massive 'shord pile' of wasters from the potteries.

One of the most important developments in the ceramics industry in the early eighteenth century took place in London. The manufacture of porcelain began at Chelsea in 1743 and at Bow in 1744; until the early years of the century it had never been made in Europe. In 1745 William Cookworthy of Plymouth discovered that kaolin, or china clay, the essential material for making porcelain, was to be found in Devon and Cornwall. By 1750 porcelain manufacture had reached such provincial cities as Derby, Worcester and Bristol.

Like the making of pottery, the burning of limestone consumed large quantities of coal. Wherever roads or navigable water linked limestone quarries and mines there were kilns where stone was burned to make lime for use as a fertilizer or in building. There were kilns in many of the coves of Cornwall, North Devon and Pembrokeshire. Near Pwlheli limestone from Anglesey was burned with coal from Flintshire. At Lilleshall and Lincoln Hill in Shropshire limestone was burned with coal from the Coalbrookdale coalfield. Dr Richard Pococke, travelling south from Oswestry in 1754, saw a hill he called 'Tana Manah' (Llanymynech) which he described as 'a limestone rock where there were a great number of kilns'. He found Clitheroe in 1751 to be 'a town chiefly supported by lime kilns' and its inhabitants 'a poor people, the nature of their business makes 'em very thirsty and giving them a habit of drinking'. Lime from Clitheroe was sold up to twenty miles away. Chalk was used for the same purposes, being quarried in particularly large quantities around the Thames Estuary in Essex and Kent, and taken by sea to East Anglia.

Stone was quarried for use in building in most parts of Britain. Most of that used in houses was found locally, and in some areas stones hardly suitable for building were employed simply because they were available. Some types of stone were of high quality and were marketed nationally. The most spectacular quarrying enterprise of the early eighteenth century, an archetypal seigniorial concern, was the quarry at Combe Down near Bath, from which in 1731 Ralph Allen built a spectacular railway past his mansion at Prior Park to the River Avon. The railway achieved a fall of about five hundred feet from the quarries to the river, and was modelled largely on Shropshire practice. Most of the buildings constructed in Bath in the mid eighteenth century incorporated stone brought along Allen's railway. A very different quarrying area was on the Isle of Portland where was produced what Defoe called:

> the best and whitest free stone . . . with which the cathedral of
> St Paul's, the Monument, and all the publick edifices in the city
> of London are chiefly built.

The island had a miserable and thinly inhabited appearance, but Defoe found no very poor people among its stonecutters. The quarrymen worked as individuals, each paying a shilling a ton royalty to the crown for all the slate they took out. A small area was reserved to be worked for public buildings. To the east of Portland numerous quarries on the Isle of Purbeck produced paving stones for London, the transport of which provided employment for many local ships and their crews. Most of the principal provincial towns had quarries within about ten miles which provided their building materials. Bristol drew its paving stones from Bristleton Common near Keynsham. Exeter obtained most of its stone from Hevitree on the outskirts of the city, but imported some of harder quality from Exmoor, some thirty miles away. Roofing materials of high quality were transported considerable distances. The slates quarried at Delabole in North Cornwall were famous, and were exported through Padstow and Port Isaac.

In the early eighteenth century most of the slate quarries of North Wales were small and situated on tracts of common. Production was steadily increasing and markets were widening—between June 1729 and December 1730 two-and-a-half million slates were exported from the four harbours of Caernarvon, Beaumaris, Conway and Holyhead—but the trade was haphazardly organized and production was spasmodic. Settlements on some of the commons became colonies of craftsmen rather than of quarrymen. The agent to the Penrhyn estate wrote in 1734:

> all the old workmen had in a manner left off, seeing that nobody took care to promote a trade, and betook themselves to cobbling, weaving and other little businesses to get bread, so that half of the houses usually inhabited by Quarrymen are now held by people that are quite strangers to the business.[14]

Bricks and roofing tiles were made wherever coal was available to fire them. In rural areas coal was often transported to a building site, and bricks made from clay dug up locally. Around every expanding town, particularly to the north of London, there were ragged skirts of brick pits and kilns.

The early eighteenth century saw a period of steady expansion in the metal mines of England and Wales, although since they were situated in remote places they often escaped the attention of travellers. The mining of copper ore in Cornwall expanded considerably. The copper industry had declined in the seventeenth century, but by 1700 ore from Cornwall was being taken to Redbrook in the Forest of Dean and to Bristol to be smelted with coal. The principal entrepreneur in the revival of the trade was John Coster, who worked the smelter at Redbrook, and in 1714 patented a water-powered system of draining mines, which enabled the exploitation of deeper lodes of ore in Cornwall. By 1720 about six thousand tons of copper a year were being produced in Cornwall, and the same year saw the erection of what was probably the first Newcomen engine in the county at Wheal Fortune. About the same time the smelting of Cornish copper ore commenced in the Swansea area. The Newcomen engine was expensive to operate at a distance from a coal source, but the engines of the Cornish copper mines were fired with Welsh coal brought by ships which returned to Swansea or Neath with cargoes of ore.

Tin mining in Cornwall was one of the most regulated branches of industry in Britain. The trade was controlled by the stannary courts which met in certain Cornish towns. It was through these towns alone that tin could be exported, and then only when it was in three hundredweight blocks bearing an official stamp. Tin was obtained by mining in the conventional way, working down a lode of ore, or by 'streaming', washing out fragments of tin from the alluvium in river valleys. Many Cornish valleys were given over to the streaming process, in which increasingly complex arrays of dipper wheels, round tables and vibrating tables were coming into use. Even the simplest form of streaming, swilling the alluvium in a pan, used considerable quantities of water, and the valleys were braided with water-courses taking water to the works for washing or for turning the waterwheels. The restored works at Tolgus, the scene of stream working for several centuries, gives a good impression of the operation.

Most of the stream tin went to old-fashioned 'blowing houses' for smelting:

> a rude structure, probably of rock and turf, with a thatched
> roof, the whole being so inexpensive that it was burned down
> to save the particles of tin which the blast had driven up into the
> thatch.

It was usually a charcoal-fired granite furnace, with bellows driven by a small waterwheel, the molten tin flowing from the furnace into granite moulds. Before 1700 there were also reverberatory coal-fired smelters in Cornwall, which became more common as the working of lode mines increased. The important smelter at Calenick near Truro was founded in 1711. Before smelting the tin ore was reduced to a powder by water-powered stamps, the appearance and noise of which were characteristic features of the Cornish industrial landscape.[15]

Celia Fiennes was much impressed by a smelter near St Austell in 1698:

> they take the ore and pound it in a stamping mill which
> resembles the paper mills, and when its fine as the finest sand

> . . . this they fling into a furnace and with it coale to make the
> fire, so it burns together and makes a violent heat and fierce
> flame, the mettle by the fire being separate from the coal and its
> owne drosse, being heavy, falls down to a trench made to
> receive it . . . I went a mile farther on the hills and soe came
> where they were diggin in the Tinn mines, there was at least 20
> mines all in sight which employs a great many people at work.

Richard Pococke, some half a century later, travelled:

> from St Blazey to Grampound, which is a tin country, we found
> the soil very indifferent, and covered with heath.

West of Truro he:

> entered on a wild heathy country, and came in three miles to
> Chasewater, a country of tin and copper. Each mine has two
> shafts divided by timbers – the ladder shaft and the wem shaft,
> with a wem or windlass for raising and lowering the tub or
> kibble, and a fire engine shaft for raising water.

In Cornwall, as in Snowdonia, the Potteries, the Black Country and
the West Riding, industry flourished on the open heaths.

Some copper was mined outside Cornwall. The mine at Ecton in
North Staffordshire was already celebrated in the early eighteenth
century, its ore being smelted at Cheadle. There were mines at Alderley
Edge in Cheshire from which ore was sent to Macclesfield and War-
rington. In 1750 Richard Pococke observed disused copper mines at
Caldbeck, west of Carlisle.

The largest metal mines outside Cornwall were those from which
lead was extracted. Lead workings were widely dispersed, in the
Mendips, the western part of Derbyshire, the Yorkshire Dales and in
every county in Wales, where Defoe found Aberystwyth 'a populous
but very dirty, black smoaky place' on account of the lead workings.
Many workings were still of a very primitive kind in the early eighteenth century. Prominent features of the landscapes of Wensleydale
and Swaledale are the remnants of 'hushes', soil dams formed on the
tops of hills. Water was released from them suddenly, to cut trenches
in the soil of the hillside below and create a pile of topsoil at the
bottom. The trench might reveal the existence of veins of ore in the hill,
while lead fragments might be found among the debris at the bottom.[16] In Derbyshire most mines remained shallow because it was
believed that ores deteriorated as lodes were pursued deeper into the
earth. Horse gins were scarce in the county in the early eighteenth

century, the most common form of winding being by a simple wind-lass. Drainage soughs in Derbyshire were highly sophisticated, and several mines had Newcomen pumping engines. Most of the mining district of Derbyshire consisted of scattered settlements on commons. One visitor to Winster observed:

> Innumerable cottages are scattered on the sides of the hills. . . .
> Culture is generally extended to the tops of the mountain. . . .
> The miners employ those hours which are not spent in subter-raneous work or necessary refreshment . . . in clearing the ground for the plough.

Ore-bearing rock was broken with hammers near the mine, and the resulting particles washed in a sieve held in a tub of water to separate the ore, and then washed again in a buddle to remove the lighter non-metallic fragments. Some Derbyshire ore was smelted in wood-fired hearths, powered by the swift streams running eastwards off the Pennines, but by the 1730s coal burning cupola smelters were in use in the county.

The rivers were the main means of inland transport in England in the early eighteenth century, and goods were carried vast distances overland to the principal river ports. Defoe wrote in about 1720 that:

> The Thames is the channel for conveying an infinite quantity of provisions from remote counties to London, and enriching all the counties again that lye near it; by the return of wealth and trade from the city.

At Reading he watched huge barges which had sailed up the river from London lightening their loads before proceeding upstream, having brought coal, salt, groceries or tobacco from the capital. The return cargoes were chiefly malt and meal, with some timber from the Berk-shire woodlands. At Marlow he noted that malt and meal from High Wycombe were loaded, together with beech wood from the Chilterns, and the varied produce of the great concentration of mills in the vicinity. He observed a similarly heavy trade on the Ouse at Bedford. At Nottingham he watched the importation of salt, hemp, flax and iron from the Baltic, and a downstream traffic in lead, coal, wood, corn and cheese. Bawtry he found to be 'the centre of all the exporta-tion of this part of the country, especially for heavy goods' among which he quoted lead, edge-tools and millstones.

The Severn was navigable for about a hundred and forty miles from the sea to Pool Quay near Welshpool, where its passage was blocked

41

by a weir built in the Middle Ages by the monks of Strata Marcella Abbey. Bewdley and Bridgnorth, the main ports on the middle section of the river, received goods by packhorse and waggon for dispatch downstream from as far away as Manchester and Hanley. Many of the Severn's tributaries were navigable, the Avon to Stratford, the Wye to Hereford and even to Hay, and portions of the Stour and the Teme.

The Great Ouse Navigation was steadily improved during the late seventeenth and early eighteenth centuries, although there was constant disagreement between those who wished to use it for commercial navigation and those who wanted to employ it to drain the surrounding fens. An act for improving the Ouse itself was obtained in 1720, but the Lark was the subject of legislation in 1700, the Cam in 1702 and the Nene in 1714 and 1725. Many of the drains were also navigable, and numerous villages in Cambridgeshire, Bedfordshire and Huntingdonshire had their own wharves or hythes where such commodities as wine, Scandinavian timber, salt and bricks were handled.[17]

Many riverside landscapes had few man-made features. Some rivers, like the Severn and the Wye, lacked even towpaths so that horses could not be used for upstream haulage. At Worcester Celia Fiennes observed the Severn 'on which were many Barges that were tow'd up by the strength of men, six or eight at a time'. On such rivers the shallows were improved only informally by the users. Navigation was only possible when the water level was sufficiently high, and long periods were spent awaiting rain. It is a measure of the relatively slow pace of economic activity that the iron trade of the West Midlands was able to accommodate the delays caused by the Severn's lack of water.

On some rivers the shallows could be passed by locks. The pound lock had been known in England in the sixteenth century, but it was still a comparatively unusual feature of the riverside landscape in 1700. While a pound lock has two sets of gates to pass boats from one level to another, a flash lock has only one, its purpose being to release a 'flash' of water to carry boats over shallows below, and to impound it to help them over the reach above. On rivers like the Thames, where there were numerous mills as well as flash locks, there were frequent conflicts between millers and boatmen over the opening of the locks. A survey in the late 1960s shows that there were as many as seventy flash locks on the Thames between London and Cricklade, although not all were necessarily in operation at the same time. While four pound locks had been built on the river in the early seventeenth century, most changes of level were still achieved by flash locks. Other navigations on which flash locks were found were the rivers running into the Wash and some of the tributaries of the Severn. Some flash locks were simply removable portions of mill weirs, with a wooden sill across the river bed and a horizontal swinging beam directly over the sill at water level. Vertical baulks or 'rimers' were set against these timbers, and square planks or paddles placed against them. The top ends of the paddle and rimer handles were controlled by a horizontal guide bar. The guide bar, the paddles and the rimers would be removed when the lock was opened for boats, and then the main beam would be swung open, letting through a great torrent of water which would carry with it boats going downstream. Boats going upstream would be hauled through with the assistance of winches. By the early eighteenth century some flash locks were neater structures with stone abutment walls.[18]

There were no locks of any kind on the Severn, but at intervals along the river were fish weirs, wickerwork dams with traps in them for catching fish. Some at least dated from the Middle Ages. It was impossible for barges to pass through such weirs and bypass channels were dug around them, creating islands which can still be seen in the river.

Many rivers were improved in the early eighteenth century by the construction of pound locks and towpaths, particularly in areas where mines and manufactures flourished. The Act of Parliament for the Aire and Calder Navigation in Yorkshire was obtained in 1689. In 1726 the River Don was made navigable upstream from Homstile near Doncaster, and in 1751 it was completed to a wharf at Tinsley near Sheffield. In the late seventeenth century Thomas Patten eliminated the shallows and weirs on the Mersey below Warrington, and in 1721 acts were obtained for the improvement of the Weaver and of the Mersey and Irwell above Warrington. To the north of London the Lea Navigation Act of 1739 improved the navigation to such places as Ware and Broxbourne. The River Tone was made navigable from Bridgwater to Taunton under an act of 1717.

Attempts were made to utilize some of the most obscure English rivers. At the confluence of the River Tern and the Severn in Shropshire a lock large enough to allow the passage of boats of 23 feet by 7 feet 8 inches was excavated in 1969.[19] It was probably constructed in the early eighteenth century to allow vessels to proceed several miles up the Tern to forges at Attingham and Upton Magna. On the Dick Brook which flows into the Severn about three miles below Stourport are the

remains of two flash locks, one of them bearing the date 1715. The
valley has a varied industrial history. A charcoal blast furnace was in
use in the mid seventeenth century. A site on the stream was used in the
eighteenth century as a fulling mill, a paper mill, a flint mill, an iron
forge and a bobbin mill. The locks are built of sandstone blocks and
would have admitted boats up to 10 feet 9 inches in beam. One of the
far reaches of the Thames was the River Cherwell where, in the first
decade of the eighteenth century, a local landowner, Sanderson Miller,
operated a service of flat-bottomed boats from Oxford to Banbury,
over twenty miles from the confluence with the Thames.

Eighteenth-century views of ports and wharves on navigable rivers
give an impression of unhurried disorder. Quaysides in towns were
often littered with casks, barrels and packages in a degree of confusion
which suggests exactly the propensity to lose goods in transit which is
found in documents relating to the river navigations. At many unloading points there were no wharves. Bulk goods were shovelled into carts
drawn by horses into shallow water, while packages were roughly
manhandled ashore.

Large quantities of goods were also conveyed by coastal shipping.
Few creeks or inlets remotely hospitable to vessels were unused, and
many places which have long ceased to be regarded as ports had quite
important overseas trading connections. All round the coast of southern England ports like Whitstable and Littlehampton sent agricultural
produce to London. In East Anglia such small ports as Wells traded
with the Netherlands as well as with the capital. Minehead, Padstow
and Cardigan shared in the Irish trade. Bridport traded with New-
foundland. There were eighteen Acts of Parliament concerned with the
improvement of harbours between 1700 and 1750, some for major
ports like Liverpool and Plymouth, but others for places as small as
Watchett and Whitby. One of the most impressive ports was Whitehaven, developed in the 1670s and 1680s by Sir John Lowther, which
continued to grow rapidly in the eighteenth century, its population
rising from 2222 in 1693 to 9063 in 1762. To the coal trade, for which
it was originally built, was added considerable overseas business,
particularly the import of tobacco. Whitehaven was built to a grid
plan, with most of the original houses having three storeys, its
piers were lined with warehouses and there was a church and a
windmill.

Not all goods were carried in boats, however. The cloth trade, in
particular, used road transport over considerable distances, even

where there were alternative waterways. Road carriage steadily increased in the eighteenth century. Many towns at road junctions or river crossings gained much of their substance from what was called the thoroughfare trade—the provision of food, horses and accommodation to travellers.

Under the Tudor statutes for the maintenance of highways the cost of maintaining roads was the responsibility of the parish, which was answerable to the Quarter Sessions. While the system was tolerably just when it applied to roads used by local residents, it was manifestly unjust to those who lived in parishes charged with the upkeep of the great main roads. In the second half of the seventeenth century a system was evolved by which the cost of such main roads was transferred from those who lived near them to those who used them. Tolls were collected at gates or turnpikes, and these roads were thus known as turnpike roads. By Acts of Parliament powers were granted to bodies of trustees to set up gates for the collection of tolls at specified rates, the income from which was to be used for the upkeep and improvement of the roads; powers were also granted for the acquisition of land and road metals. Some thirty-seven such acts were passed before 1720, of which twenty-five applied to roads within forty miles of London. There was a boom in turnpiking in the 1720s, when forty-six acts were passed. These early acts applied mostly to the radial roads from London to the main provincial centres, almost all of which were controlled by turnpike trusts by 1750. During the 1720s the first 'town-centred' trusts were set up, controlling networks of roads radiating from such market towns as Bristol, Worcester and Hereford. Only twenty-four new acts were passed in the 1730s, but there were thirty-nine in the following decade.[20]

To what extent the early turnpike trusts altered the landscape is uncertain. Defoe regarded them as successful. 'Very great things are done by them,' he wrote, and he described the routes from London to Harwich and Ipswich:

> These roads were formerly deep, in times of floods dangerous, and at other times, in winter scarce passable; they are now so firm, so safe, so easy to travellers, and carriages as well as cattle, that no road in England can yet be said to equal them.

It is doubtful whether many turnpike trusts used their powers to construct entirely new roads before 1750. Most of the routes they took over were ancient and well-established, and beyond the improvement of surfaces by metalling and draining, and perhaps a little embanking and cutting, the appearance of the roads was little altered. Cottages were built for toll collectors alongside the gates, and most turnpike roads were lined with milestones. Road travel remained very slow. In spite of the turnpiking of the main roads from London it still took several days in 1750 for a carriage to travel to a city a hundred and fifty miles away, and a heavy waggon often needed as much as two weeks for a similar journey.

Many of the goods which people used—the clothes they wore, the shoes on their feet, the tools they used in their trades, the plates and pots in their kitchens—were made in market towns. In 1700 there were between forty and fifty towns in England with populations between 2000 and 5000, and about thirty with more than 5000. Most towns in the latter category were concerned with the supply of goods of some kind to markets beyond their own hinterlands. There were shoemakers, tailors and blacksmiths in most towns, but in London and the main provincial centres like Exeter, Norwich and Bury St Edmunds there were more sophisticated trades, pewterers, makers of tinware and sword cutlers. Brewing and malting prospered in most market towns, and the London breweries were probably the largest manufacturing enterprises in Britain making a product which was actually sold to customers.

The leather trades were particularly well-established in towns in regions where there was extensive pastoral farming and where there were woodlands to yield large quantities of bark. Tanning in towns like Liskeard, Kendal, Bewdley and Burton on Trent was of more than local significance. Tanneries with pits for the washing and liming of skins, yards with stone tables for scrubbing and warehouses for drying skins were among the most commonplace manufactories of early eighteenth-century towns. Francis Chaplain of Lichfield, who died in 1671, left in his tanyard 'in the cisterns, handlers, masterings and lymes, and ready dryed lether worth two hundred and twenty foure pounds', as well as bark worth £20 and hand tools worth £2. Some tanners worked in rural areas. John Waylett of Writtle in Essex, who died in the late 1680s, left skins worth over £400 in his tanyard, with wheelbarrows, knives, weighbeams, a grindstone and a pile of horns. Sometimes such horns were used to build boundary walls. John Higgins from Richards Castle in Herefordshire, who died in 1726, had a tanyard alongside a stream which flowed towards the River Teme at a point where it was crossed by a main road. He left skins and leather worth over £200 in and about the tanhouse, together with horns and hair, weights and scales and a bark mill.[21]

The English and Welsh woodlands were a source of raw materials for many manufacturing processes. The best timbers were used for shipbuilding and house construction, and were taken from the remotest parts of the country by road to the coast or the nearest navigable water. Defoe records that quantities of oaks were floated down the Arun, and taken on the Test and Itchen to Southampton. Rafts made up of Welsh oaks were frequently floated down the Severn. In the Wyre Forest oak bark was taken to the tanneries of Bewdley, and oak timbers hauled there for boatbuilding. Oak and birch were coppiced on cycles of about eighteen years for charcoal burning, as in many other parts of Britain. Brooms and brushes were made of birch

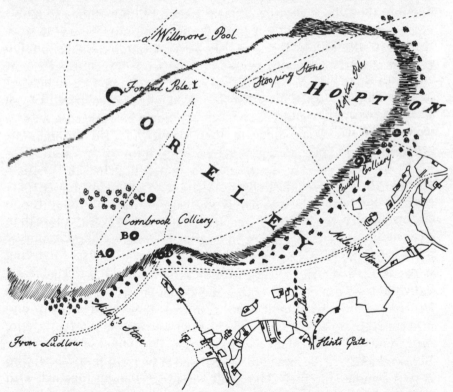

Figure 3 Coal mining on the common in the parish of Coreley on Titterstone Clee Hill, Shropshire, c. 1770. The dotted line from left to right is the turnpike road from Ludlow to Cleobury Mortimer and Bewdley. The Forked Pole is still a prominent landmark on the hill.
(*Redrawn from the Craven Estate Map*)

twigs, and small pieces of oak were split to make skets for use in the mines of the Black Country. Crates were made for the North Stafford-shire potters and sent as return loads on waggons which brought wares from Hanley to Bewdley. In Hertfordshire alders were grown in water meadows and the wood from them was used for turning dishes and bowls, making clogs, and for hurdles and chair frames. A Swedish visitor to the Home Counties in 1748 noted the use of holly for toys, and the handles of whips and knives, and observed the cultivation of box trees on the Duke of Bridgewater's estate in the Chilterns for sale to the London turners.

The open commons provided accommodation for workers in mines, ironworks and other major manufacturing concerns. They were also areas where consumer goods were made. The process of squatting on common land began in the sixteenth century. Sometimes squatters erected cottages in plots on the side of a common, sometimes on 'islands' in the middle. It was widely believed that if a house could be erected in one night, with smoke coming from the chimney before sunrise, the cottager had established a right to remain. Often the lords of manors tacitly encouraged such settlement, particularly if labour was needed in the vicinity. Squatters could not be charged a rent for the use of common land, but they could be fined annually for encroachment. Their cottages were usually set in plots of about an acre, enclosed by a hedged earthen bank in which such useful plants as the damson, the hazel, the holly and the rowan would be planted. Such settlements became the nuclei of large-scale industries in areas like the Black Country, the Forest of Dean and the Potteries. Others remained as service centres, providing goods and such services as well-digging or carting for the surrounding areas.

Squatters made their living from a variety of sources. They culti-vated their own plots and grazed their own beasts on the commons, but they could also exploit other resources there. In Cartmell com-moners were able to take bracken, furze, wood, peat, clay, rushes, nuts, juniper berries, slate and limestone. On Ivinghoe Common in Buckinghamshire they dug flints, quarried gravel, cut furze and bound it into bundles for fuel. Above all squatters were craftsmen. They became shoemakers, tailors or weavers. They dug pebbles from under the clay. They filled carts with sand and took it to building sites. They kept bees and sold the honey. Their wives baked cakes and acted as midwives. Such communities were of great importance in the estab-lishment of major industries.

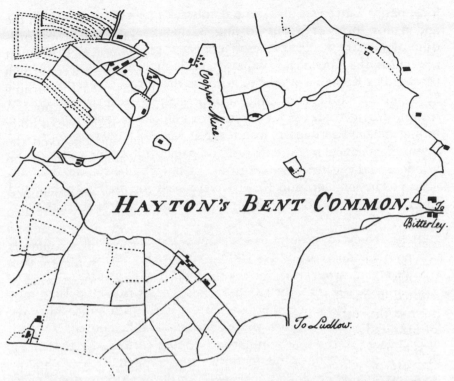

Figure 4 The landscape of industrial squatter settlements: Hayton's Bent Common in the parish of Stanton Lacy, Shropshire, *c.* 1770. Several squatters' cottages in small enclosures are scattered around the edges of the common, and there are two 'island' encroachments in the middle. The small copper mine doubtless provided employment for some of the squatters. *(Redrawn from the Craven Estate Map)*

By contrast many enterprises of the early eighteenth century were promoted by landlords. At Malton Celia Fiennes noted that her kinswoman, Mary Palmes, had used the outbuildings of a demolished mansion 'for weaving . . . having set up a manufactory for Linen which does employ many poor people'. At Ashridge in Buckinghamshire the Duke of Bridgewater had a large brickyard, where beech twigs and bracken bound in bundles were used as fuel. Lord Burlington was responsible for building a smelting house for the lead mines outside Girsington in Yorkshire.

Water was perhaps the most characteristic feature of the industrial landscape of the early eighteenth century. River barges and coastal shipping carried most goods which were marketed on more than a

49

local basis. Water was an essential source of power for many mines and in most forms of manufacturing. Many of the greatest concentrations of industry were at places where water power was abundant. In the 1720s the Greenfield Valley near Holywell in Flintshire was thronged by Roman Catholic pilgrims to the miracle-working well of St Winifred, but the cold, mineral-impregnated stream which flowed from it provided power for three corn mills, two snuff mills and a fulling mill, and perhaps an iron forge as well.[22] Defoe was impressed by the great concentration of corn and paper mills in the valley of the Loddon, and the remarkable group of brass mills on the Thames nearby. The mills around Kendal were used for making paper and snuff, rasping logwood and grinding box irons cast at the Lakeland ironworks.

By 1750 most of those areas which were to become major centres of mining or manufacturing by 1800 were already industrialized to a considerable degree. There were some industrial units of considerable size: Lombes' silk mill, the Coalbrookdale ironworks, the Tean tape mills, the Tanfield Lea collieries. In areas like South Lancashire, the Black Country, the Potteries, the hills around Halifax and the Redruth district there were large populations almost entirely dependent for their livings on mines and manufactures, even if they worked in relatively small units and maintained some links with farming. There were, nevertheless, few districts where mines and manufactures dominated the landscape, and few which were noticeably polluted. Trades and manufactures were normally seen as socially useful activities which ensured that the poor could find a living. Dr Richard Pococke described Prescot in Lancashire as:

> a little town delightfully situated on a hill, its steeple, windmill, glasshouses and earthenware houses render it a very beautiful point of view at two or three miles distance.

To foreign visitors in the early eighteenth century Britain appeared to be a busy, thriving, trading and manufacturing nation—but there were few sights in its manufacturing regions which would have been altogether unfamiliar to a Walloon, a Silesian, an Alsatian, a Dalarnan or any other traveller from industrialized provinces. It was in the decades after 1750 that the landscape of industrial Britain became one which was, for a time, altogether unique.

References

1   A.P. Wadsworth and J.de L. Mann, *The Cotton Trade and Industrial Lancashire 1600–1750* (1931, rep. 1965).
2   S.D. Chapman, *The Early Factory Masters* (1967).
3   A.H. Shorter, *Paper Making in the British Isles* (1971).
4   Ernest Straker, *Wealden Iron* (1931, rep. 1967).
5   David Hey, *The Rural Metalworkers of the Sheffield Region* (1972).
6   Knight Papers, Kidderminster Public Library.
7   E. Wyndham Hulme, 'The Statistical History of the Iron Trade, 1717–1750' in *Transactions of the Newcomen Society*, XI (1928–9).
8   Norman Mutton, 'Charlcott Furnace' in *Transactions of the Shropshire Archaeological Society*, LVIII (1965–8).
9   Barrie Trinder, *The Industrial Revolution in Shropshire* (1973).
10 M.J.T. Lewis, *Early Wooden Railways* (1970).
11 Probate Records, Hereford Record Office.
12 J.S. Allen and L.T.C. Rolt, *The Steam Engine of Thomas Newcomen* (1977).
13 A.W.A. White, *Men and Mining in Warwickshire* (1970).
14 Jean Lindsey, *The History of the North Wales Slate Industry* (1974).
15 D. Bradford Barton, *A History of Tin Mining and Smelting in Cornwall* (1967).
16 Arthur Raistrick, *The West Riding of Yorkshire* (1970).
17 Dorothy Summers, *The Great Ouse: the history of a River Navigation* (1973).
18 M.J.T. Lewis, W.N. Slatcher and P.N. Jarvis, 'Flashlocks on English Waterways: a survey', *Industrial Archaeology*, VI (1969).
19 J.H. Denton and M.J.T. Lewis, 'The River Tern Navigation', *Journal of the Railway and Canal Historical Society*, XXIII (1977).
20 William Albert, *The Turnpike Road System in England 1663–1840* (1972).
21 D.G. Vaisey, *Probate Inventories of Lichfield and District 1568–1680* (1969).
22 K. Davies and C.J. Williams, *The Greenfield Valley* (1977).

3 A Landscape of Economic Growth, 1750–90

Before 1750 the impact of mines and manufactures on the English landscape scarcely differed in kind from what could be seen in other prosperous parts of Europe. By 1790 foreigners visited Britain in order to see evidence of industrial growth on a scale which seemed altogether remarkable and the subject of wonder. However much the arguments about the origins of the Industrial Revolution may be qualified, no one could deny that considerable structural changes took place between 1750 and 1790. Population began to increase at a faster rate. A new pattern of financial institutions, particularly the linked network of country banks, was established. Foreign trade started to grow, especially after the conclusion of the American War of Independence. The pace of innovation in manufacturing industry began to quicken.

Similar changes may be observed in the history of the English landscape. Whether or not there were industrial landscapes before 1750 is a matter of debate and definition. By 1790 there were areas wholly given over to manufacturing where kilns, furnaces, engine houses, headstocks, railways, canals and workers' housing totally dominated the landscape. Many of the characteristic features of the landscape of the Industrial Revolution first appeared during the forty years after 1750; the cotton mill, the narrow canal, the iron railway, the Boulton and Watt steam engine. Some changes were the direct consequence of technological innovation. Others occurred because of the uneven pace of growth. One section of an industry might expand established ways of working in order to keep pace with increased production resulting from innovation in a related sector. The development of cotton spinning mills vastly increased the numbers of domestic handloom weavers. For a time the multiplication of coke-fired, steam-powered blast furnaces stimulated the building of charcoal-using, water-powered forges. Other changes in the landscape were the consequence of new forms of organization rather than of new

52

technology. There were few tasks performed at Matthew Boulton's great Soho Manufactory in Birmingham which could not have been undertaken in one of that town's water mills or back street workshops. What was new was the work discipline, the control of quality and the new potential for marketing which came from organization in a larger unit.

During the second half of the eighteenth century mines and manufactures were seen in a new light,—as objects of curiosity, as sources of national wealth, as picturesque vistas which could inspire horror in the same way as mountains or rocky seashores. William Bray, during a tour of the Midlands in 1777, noted that the Lombes' silk mill at Derby then employed two hundred people 'to the great relief and comfort of the poor'. In his second edition, written in 1783, he observed that so many visitors went to the mill that money was collected from them:

> the money given by strangers is put into a box which is opened the day after Michaelmas Day and a feast is made; an ox is killed, liquor prepared, the windows are illuminated and the men, women and children employed in the work, dressed in their best array, enjoy, in dancing and decent mirth, a holiday, the expectation of which lightens the labour of the rest of the year.

Numerous travel books were published in the closing years of the eighteenth century. Robert Southey observed that every Englishman who spent the summer in any of the mountainous provinces or went to Paris for six weeks published an account of his travels, and in many such accounts there are also descriptions of the great visitor-attractions of early industrial Britain—Etruria, Soho, Coalbrookdale, the Bridgewater Canal or New Lanark. Artists paid increasing attention to industrial subjects and many of their pictures were engraved and widely sold. It was in this period that the industrial landscape was recognized and defined.

The construction of canals had the most wide-ranging effect on the landscape of this period. William Bray remarked of the Trent and Mersey Canal:

> these undertakings strongly mark the spirit of enterprise, so characteristic of the present age. Their advantages to trade are immense, and in different respects every country is benefitted through which they pass.

The building of navigable canals came late in Britain. The first major artificial water in Britain, the Newry Canal, was constructed in Ireland between 1730 and 1744, well over a decade before there was any comparable waterway in England. The development of English canals began in Lancashire. An Act of Parliament was obtained in 1755 on the initiative of some Liverpool merchants, ostensibly to improve the navigation of the Sankey Brook, but in effect to build a canal from the mining area subsequently called St Helens to the River Mersey, a work completed in 1757. Parliamentary hostility to the building of new cuts led to the pretence that the work was a river improvement, but by any sensible definition it was a canal. However, the new waterway did closely follow the line of the brook. By contrast the Bridgewater Canal from Worsley to Manchester, which received parliamentary sanction in 1759, cut across the natural routes.

The Bridgewater Canal was a seigniorial enterprise, an attempt instigated by John Gilbert, agent to Francis Egerton, third Duke of Bridgewater, to increase the income from his master's estate and thereby reduce the burden of debts which the Duke had acquired in his youth. The mines on the Worsley estate to the north-west of Manchester were old-established and were drained by inadequate soughs. The canal was part of a wide-ranging scheme of improvement. It was completed to Manchester in 1761, cutting across Trafford Moss, an ill-drained area where lost cattle were occasionally swallowed up, and triumphantly bridging the River Irwell at Barton. At Worsley the canal ran right into the mine workings while at Castle Field, on the edge of Manchester, it ran beneath a hill; containers of coal were lifted from the boats in the tunnel up a shaft to the terminus at the top of the hill by means of a windlass powered by a waterwheel. In 1762 a further Act of Parliament was obtained to build a canal from a junction with the existing line at Longford Bridge, Stretford, to the River Mersey, providing a route to Liverpool, the first artificial waterway to be of regional rather than purely local significance.

The Bridgewater Canal became an object of admiration, a scene to be visited and described, particularly after 1766 when passenger boats began to carry tourists from Manchester to explore the mines at Worsley. Jean-Jacques Rousseau and the King of Denmark were among foreign visitors who made the journey. After the canal was completed to a junction with the Trent and Mersey at Preston Brook in 1776, a passenger service was established between Liverpool and Manchester. A tourist who travelled in the Duke's passage boat in

1785 noted that there were two cabins for the accommodation of different classes, and that in the event of improper conduct by passengers, the master was under instruction to set them down on the bank and return their fares.

The Bridgewater Canal set the pattern for two distinct types of waterway which were constructed during what may be described as the first canal age. This lasted until about 1790, and about a thousand miles of canal were built. The Bridgewater Canal's first section, from Worsley to Manchester, was essentially a local concern, built to carry coal from the mines to the market place, and while it was authorized by an Act of Parliament, since it crossed properties other than the Duke's, it was in effect a private waterway serving the estate. By contrast the line to the Mersey was of regional, even national, significance, for it provided a connection far superior to the existing Mersey and Irwell Navigation between the centre of the expanding cotton industry and its principal port.

Many of the canals built before 1790 were, like the first portion of the Bridgewater, of no more than local significance, even if they served mines and manufactories of national importance. Frequently such canals were constructed by individual landlords or industrial partnerships purely for their own purposes. The Donnington Wood Canal in the Shropshire coalfield was a tub-boat system built in the mid 1760s by Bridgewater's brother-in-law Earl Gower, his agent John Gilbert and Gower's agent Thomas Gilbert; it linked Gower's mines at Donnington Wood with his limestone quarries at Lilleshall and with a retail coal wharf at Pave Lane on the Newport–Wolverhampton road. The canal was the first of a series of tub-boat waterways which crossed the Coalbrookdale coalfield by the mid 1790s, linking its principal ironworks with the Severn Navigation. Sir Nigel Gresley's Canal was built in 1775–6 to connect collieries at Apedale with Newcastle under Lyme, three miles away. Sir John Glynne's Canal, built in 1768, carried coal from mines in Flintshire into the city of Chester. The St Columb Canal was constructed in the 1770s to take sea sand for use as manure to improve 'many thousand acres of barren and unprofitable ground' on the north coast of Cornwall. The three-mile-long Kymers Canal, built in the late 1760s, took coal from Pwllyllgod in the coalfield west of Llanelly to the town of Kidwelly. Such canals carried boats of limited size, and in most cases were built cheaply, with few if any locks or other major engineering works.

55

Long before the Liverpool line of the Bridgewater Canal was completed it was linked with other schemes, which by 1790 created the much-heralded 'Silver Cross' linking the four main estuary navigations of southern Britain. In 1766 an Act of Parliament was obtained for the Trent and Mersey Canal, which was eventually opened eleven years later, extending over ninety-three miles from a junction with the Bridgewater at Preston Brook near Runcorn to Derwent Mouth on the navigable Trent. The initial impetus for the canal had come from the Potteries, where Josiah Wedgwood and other master potters sought improved communications with the Mersey, the Humber and the Severn. The concern was supported by Earl Gower, whose Trentham estate lay along its route, and by Birmingham and Liverpool interests as well as by the Duke of Bridgewater. Its engineer, until his death in 1772, was James Brindley. At Great Haywood near Stafford the Trent and Mersey was joined by the Staffordshire and Worcestershire Canal, extending over forty-six miles to Lower Mitton on the River Severn, close to the confluence of the Worcestershire Stour, where the new town of Stourport subsequently grew up. The Staffordshire and Worcestershire was opened in 1772, being joined outside Wolverhampton by the Birmingham Canal, which had received parliamentary sanction in 1768 and been opened as far as Wednesbury the following year, amid much celebration of the cheap coal which it carried to Birmingham from the Black Country:

> So quick in performing this mighty affair,
> So great was the industry, prudence and care,
> Eighteen months have scarce run
> Since the work was begun.
> How pleasing the sight!
> What a scene of delight!
> As the barges come floating along.
>
> What relief in the fare
> Of all heavy ware,
> When the whole undertaking is finished!
> In affairs what a turn,
> When cattle and corn
> In their rates shall be greatly diminished.
>
> Since by the Canal Navigation
> Of coals we've the best in the nation,
> Around the gay circle your bumpers then put,
> For the cut of all cuts is the Birmingham cut.[1]

At Fradley Junction near Lichfield the Trent and Mersey was joined by the Coventry Canal, authorized in 1768 and extending thirty-two miles to the city of Coventry. At Longford this was joined in turn to the Oxford Canal, also sanctioned in 1768, which linked it with the River Thames at Oxford. The building of the Oxford Canal was much delayed, and it was not until 1790 that the first vessels sailed through to the Thames. By that year all the four principal estuary navigation systems—the Mersey, the Humber, the Thames and the Severn—were linked by inland waterways. The two latter rivers were directly connected by the Thames and Severn Canal, completed in 1789, which, with the Stroudwater Navigation, enabled broad-beamed vessels to sail from Framilode below Gloucester to Lechlade above Oxford. The Mersey and Humber were in process of being connected by the Leeds and Liverpool Canal, authorized in 1770. It was not completed until 1816, although some portions became important local waterways long before through-navigation was possible. Most of these waterways could only accommodate boats with a seven-foot beam, while most river navigations were worked by vessels up to fourteen feet wide. This narrow gauge hampered the efficient operation of the waterways system since it meant that goods had to be transhipped at the points where the narrow canals joined the river navigations. However, it might never have been possible to raise sufficient capital to build some canals to a broad gauge.

The trunk canals were linked by numerous branches to important mining and manufacturing centres. The Dudley and Stourbridge Canals, built in the late 1770s, connected some of the richest mining areas of the Black Country with the Staffordshire and Worcestershire Canal. The Cromford and Erewash Canals linked the navigable Trent with some of the important cotton mills in the Derwent Valley. The Chesterfield Canal connected the same river to the town from which it took its name, and was opened to traffic in 1777. The Caldon Canal, completed in 1779, ran seventeen-and-a-half miles from a junction with the Trent and Mersey in the Potteries to the great limestone rocks at Caldon. Some market towns were linked with navigable water by short dead-end canals: Driffield, for example, gained access to the River Hull by a five-mile-long canal built in 1770. Canals built in this period which served neither a source of mineral wealth nor the needs of long-distance navigation rarely prospered. The Chester Canal between Chester and Nantwich, completed in 1779, had a difficult struggle for existence before it was connected with other waterways.

THE 'SILVER CROSS' CANALS

Manchester
Runcorn
BRIDGEWATER
Preston Brook
R. Trent
TRENT
AND
MERSEY
Nottingham
Shardlow
Great Haywood
Derwentmouth
Fradley
Aldersley
Fazeley
R. Severn
Birmingham
COVENTRY CANAL
Stourport
OXFORD CANAL
Framilode
Stroud
Lechlade
Oxford
London
THAMES
AND
SEVERN
R. Thames

Kms 0   30   60   90   120
Miles 0   30   60

Figure 5 The 'Silver Cross' canals which linked the four main English river estuary navigations, the last link of which was completed in 1790

The impact of the first generation of canals on the landscape was considerable. Most narrow canals twisted around the hills to such an extent that some needed to be straightened in subsequent generations. They crossed river valleys on embankments and lumbered over rivers on brick or stone aqueducts made somewhat ungainly in appearance by the three or four feet of puddled clay needed to seal their bottoms from leakages. They climbed watersheds by pound locks, sometimes grouped in staircases, like the great flight of twenty-two on the Birmingham Canal near its junction with the Staffordshire and Worcestershire at Aldersley, and sometimes widely scattered. They were crossed by main roads on arched brick or stone bridges, and by farm tracks on accommodation bridges of various kinds—lifting bridges on the Oxford and cantilevered split bridges on the Staffordshire and Worcestershire. Thomas Pennant wrote of the Trent and Mersey Canal about 1780:

> The cottage, instead of being covered with miserable thatch, is now secured with a substantial covering of tiles or slates, brought from the distant hills of Wales or Cumberland. The fields, which before were barren, are now drained, and by the assistance of manure, conveyed on the canal toll-free, are cloathed with a beautiful verdure. Places which rarely knew the use of coal, are plentifully supplied with that essential article upon reasonable terms; and, what is of still greater public utility, the monopolizers of corn are prevented from exercising their infamous trade.

The village canal wharf with its paved or setted surface, its piles of coal, its small warehouse, its lime kiln, its weighbridge and its little crane became an unexceptional feature of the English landscape. In towns canals were lined with warehouses, stables for boat horses, boatbuilding yards, pubs and cottages for boatmen and manufacturing concerns using coal or other raw materials brought by the boats. At isolated junctions like Fradley small communities of canal workers grew up, with short terraces of cottages, often grouped around a public house. Canal towns became established at points where the narrow canals joined the river navigations, distinctive settlements, with many features in common.[2]

At Runcorn, where traffic from the Bridgewater and Trent and Mersey Canals reached the Mersey, basins and quays were constructed at the top of the flight of ten locks which went down to the river. Warehouses were built, and cottages for workpeople, and the whole was overlooked by Bridgewater House, an elegant red brick dwelling of three storeys from which the Duke supervised the construction of the locks, and where he stayed on subsequent visits to the town. For a time Runcorn became a fashionable bathing resort, and as late as 1834 was described as 'the Montpellier of England'. At Stourport basins were constructed in which goods could be transferred between the narrow boats from the canal system and the broad-beamed barges from the Severn. Large warehouses and stables were built, a new bridge was erected over the Severn and at the centre of the new port stood the substantial Tontine Hotel. Around the docks there grew up, apparently with a minimum of planning and co-ordination, a town of the most delightful Georgian vernacular houses. Stourport, like Runcorn, was temporarily a resort, with the county newspaper reporting in 1775:

> This place is become the Resort of People of Fashion from Worcestershire and the adjacent counties. The Beauty of the Country about it, the fine navigable Canal now completely finished, the spacious Bason for the Vessels, the River Severn and the New Bridge over it, form altogether a very pleasing Scene. The large Public House there is capable of accommodating great numbers of people. Scarcely a day passes but several Parties of Ladies and Gentlemen come there in their Carriages. Regattas (a fashionable term for Water Parties) are not unusual.

At Shardlow, about a mile from the junction of the Grand Trunk Canal with the River Trent, where it was crossed by the main road from London to Manchester, basins and warehouses were constructed where goods were transhipped between river and canal craft, and rope walks, smithies and boatyards serviced the vessels.[3] Lord Torrington wrote in 1789 of:

> the navigation of the Trent to the Mersey, around which, at Shardlow, are built so many merchants' houses, wharfs &c. sprinkled with gardens, looking upon the Trent and to Castle Dunnington Hill, form as happy a scene of business and pleasures as can be surevy'd.

In terms of administrative change, the third quarter of the eighteenth century was a period of rapid progress in road improvement. In the 1750s 184 Acts of Parliament were passed creating new turnpike trusts, and 193 trusts were authorized in the following decade. In 1773 Thomas Gilbert's General Turnpike Act regularized the conditions under which trusts operated, allowing them to erect weighing machines and to construct side gates, among other powers. Almost every individual act allowed the trust concerned to buy land and divert roads. To what extent this legislation actually altered the landscape is uncertain. The effect of it was to place under the control of turnpike trusts almost every road in England and Wales which was of more than local consequence, so that milestones and tollgates, weighing machines, boards marking the lengths of hills on which extra horses could be attached to vehicles free of charge, and toll collectors' cottages, became familiar features of the landscape. In regions which have been studied closely it seems that before 1800 turnpike trusts undertook relatively little building of new roads, being content to improve in a piecemeal fashion the routes entrusted to them, constructing embankments over some marshy stretches, cutting through the summits of some hills and straightening the occasional corner, but not creating totally new lines. Many of the structures of this generation of turnpike roads were ephemeral. In Devon, one tollhouse still survives at Newton Poppleford, dating from the creation of the Lyme Regis trust in 1758, but the great majority of tollhouses in the county were built after 1800, whatever the dates of the roads on which they stand.[4] Many of the roads turnpiked in the 1750s and 1760s were networks based on market towns, like the trusts at Truro created in 1754, Droitwich in 1755, Much Wenlock in 1756, Frome in 1757 and South Molton in 1759. In some cases there appears to have been an element of regional co-ordination by which the simultaneous creation of several trusts had the effect of turnpiking lengthy through-routes. In 1769–70 five trusts were authorized in the Norwich area. In 1756–8 three trusts radiating from Shrewsbury were created, together with one based on Ludlow which formed an end-on junction at Church Stretton with one of the Shrewsbury roads. The number of new acts in the last quarter of the eighteenth century declined substantially, doubtless because most of the existing main road system was already subject to the control of turnpike trusts. Some of the acts in this period related to secondary or even minor roads, and may have been passed only to prevent the use of such routes to avoid tollgates on main roads. Other new acts were related directly to industrial enterprises. In North Shropshire the Wem-Bron-y-Garth road, turnpiked in 1771, and that from Burlton to Llanymynech, for which an act was obtained in the following year, both linked limestone rocks on the Welsh border with areas with acidic soils where agricultural improvements were taking place and lime was in heavy demand.

Stage coach services grew from a few scattered routes in 1750 to a national network, with a sophisticated series of connections, by 1790. Numerous inns were built, often with extensive stabling to provide horses for stage coaches, and more particularly for post coaching purposes. Many were in towns, and places like Daventry and Lichfield came to depend upon the thoroughfare trade. It was the general practice for coaches to change horses every ten to fifteen miles, and where gaps between towns were greater than this, as in the Welsh hills on the road to Holyhead, new inns appeared in isolated situations in the countryside.

No branch of manufacturing grew more rapidly between 1750 and 1790 than cotton textiles, and none had a more widespread effect on the English landscape. Cotton manufacturing was already well-established in Lancashire in the early eighteenth century, with a skilled and experienced workforce and a mature form of capitalist organization. Changes came about through two related factors: technological innovation—the development of powered machines to do what had previously been done by hand—and the organization of production in such a way that work could be concentrated in a single large building. Tasks could then be broken up, so that limited operations could be undertaken by unskilled labour; and mechanical power could be applied where appropriate, whether to power a new machine like a water frame or a mule, or an ancient device like a pulley hoist which, in a large building, could be used to do work which had to be done manually in a domestic setting.

The man principally responsible for the revolution in the cotton industry was Richard Arkwright, a sparsely educated barber and wigmaker, who was born at Preston in 1732. Arkwright's claim to have invented the water frame, the powered machine for spinning cotton yarn which was an essential element in his success, has been much debated, but the question is largely irrelevant in a study of landscape history. Arkwright's significant skill lay in the organization of production, in his combination in a single building of several machines which transformed raw cotton—carding, roving and spinning it—into yarn which could be used by a weaver. He solved many of the problems which arose when large numbers of people were concentrated in one building by installing warm-air heating and columns of lavatories within the staircase blocks or turrets of his mills.[5] As an aid to gaining acceptance for the revolutionary notion that his employees should work regular hours, most of his mills were topped with a cupola containing a bell to summon them to work. Arkwright brought to cotton manufacture:

> a system of industry, order and cleanliness, till then unknown in any manufactory, where great numbers were employed together, but which he so effectually accomplished that his example may be regarded as the origin of almost all similar improvement.

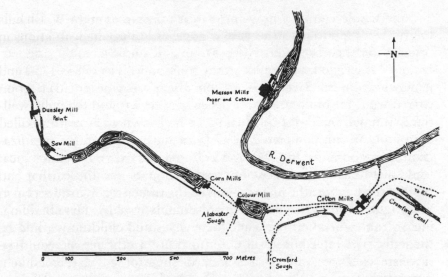

Figure 6 Water power at Cromford. To the left is the Bonsall Brook which powers a succession of mills before running on the waterwheels of Arkwright's mill, which also drew some of its water from the Cromford Sough. The Masson mills drew their power from the River Derwent

Arkwright patented the water frame spinning machine in 1769, the year in which he established a cotton mill in Nottingham, to which city he had moved in 1768. The machines were driven by horse gins, and a large proportion of the textile factories of the late eighteenth century were similarly small, often urban establishments, utilizing the power of horses. The Nottingham factory prospered, however, and by 1772 it was a four-storey building employing three hundred people.

In 1771 Arkwright, with his partners John Smalley, Samuel Need and Jedediah Strutt, set up the first water-powered cotton mill at Cromford in Derbyshire, a district which he probably knew from a period he had spent living in nearby Wirksworth, and one in which water power had been used in sophisticated ways to power mills for dressing lead ore and grinding colours. At the site of his first mill, near the confluence of the Bonsall Brook and the River Derwent, it proved possible to increase the power gained from the brook and from the Cromford Sough, which drained local lead mines, over a period of some twenty years. The first mill was a five-storey stone building ninety-seven feet long and thirty-one feet wide. A second, adjoining seven-storey mill was constructed in 1776–7, and a combined mill and warehouse in about 1785. Other buildings were added up to 1791,

63

and the whole complex now encloses a massive courtyard, a most impressive memorial to the vast change of scale which Arkwright brought to the cotton industry. Less than half a mile from the original factory Arkwright built the six-storey Masson Mill in 1783–4, taking its power from the River Derwent, on which was constructed a long, curved weir. He built homes for his employees around the mills, and the communal buildings essential to a small town or large village—a corn mill, an inn completed in 1778, a market place, for which a charter was obtained in 1790, and a church erected on the site of four lead smelthouses. The most interesting houses are the earliest, in North Street, where the upper rooms of the three-storey cottages have 'long light' windows, which were presumably used by men for weaving or framework knitting while their wives and children worked in the mills. The later houses in Cromford are a mixture of two- and three-storey types, all of a standard superior to that of much nineteenth-century urban housing. Overlooking the village is Willersley Castle, a mansion which Arkwright began to build in 1788.

Cromford became one of the curiosities of the age and was visited by numerous travellers. William Bray wrote in 1783 that the mill employed two hundred people, most of them children, who worked by turns day and night. He noted:

> another mill as large as the first is building here, new houses are rising around it, and everything wears the face of industry and cheerfulness.

Two years later Thomas Newte recorded:

> At Crumford . . . the road is cut through a rock just wide enough for a carriage to pass. As soon as you get through this, the view which presents itself is highly curious and romantic. . . . At Crumford are two very large cotton mills.

In 1789 Lord Torrington commented:

> Below Matlock a new creation of Sr Rd Arkwright's is started up, which has crouded the village of Cromford with cottages, supported by his three magnificent cotton mills. There is so much water, so much rock, so much population, and so much wood, that it looks like a Chinese town.

The following year he wrote:

> Speaking as a tourist, these vales have lost all their beauties; the rural cot has given place to the lofty reed mill, and the grand

houses of overseers; the stream perverted from its course by sluices and aqueducts will no long ripple and cascade. Every rural sound is sunk in the clamours of cotton works; and the simple peasant (for, to be simple we must be sequester'd) is changed into the impudent mechanic: the woods find their way into the canals; and the rocks are disfigured for limestone.

Arkwright's success was copied elsewhere in Derbyshire. He himself was concerned with mills at Cressbrook, Bakewell and Wirksworth where, in 1780, he installed a Newcomen pumping engine, the first to be employed in a cotton mill. At Rocester in Staffordshire he built a cotton factory on an old mill site in 1781. His partner Jedediah Strutt built mills from 1773 onwards downstream from Cromford on the Derwent at Milford and Belper. Strutt and his sons also created colonies for the accommodation of their workpeople. Just as at Cromford there were weavers' or knitters' attics to provide employment for the husbands of women working at the mills, so there are nailmakers' workshops amid the Strutts' cottages at Belper. The north mill at Belper, built just after 1800, had a colossal waterwheel, twenty-three feet wide. It became, through Rees's *Cyclopaedia*, one of the most celebrated features of the English industrial landscape. Thomas Evans constructed a cotton mill still further down the Derwent at Darley Abbey, on the edge of Derby, in 1783. The Evans family was also concerned with banking, with an iron forge and a paper mill. In 1787, when trying to attract families to work in the cotton factory, they quoted their ability to provide employment for men in their other enterprises as well as offering houses and a milking cow for each family. The lofty three-storey terraces in Darley Abbey are among the most impressive dwellings in any cotton factory colony.

The water-powered cotton mill was a novelty, both for its size and in the concentration of capital which it represented. A mill cost no more than a large integrated ironworks or a series of lead smelthouses, but such establishments were usually dispersed, whereas the whole value of a cotton mill was concentrated in one multi-storeyed building. Mills often brought an element of drama to the landscape and, as Dr Jennifer Tann has observed, they frequently drew architectural inspiration from contemporary country houses. Samuel Oldnow's mill at Mellor, the Masson Mill at Cromford, and perhaps above all the Palladian Cressbrook Mill in Millers Dale all displayed features derived from polite architectural practice.[6]

Cotton spinning spread from Derbyshire across the Midlands.

There were particular concentrations around Mansfield, as a result of the enterprise of Arkwright's associate Samuel Unwin, and on the northern side of Nottingham where a group of five or six mills was built by G. and J. Robinson from the late 1770s onwards. There were spinning factories in Northampton, Wolverhampton, Lutterworth, Warwick and Shrewsbury, and at remote country sites like Stramshill near Uttoxeter and Wild Boar Clough in the Pennines. The industry also spread to Scotland and Wales. In 1784 Arkwright went to Glasgow where he met David Dale, who took him to see the Falls of Clyde. The following year Arkwright and Dale built the first of the mills below the falls which, as New Lanark, was to become one of the most celebrated sights of industrial Britain. John Smalley, one of Arkwright's original partners, set up a cotton mill in the Greenfield Valley near Holywell in Flintshire in 1777. Since it was constructed of stones from the ruins of the medieval Basingwerk Abbey it was called the Yellow Mill. Smalley's sons built further factories in the valley, the Upper Mill in 1783, the Lower Mill in 1785 and the Crescent Mill in 1790. The Arkwright-style mill was usually about a hundred feet long and thirty feet wide, and was up to six storeys high. It was normally powered by water, and frequently had a reservoir in its immediate vicinity, and sometimes a steam engine to return used water to it. The larger mills had clocks in their classical pediments and were frequently surmounted by cupolas containing bells, visible and audible symbols of the discipline and organization associated with the new ways of working which Arkwright had brought to the textile industry.

By 1797 there were some nine hundred cotton mills in Britain, but only about a third used Arkwright's system. Most of the remainder were smaller mills employing the spinning mule, the invention of Samuel Crompton in 1779, which could be used to produce finer qualities of yarn than could be made on a water frame. There were fifty such mills in Stockport alone by 1795. In 1782 Arkwright attempted to work his mill in Manchester with a rotative atmospheric engine, supplied by Thomas Hunt of London, but without success. The first Boulton and Watt engine to work a cotton mill by rotative motion was installed at Papplewick, Nottingham, in 1785, and ten years later a similar engine was successfully used to power a mule mill. Nevertheless, while many of the new mills built after 1790 were steam operated, water remained the principal source of power for cotton spinning for another two decades.

The technology of applying power to weaving lagged far behind its application to spinning, and the vast growth in spinning capacity greatly increased the numbers of hand workers utilizing the yarns. In the East Midlands such workers were mostly stocking knitters, and many cottages with workshops in which frames could be situated were built in Nottingham and surrounding districts in the late eighteenth century. In Lancashire, where the numbers of handloom weavers grew prodigiously, numerous cottages were built to accommodate them. There were several varieties of weavers' cottages, the most easily recognizable of which had 'long lights', mullioned windows extending for almost the whole width of the building, on the first or second floors. However, many had 'loomhouses', or rooms for weaving, on the ground floor or in a cellar. The teetotaller Joseph Livesey was brought up in a cottage with a cellar loomshop at Walton-le-Dale near Preston. The cottage of Samuel Bamford's uncle near Middleton:

> consisted of one principal room called 'the houses'; on the same floor with this was a loom-shop capable of containing four looms, and in the rear of the house on the same floor, were a small kitchen and a buttery. Over the house and loom-shop were chambers; and over the kitchen and buttery was another small apartment, and a flight of stairs. The whole of the rooms were lighted by windows of small square panes, framed in lead . . . those in the front being protected by shutters.

A survey by Mr J.G. Timmins has shown that in Central Lancashire—the area bounded by Accrington in the east, Bolton in the south, Longridge to the north and the edge of the textile districts to the west—many hundreds of former handloom weavers' cottages which had cellar or ground floor workshops still remain, but the condition of the majority has been altered beyond recognition.[7] Many had triple windows on the ground floors, which have been filled in, and some of the larger cottages have been converted into pairs of separate dwellings. Many such cottages were built in groups, forming colonies of weavers, who had distinctive ways of life.

By 1790 the landscape of the Manchester region was being transformed by the cotton industry. John Aikin estimated that in 1788 there were forty-one water-powered mills in Lancashire, eight in Cheshire and twenty-two in Derbyshire, some of which were in the west of the county within the Manchester region. By 1795 there were a hundred such mills within ten miles of Ashton under Lyme. Manchester itself was booming, as merchants built elegant houses on its outskirts at places like Ardwick Green, but the River Irwell was by then destitute of fish, as a result of pollution by effluents from the dye-houses. The merest hamlets in the Pennine foothills grew to industrial settlements of considerable size. Mottram, which about 1750 had been a cluster of houses on top of a hill around a church, was by 1795 a long street of 127 houses, most of them built of thick flagstones and roofed with heavy slates, although the more recent buildings were of brick. The hamlet served as a market, and many of the houses were occupied by shopkeepers and publicans. Within a small circuit of Mottram church were twelve water-powered cotton mills, besides many smaller mills turned by horses or lesser streams. Mills were constructed in the most remote surroundings, and aroused equivocal feelings among those who saw them. Aikin remarked of the cotton mill built about 1790 near Broad Bottom Bridge over the Mersey by Kelsall and Marsland, 'This pile of building has much injured the picturesque beauty of the view, concealing a fine wood in which the river loses itself'; but others saw mills as sources of prosperity, and as structures which were romantic in their own right.

The development of the silk industry paralleled, on a lesser scale, that of the cotton trade, and silk factories became a familiar feature of the landscape of such northern towns as Macclesfield and Stockport, as well as in various parts of southern England. Mechanical means of spinning woollen yarn developed more slowly, and the factory was a relatively rare sight in the West Riding or in other woollen districts before 1790. The most impressive additions to the landscape of industrial Yorkshire in the period were the cloth halls, the most imposing of which was the Piece Hall in Halifax, completed in 1779, where cloths were brought for purchase by middlemen.

If the cotton industry had the most wide-ranging effects on the landscape of the late eighteenth century, mining and especially the smelting of metal ores made the most devastating impact on the areas where they flourished. The iron industry underwent a period of remarkable growth between 1750 and 1790, profoundly affecting every other major industry. Much of this growth, and most of the principal innovations of the period, took place on the Coalbrookdale coalfield in Shropshire, but by 1790 the patterns of activity established there were being copied in other districts, where more extensive mineral resources gave the potential for greater growth.

The discovery that coke could be used instead of charcoal to smelt iron in a blast furnace, made at Coalbrookdale in 1709 by the first Abraham Darby, was for a long time of limited value. Darby's own

1 The impact of boundaries upon the industrial landscape in the Clee Hills,
Shropshire. The stream in this valley is the boundary between the parishes of
Abdon on the left and Clee St Margaret on the right. On either side slopes lead
up to Abdon Burf and Clee Burf, the two summits of the Brown Clee Hill, just
under 1800 feet above sea level, where coal and iron ore were mined. Abdon
was enclosed in the early nineteenth century and is not neatly divided into
fields. The common land of Clee St Margaret has never been enclosed and on
the horizon a sea of bracken stretches to the shoulder of the hill. The
irregularly shaped fields in the right foreground are squatter enclosures set up
around cottages where miners who worked in the pits on the hilltops made
their homes, along with weavers, blacksmiths, shoemakers and other
craftsmen. In the Middle Ages the road up the valley was used by 'strakers'
who had grazing rights on the summit of the hill. In the seventeenth and
eighteenth centuries it was the route by which packhorses brought down coal
and iron ore

2 A dramatic landscape
created by the waste products
of industry. Heaps of spoil
from china clay workings
near Bugle, Cornwall, are
swept by a thunderstorm

3 An isolated terrace of weavers'
cottages, called Antioch, at
Rakewood on the Lancashire side of
the Pennines. Their situation recalls
the landscape of the textile districts
in the time of Defoe, although the
buildings themselves are probably of
a later date. Some of the 'long light'
windows of the first floor loomshops
have been partially filled in

4 The Lombe brothers' silk mill at Derby, 1794, from a drawing by J. Nixon,
engraved by Walker and Storer. The five-storey mill in the centre dates from
c. 1717. The building with the pitched roof to the right is an earlier mill of
1702

5 Bringewood Forge Bridge on the River Teme on the borders of Shropshire and Herefordshire. The stone bridge was built in 1772 in the midst of what was one of the densest concentrations of ironworks in Britain before the mid eighteenth century. The arch on the far side of the bridge accommodated the tail race from the waterwheel which powered the furnace bellows. The surveyor for the bridge was Thomas Farnolls Pritchard, designer of the Iron Bridge

6 Hetton Staithes: roofed staithes of a type used in the North-East by the beginning of the eighteenth century (*From a drawing by J.D. Harding*)

7 'A View of the Tanfield Arch in the County of Durham.' The 105-foot stone railway bridge known as the Tanfield, or Causey Arch, completed in 1727, was one of the first industrial monuments to attract the attention of artists (*From a drawing by Joseph Atkinson engraved by J.C. Stadler*)

8 William Williams's painting 'A View on the River Severn at Madeley near Coalbrookdale where the iron bridge is to be built', *c.* 1777. The scattered, haphazard landscape of the Severn Gorge in Shropshire is well-captured in this painting. The chimneys on the left bank are part of a lead smelter. The primitive nature of the moorings of the Severn barges makes an interesting contrast with the vast installations on the Tyne, shown in Pl.6

9 One of the new features of the industrial landscape of the early eighteenth century. A Newcomen steam engine from J.T. Desaguliers, *A Course of Experimental Philosophy*, published in 1744

10 A map of Burslem, Staffordshire, in 1750. The maypole stands in the centre of the village, in which there are numerous small potworks with bottle ovens. To the left of the maypole is a large 'Shord Pile' of wasters from the potteries. The map shows clearly the rural setting of the Potteries in the early eighteenth century, and the scattered nature of settlement

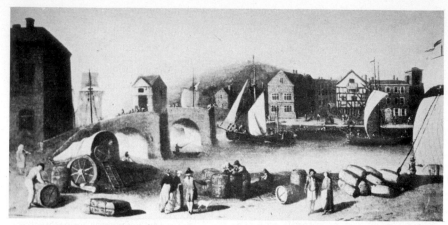

11 The unhurried disorder of a riverside quay at Bewdley, Worcestershire, in the mid eighteenth century

12 The first milepost on the Trent and Mersey Canal at Shardlow, cast in iron by Rangeley & Dixon of Stone, Staffordshire

13 The eastern portal of Sapperton Tunnel through which the Thames and Severn Canal passed beneath the Cotswold Ridge. It might almost be a folly in the grounds of a great house

14 The Oxford Canal at Banbury, opened in 1772. The wharf on the right was acquired in 1825 by the town's Paving and Lighting Commission and used for unloading roadmaking materials. It was subsequently used by the successors to the Commission, the Board of Health and the Borough Corporation, and remained a depot for building and road maintenance until 1974

15 A south-west prospect of Stourport, 1776. The newness of the canal town of Stourport is very evident in this picture, drawn four years after the opening of the Staffordshire and Worcestershire Canal. The Tontine Hotel is in the centre, with stables for canal boat horses to the right. To the left is the basin where goods were transferred from river barges to canal narrow boats.

16 Cromford Mill from the upstream side. This was the first water-powered cotton mill, built by Richard Arkwright in 1771. Originally it had five storeys: the top two floors were destroyed by fire in the nineteenth century

17 North Street, Cromford: the earliest houses built by Richard Arkwright in Cromford, c. 1777. The top storeys have 'long light' windows and were used for weaving or framework knitting. The school at the end of the street was built in 1832

18 Masson Mill, Cromford, the earliest parts of which were built by Richard Arkwright in 1783–4. It is still used for the manufacture of thread. The cupola over the main entrance was restored in 1975

works at Coalbrookdale prospered as a foundry, and a close-knit community of moulders, pattern makers and grinders grew up around it. It was at Coalbrookdale in the 1740s that a steam engine was first used to recirculate the water between the pools of an ironworks. About 1750 a wooden railway was built to carry ore and coal to the works and, by experiments not now fully understood, the second Abraham Darby learned how to make iron which could be forged into wrought iron, using coke as his fuel. In 1754 Darby, with his partner Thomas Goldney, leased the mining rights in the township of Great Dawley, and they took over an old corn mill at Horsehay where they built a blast furnace. A dam was constructed, creating a large pool to store water to power the wheels which worked the furnace bellows. A hostile observer noted in December 1754 that 'a great part of the Mighty dam is Tumbled down', and counted about sixty men plugging the leaks in the remainder with coke and charcoal dust. A steam engine was built to pump water back over the dam, and building materials, timber, firebricks, blocks of sandstone for the furnace hearth and alabaster were brought to Horsehay from all directions. Wooden railways were constructed to bring in limestone, coal and iron ore, and to take the pig iron to the River Severn, about three miles away. The blast furnace, blown in during May 1755, was immediately successful and a second furnace came into operation at Horsehay two years later. This occasion was celebrated with a dinner for three hundred people, and the food—a cow and calf, hams, ten large plum puddings and two hogsheads of ale—was delivered by railway waggons.

Encouraged by the demands for iron created by the Seven Years War, Darby and his partners built two other furnaces at nearby Ketley, and by 1759 five more had been constructed in the vicinity by other partnerships. The Coalbrookdale coalfield became in a short space of time the leading iron-producing area in Great Britain—and its landscape was totally transformed. Areas which had been fields or woodland were dotted with horse gins at the heads of mine shafts, from which coal and ore were brought up. The ore had to be separated on the surface from the clays and shales in which it was found. This task was undertaken by gangs of women, and caused the clay mounds which still dominate much of the district's landscape. Around the furnaces was flat land where iron ore was calcined in open heaps, and coal was converted by the same methods into coke, both processes producing vast quantities of sulphur-laden smoke. The ironmaking companies leased quarries and mines from which they obtained limestone. Some was taken to be used as a flux in their blast furnaces. The rest was burned in kilns, with coal from the companies' mines, to make lime which was sold for building and agricultural purposes. The companies also set up brickworks, to provide the bricks which were used in vast numbers in their own ironworks and mines, and also for general sale. The bellows of all the new furnaces of the 1750s were worked by waterwheels, necessitating the digging of pools and the building of Newcomen engines to recirculate the water. Numerous horses drew waggons along a dense network of railways, conveying raw materials to and from the various works, and taking coal, iron and bricks to the Severn barges.

One of the new ironworks in the area was that of the New Willey Company, whose chief partner was John Wilkinson. In 1776 Wilkinson for the first time used a steam engine to work the bellows of a blast furnace directly, rather than pumping water back over a waterwheel, and this had the effect of freeing the builders of ironworks from the necessity of excavating large pools and digging complex leets. The following year Wilkinson built the Snedshill Ironworks at Oakengates, the first group of blast furnaces to be independent of water power. In the early 1780s rotative steam engines were employed to work hammers and rolling mills in iron forges. New methods of forging wrought iron, using coal instead of charcoal, were perfected by John Wright and Richard Jesson of West Bromwich in 1773, and by Henry Cort of Fontley, Hampshire, in 1784. These developments made it possible to locate forges alongside the blast furnaces which provided them with pig iron, and greatly increased the sizes of the principal ironworks. Forges were large buildings with steam engines working rolling and slitting mills, usually installed in high engine houses which towered over the low roofs of the other buildings. Within the forge would be banks of puddling furnaces from which protruded high chimneys. The Wright and Jesson process utilized refractory clay pots, and forges where it was employed normally had several conical pottery kilns where such pots were made. The waste tips of these works consisted of broken fragments of yellow vitrified pots, as well as the usual slags. From the 1770s onwards experiments were made at a number of ironworks with ovens for the manufacture of coke, which saved some of the valuable products lost when coal was coked in open heaps. In Shropshire the ninth Earl Dundonald constructed ranges of ovens at the ironworks at Benthall and the Calcutts which added a new element to the landscape of ironworks—the conical tops of the ovens themselves, and the long chimneys arising from the condensers where tar was extracted from the smoke led off from the kilns. At works where there were foundries for the manufacture of cast iron objects there were ranges of workshops for making patterns and moulds, devices for breaking large pieces of scrap iron, grinding shops, and, if cannon or steam engines were made, boring mills which might be steam- or water-powered.

Complex works of this kind came to dominate the landscape of every ironworking region in the British coalfields. Nevertheless, there were only a few such works by 1790. The expansion in Shropshire in the 1750s had been followed by a second period of furnace building during the American War of Independence in the 1770s and 1780s. Ironworks of this type were established in South Wales, particularly along the northern rim of the coalfield where the seams of iron ore outcropped and where supplies of limestone were near at hand. The first coke-fired furnace in the region is generally accepted to have been that at Hirwaun near Aberdare. Others were built in the Merthyr area, at Dowlais in the late 1750s, the Plymouth and Cyfarthfa works in the 1760s and the Penydarren furnaces in 1784. The Sirhowy and Cefn Cribwr furnaces were blown in during the 1770s. In South Staffordshire John Wilkinson's ironworks at Bradley, where the first furnaces were blown in about 1766, was one of the largest and most complex in Britain, and saw many innovations in the application of steam power to the forging processes. During the 1780s five new works with coke-fired blast furnaces blown by steam engines came into operation in the region. Works of a similar kind were also built in Derbyshire and South Yorkshire, around Chesterfield and Rotherham; and the Carron works in Scotland, founded in 1760, was one of the largest and most innovative ironmaking concerns in Britain. By the 1790s the foundations for the growth of vast ironworking regions had been created in South Wales and the Black Country, but in terms of production the tiny Coalbrookdale coalfield remained dominant. Of the 48,200 tons of pig iron produced by coke-fired furnaces in England and Wales in 1788, 23,100 tons were smelted in Shropshire; and twenty-one of the fifty-three blast furnaces then in operation were sited there.

The older ironworks and ironworking methods were far from extinct in 1790, however. In 1788 there were still twenty-four charcoal-fired blast furnaces in operation making some 13,100 tons of pig iron a year. The number of furnaces in the Weald declined during the second half of the eighteenth century, only two or three surviving after 1790, and only one remaining at work into the nineteenth century. The forges in the region similarly declined. The lack of coal meant that it was impossible to work steam engines economically in Kent and Sussex; the furnaces and forges could only operate at those times of the year when streams were flowing. The manufacture of cannon, in which some of the Wealden works had specialized, was gradually taken over by foundries in the coalfields, particularly by the Carron works in Scotland. In 1777 it was noted that the Darvel Furnace had ceased work on the conclusion of the last peace with France and Spain, that it was decaying, and that the manufactory at Carron would probably prevent its revival. In other areas water-powered forges continued to prosper. About 1760 the Coalbrookdale Company converted the Bridgnorth town mills at the confluence of the Worfe and the Severn into a forge; and other partnerships built forges on the banks of the Severn, powered by its tributary streams, at Eardington and Hampton Loade between Bridgnorth and Bewdley, which utilized pig iron brought down the river from the Coalbrook-dale area. The same source of supply sustained the forges in mid Wales. In spite of the development of the coal-using, steam-powered forging process, Thomas Telford still regarded water as the normal source of power for a forge as late as 1800.

The iron industry was closely involved with the development of the steam engine. Without the growth in overall iron production and the spread of foundry skills, the steam engine could not have multiplied as it did in the last quarter of the eighteenth century. Without the steam engine, ironworks would have remained tied to sites where there was water power. The year 1800 is a more significant date in the history of the steam engine than 1790, and it is probably not too wild an estimate to suggest that there were then about two thousand engines at work in Britain, but this followed a decade of hectic engine building, and the number in 1790 would certainly have been much lower. Many of the engines built in the late eighteenth century were Newcomen engines, 'common' engines as they were often called. Their thermal efficiency was low, and their ability to drive complex machinery smoothly was uncertain, but for many tasks in the coalfields, where the cost of fuel was of little consequence, they were quite adequate.[8] 'Almost every coal mine' wrote one observer in 1778, with a degree of exaggeration, 'is provided with one or two steam engines and every proprietor has attempted some improvement.'

The great changes in the operation of steam engines in this period were due to James Watt, a scientific instrument maker from Glasgow, who began experiments to improve the efficiency of the Newcomen engine in 1765. He discovered that efficiency would be improved if the cylinder was kept warm in a steam jacket, and if steam was ejected from the cylinder to a separate condenser; and in 1769, he patented the idea of the separate condenser. In 1774 he was persuaded to move to Birmingham, to enter into a partnership with Matthew Boulton. Boulton had erected the Soho Manufactory on the north side of the town in 1761–2. Using water power for some processes he made buttons, steel jewellery, Sheffield plate and the other intricate metal items for which Birmingham was well-known. Under Boulton's guidance Watt's patents were extended to last until the end of the century. In 1776 the first working Watt engines were constructed, using cylinders made by John Wilkinson, which were bored by a machine adapted from one Wilkinson had patented for boring cannon. The first engine was employed to pump out a mine at Tipton, while the second blew Wilkinson's furnace at Willey in Shropshire. The Watt engine offered great economics in fuel consumption, but to operate one honestly was expensive. Boulton and Watt did not, until 1796, provide any of the parts except the valves, which were intricate devices the Soho Manufactory was well-suited to manufacture. Customers were provided with sets of drawings and the services of an erector. Cylinders were acquired from Wilkinson, or in some cases from other foundries. Timber for beams and other parts were acquired locally. When the engine was erected and operating, the owners had to pay Boulton and Watt a third of the estimated savings in fuel costs, as compared with a Newcomen engine of the same power. In 1782 Watt patented an engine which could be used to provide rotative action, and thus to power machinery, refining the process still further with the development of his parallel motion for connecting the beam to the piston rod in 1784, and the centrifugal governor in 1788. By 1790 there were few purposes for which the Watt engine was used for which Newcomen or 'common' engines were not also being employed. A Newcomen engine with a crank to enable it to turn machinery was built by James Pickard in 1780, before there was a Watt rotative engine. Wilkinson had found that he needed a regulator to control the entry of air into the blast furnace in order to blow it evenly; once a regulator had been designed it enabled the Newcomen as well as the Watt engine to be used to work furnace bellows. While the Watt engine was expensive to use, some engineers sought to gain the same degree of efficiency without infringing the patents, so that numerous 'mongrel' engines appeared in the late eighteenth century. Others, less scrupulous, built engines of the Watt type without paying the necessary premiums.

The implications of the steam engine's improvement for the landscape were many. The rate of building of both the common atmospheric and the Boulton and Watt engines accelerated in the closing decades of the eighteenth century. In mining districts remote from the coalfields, particularly in Cornwall, the improvements in efficiency which came with the Boulton and Watt engine made feasible the use of steam in many places where mining had hitherto proved unprofitable. Gradually the improved efficiency of steam engines enabled the production of smaller machines, which could be used for purposes like grinding grain or winding coalpits.

In many areas the coal industry was closely linked with the iron trade. Overall production increased substantially between 1750 and 1790. Exports from England and Wales grew from less than 200,000 tons per annum in the 1750s to over 600,000 in 1790. Dispatches by coastal and overseas shipping from Newcastle and Sunderland rose from between 400,000 and 500,000 fifty-three-hundredweight chaldrons a year in the 1750s to more than 700,000 a year by 1790. In most coalfields of consequence there was substantial investment in steam engines. Around Bristol there were about twenty engines working at coal mines by 1770. In most areas where iron was made only a few seams produced good coking coal for use in blast furnaces, and of the other coal mined only a limited proportion could be used to fire the boilers of steam engines and in other ironmaking processes. Substantial quantities were therefore available for outside sale.

There were several new features in the landscape of the coalfields in the late eighteenth century. About 1760 screens were introduced at many collieries in Northumberland and Durham, sloping platforms with gratings at intervals, with bars spaced according to the size of coal required to pass through them. From the gratings the coal was guided by wooden shutes into waiting railway waggons. The screens enabled mines producing coal of inferior quality to bring their product up to the standards of the better collieries by separating the large lumps from the rest. From about 1780 it became the practice in the North-East to have waterwheels to power winding apparatus, using water pumped from the pits by steam engines. Railways multiplied in most mining areas. In 1767 iron rails were employed for the first time in the Coalbrookdale region: slabs of cast iron, about one-and-a-quarter inches thick, were laid on the tops of wooden rails. About 1787 John Curr of Sheffield invented a flanged rail, often called the plate rail. It was intended for use underground but was soon employed on the surface, and plateways were laid in many coalfields. Many canal companies used railways to connect with collieries or other sources of minerals which could not be reached by a waterway, except by extensive locking. The Chesterfield Canal Company reached the Norbriggs colliery with such a line in 1778. In 1783 a railway was built to link the Erewash Canal with pits at Ilkeston. In 1779 the owners of the Trent and Mersey Canal built a railway from the terminus of their Froghall branch to the Caldon Low limestone quarries in Staffordshire. Other railways ran to the Douglas Navigation in Lancashire, and to the completed portions of the Leeds and Liverpool Canal in Yorkshire.

No coalfield changed more dramatically during this period than that in South Staffordshire and North Worcestershire. The increased availability of wrought iron, first from Shropshire and then from furnaces and forges within the coalfield itself, multiplied the numbers of metalworkers living on the commons and heaths. The establishment of blast furnaces vastly increased the demand for coal. The Birmingham Canal, whose circuitous course enabled it to serve many collieries, improved the prospects for selling coal, at first in Birmingham itself and later, with the completion of other canals, to large parts of southern England. In 1776 Arthur Young left Birmingham, passed the Soho Manufactory and went through West Bromwich towards Wolverhampton:

> The road is one continued village of nailers. . . . About Wednesbury the whole country smoaks with coal-pits, forges, furnaces, &c., towns come upon the neck of one another, and large ones too. Darliston, where gun-locks are made. Bilston, a considerable place, and quite to Wolverhampton from Birmingham, I saw not one farm-house, nothing that looked like the residence of a mere farmer.

In 1792 Lord Torrington wrote:

> by a lane came to Wednesbury, another overgrown village, blacken'd with its trees and hedges by the forge fires; nay, even the sun itself is obscured by them! Every field is scoop'd by collieries and canals; and the iron stone (happy distribution)

> lays under the coal. Iron foundaries around are numberless;
> and the roads are made of the iron dross.

It was easy to conclude, as Young did in 1792, that 'All the activity and industry of this kingdom is fast concentrating where there are coalpits'. Young failed to understand the continued importance of water power in the textile industry and, to some extent, in ironmaking. Nor did he show any real awareness of the changes taking place in the remoter uplands of Britain where there was little or no coal, but where there were rich deposits of other minerals. Such deposits stimulated changes in the landscape of the uplands, and indirectly transformed some of the lowland coalfields.

The copper industry grew rapidly in the mid eighteenth century and its effect on the landscape of four widely separated but closely connected areas was dramatic. Exports of wrought copper, which did not exceed 100 tons per annum in the first decade of the century, varied between 353 and 568 tons during the 1750s. By 1790 they exceeded 3000 tons. Such figures only give an inadequate impression of the industry's growth, the main stimulus to which came from the increasing use of copper sheathing on the hulls of ships and, after 1783, from the use of copper bolts in shipbuilding, as well as from a growing trade in brass.

Between 1750 and 1770 the main growth of copper mining was in Cornwall, where production almost trebled in those two decades, to reach about 29,000 tons a year. There were about ninety mines producing copper in the county, about twenty of them of significant size. The expansion of mining in the parish of Gwennap, south-west of Truro, was particularly marked. In the 1750s smelthouses for copper were established on the coast at Hayle. Costs were higher than in Wales, but the Cornish Copper Company improved the harbour, utilizing blocks of copper slag for building piers, and imported coal, timber and iron for the mines, as well as exporting copper. The costs of working steam engines in Cornwall were high. Nevertheless, about forty Newcomen engines were working there in 1770, the majority in copper rather than tin mines. When the Boulton and Watt engine was introduced into the county in the mid 1770s the Cornish copper trade was depressed, because of competition from Anglesey, and it urgently needed the improvements in efficiency which the new engine promised. The first Watt engine in Cornwall began to work at Chacewater in September 1777, and the second at Ting Tang, Gwennap, early in

1778. The engines were successful, and twenty of similar design were in operation by the end of 1783. Boulton and Watt were much resented in Cornwall, and Cornish engineers sought to improve the efficiency of the steam engine by their own devices. Three foundries were established in the county by 1791.[9]

The depression of the Cornish copper trade was caused by the discovery of easily accessible deposits of ore on Parys Mountain in Anglesey. Charles Roe of Macclesfield had taken a lease on part of the mountain in 1764, but it was not until 2 March 1768 that the Golden Venture, the rich seam which made the area famous, was discovered. Roe and Company continued to control the eastern part of the hill until 1785 but a new concern, the Parys Mountain Company, was formed to exploit the ores which lay to the west of Roe's land. The latter company began to operate properly in 1778. It was controlled by an Anglesey solicitor, Thomas Williams, who became the dominant figure in the British copper industry. After Roe's lease expired in 1785 a concern called the Mona Company, effectively under Williams's control, took over the eastern part of the hill, so that Williams was responsible for working the whole mountain.

Parys Mountain was worked by a mixture of quarrying and mining methods. A map of 1786 shows 145 shafts. From the rim of a vast pit, a hundred yards long and seventy feet deep, men swung on ropes attached to windlasses to set explosive charges. The displaced rock was lifted to the top in kibbles and broken by gangs of women and children before being put into bags to be conveyed to the coast. Rectangular kilns for calcining the ore were first built about 1778 by the Macclesfield company. They were between ten and twenty yards wide, as long as forty or fifty yards, and the walls were four feet high. The kilns were filled with ore which was covered with flat stones and sealed with clay. The calcining process took as long as six months. The fumes were drawn through condensers where some of the sulphur they contained was deposited. Later kilns were conical and usually about twenty-seven feet high. Copper was also produced by dipping scrap iron in pits, measuring forty by twenty feet, filled with water pumped out of the mines. The copper sulphate in the water caused the iron to dissolve, leaving a copper-bearing sludge on the bottom of the precipitation pit. The copper ore was exported through the port of Amlwch where, as early as 1786, the area around the harbour was lined with calcining kilns. An Act of Parliament of 1793 made possible the improvement of the port. According to the topographer Thomas

Pennant some 1500 people were employed in the Parys Mountain mines. The copper produced there became a factor of major importance in the British economy, and by 1790 the mountain had become one of the country's most visited industrial sites.[10]

The traditional place for smelting Cornish copper ore was around Swansea and Neath: coal was cheap and the Cornish coast could easily be reached by sea. Coal for pumping engines in Cornwall was always available as a return cargo for the ships which had arrived with copper ore. From the late 1770s ore from Parys Mountain was also smelted in this area. About 1799 Thomas Williams purchased the Upper Bank works, originally established in the 1750s, and began to send a proportion of the Anglesey ore there. By the late eighteenth century the banks of the Tawe and the River Neath were lined with smoking copper smelthouses, which caused some of the most noxious pollution to be found in Britain. As early as 1768 Robert Morris had laid out the model industrial village of Morriston. Like Parys Mountain, the area came to be an object of wonder and amazement for visitors.

Parys Mountain ore was also smelted in south Lancashire, where there were old-established smelthouses for copper near Warrington, which had used ore from Alderley Edge. In 1779 the Parys Mountain Company leased land at Ravenhead, on the estate of John Mackay, and within five years had erected forty-eight reverberatory furnaces for the smelting of copper. At much the same time the Mona Company established the Stanley Smelting Company in the same area. Forty-ton flats could sail direct from Amlwch via the Sankey Canal to Ravenhead, and the refined copper could be distributed through Liverpool or by the national canal network. Mackay had moved to the Lancashire coalfield from London in the 1760s, on account of his interests in the Cheshire salt trade. He became heavily involved in mining and, as well as introducing the smelting of copper ore to the district which became known as St Helens, he also laid the foundations of the local glass industry when he established the British Cast Plate Glass Company.[11]

The Greenfield Valley in Flintshire was the other area to be profoundly affected by the rapid growth of the copper industry. Copper working began in the valley as early as the 1740s, when land was leased there by Thomas Patten who had smelthouses at Bank Quay, Warrington. His concern in the Greenfield Valley was known as the 'Warrington Company', and his installations as the Battery Works. Patten was concerned with plating and rolling copper into a state in

78

which it could be used by smiths to make useful objects, and his interests in the valley steadily expanded. Pools were excavated, new areas of land leased and the production of brass began, using locally mined zinc ores. After the discovery of the Golden Venture on Anglesey, the Warrington Company began to roll copper smelted in Lancashire from Roe's Parys Mountain ores. The smelthouses set up by Thomas Williams's Parys Mountain Company at Ravenhead were remote from any satisfactory source of water power, and in 1780 Williams completed the building of a rolling mill at the lower end of the Greenfield Valley, the first of several concerns worked by his Greenfield Copper and Brass Company. A new hammer mill for the manufacture of copper bolts was set up in 1783, and two years later his company took over the installations of the Warrington Company. A second new rolling mill, eighty-six feet long and sixty-nine feet wide, with three cast iron waterwheels and, appropriately, a copper roof, was built in 1787, to be followed in 1788 by the Meadow Mills, where rollers for printing textiles were made. By 1796 Williams had six smelters in the valley as well as the mills. The Greenfield Valley was a classic water-powered site which had known a variety of manufactures long before the mid eighteenth century. Nevertheless, its landscape was transformed by the sheer scale of the textile and copper works built there from the 1770s onwards.[12] Thomas Pennant wrote of the valley in that decade:

the stream formed by this fountain runs with a rapid course to the sea, which it reaches in little more than a mile's distance. The industry of this century hath made its waters of much commercial utility. The principal works on it at this time are battering mills for copper, a wire mill, a coarse paper mill, a snuff mill, a foundery for brass and a cotton manufactory is now establishing.

An account some years later acknowledged the scale of the changes:

Thomas Williams, esq., that useful and active character, with unparalleled speed, covered the lower part of the stream, or that next the sea, with buildings stupendous in extent, expense and ingenuity of contrivance. These great works are under the firm of the Parys Mountain Company. The buildings were completed in the year 1780.

Another important source of copper, the Ecton mine in North Staffordshire, was described by William Bray in 1777 as 'one of the richest copper mines in Europe'. It was taken under the direct control of the Duke of Devonshire in 1760, and was said in its most prosperous years to have realized a profit of £30,000. A Boulton and Watt steam engine was installed to improve drainage from the mine. Most of the ore was conveyed from the workings through an adit in small horse-drawn carts. Some copper mining continued at Alderley Edge in Cheshire, and smelters remained at work at Cheadle and Macclesfield, the latter impressing Lord Torrington in 1792 as 'a most unwholesome employ'.

The tin mining industry in Cornwall, unlike the copper industry, was relatively static in the second half of the eighteenth century. Only five tin mines were equipped with Newcomen pumping engines. The chief increase in activity was in the St Austell area, described by a traveller in 1788 as 'the Peru of Great Britain'. Much of the production came from stream workings on Hensbarrow Moor; it was smelted in the old-fashioned blowing houses and exported through the port of Par. In western Cornwall more of the tin was mined, and the ore was smelted around the main coinage towns of Penzance and Truro.

Britain was probably Europe's chief source of lead in the late eighteenth century. It was utilized in building, in pewter—still common in all but the very poorest households—in printer's type and in shot. Both red and white lead were used in making paints, and red lead was employed in glassmaking. Lead mining was an industry of the uplands. The principal source of lead in the mid eighteenth century was Derbyshire where, in the decades after 1750, coal-using cupolas displaced older methods of smelting ore. New smelting works of this kind were established, with tall chimneys, extensive flues and weighhouses at various sites, among them Totley on the River Sheaf, Wirksworth, Lea Green on the Cromford Canal and Stonedge near Chesterfield, where there are still extensive remains. The landscape of the lead mining region was impressive. Lord Torrington noted in the Winster area in 1790 that 'All the country is scoop'd by lead mines and their levels'. Pastor Moritz was told in 1782 that the cavern at Castleton, one of the great natural curiosities of the Peak District, was nothing compared with the nearby mines. Steam engines were introduced to drain many Derbyshire mines, and Charles Hatchett noted in 1796 that most mineowners preferred common atmospheric engines to those from Boulton and Watt. Drainage systems became more complex, and for a time the level at the Speedwell mine was navigable. Calamine was also mined in Derbyshire in the Wirksworth and Bonsall region, and sent to Birmingham to be used in the manufacture of brass.

The hills of Clwyd remained a mining region of considerable importance in the late eighteenth century. As well as lead, calamine was mined near Holywell, and it was calcined and combined with copper to make brass in a works at the seaward end of the Greenfield Valley. Richard Warner noted in 1798 that some seven hundred miners were employed in the area. As early as the 1770s Thomas Pennant wrote of the Holywell area, 'The hilly part of our parish, has been for a succession of years rich in mines of lead and calamine', and the coast road near Flint was, he said, 'blackened with the smoke of smelting houses'. The scale of activity was increasing at the end of the eighteenth century as such eminent entrepreneurs as John Wilkinson and Thomas Williams became interested in the region. New mines were sunk, steam engines installed and levels dug to drain them.

A relatively new source of lead in the second half of the eighteenth century was the Stiperstones range of hills in South Shropshire. Lead had been extracted in the vicinity since Roman times, and one concern was sending ore from the region to be smelted in the Severn Gorge as early as the 1730s, but it was not until the 1760s that large-scale development began. Between 1760 and 1790 all of the largest productive mines in the region were sunk or extended, Boulton and Watt engines were installed and new levels dug. The proprietors of the richest mine, at Snailbeach, which was 180 yards deep by 1797, leased a coal mine at Pontesford, on the edge of the hills, and set up a smelthouse nearby.[13]

Lead mining was also increasing in importance in the northern Pennines. The most eminent concern in the industry in the mid eighteenth century was the London Lead Company, often called the Quaker Lead Company, which had mines in many parts of the country. In the 1790s the company sold off its interests in Derbyshire and Wales and began to concentrate its activities on Alston Moor and in Teesdale.

In most metal mining districts the late eighteenth century saw a period of rapid change in the landscape. Steam pumping engines were installed in considerable numbers. New types of coal-fired smelters were erected. New levels were cut out. Many other changes are less easily defined. Streams were dammed to store water for dressing ores. Encampments of flimsy wooden buildings grew up around the principal shafts. Tracks were worn by packhorses taking away the ore. In

81

some areas miners were accommodated in company-built 'barracks', going to their homes at the end of each week's work. Elsewhere miners were allowed to build their own cottages in rough enclosures on the waste. The effects of the Industrial Revolution upon the English landscape were not confined to the manufacturing towns; they were equally to be seen in some of the remotest uplands.

The quarrying of slate in North Wales was another upland industry in which revolutionary changes began between 1750 and 1790. The ill-organized digging of slate by cottagers on the open commons was steadily suppressed, and large-scale quarries were opened by land-owners and entrepreneurs, who also took active roles in marketing the slate, and in transporting it to the coast. In the area where the town of Bethesda now stands the workings were taken over in the mid 1780s by the landowner Richard Pennant, son of a Liverpool merchant, who had married Anna Warburton, heiress to the estate, and was created the first Baron Penrhyn in 1783. His agent William Williams directed the start of working at what came to be known as the Penrhyn Quarry. Pennant leased land on the fringe of his own estate from the Crown and from other landlords, and by 1790 had commenced the construc-tion of a harbour for the export of slate and a road to link it with the quarries. Similar developments took place in the 1780s on the manor of Dinorwic near Llanberis, where three entrepreneurs took over old workings on lands owned by the Assheton Smith family. The most dramatic changes in the landscape of the slate-quarrying region took place between 1790 and 1810, but the pattern of development had been set by 1790.[14]

The pottery industry underwent revolutionary changes between 1750 and 1790, partly as a result of the introduction of new tech-nologies. The manufacture of porcelain, which had already reached the provinces from London by 1750, was established in several large towns, including Bristol, Derby, Plymouth, Lowestoft and Worcester. In North Staffordshire new forms of earthenware, like Josiah Wedg-wood's Queensware and Jasperware, were developed which, like porcelain, required raw materials from several areas of the country. The expansion of the industry was in part a response to increased demand, and in particular to a great increase in tea drinking. While master potters gained prestige from supplying wares to the crowned heads of Europe, they became prosperous because they produced cups, saucers, plates and ornaments cheaply enough for them to be bought by all but the very poor. The growth of the industry was also due to new forms of organization, comparable with those effected by Richard Arkwright in cotton spinning, and these transformed the landscape of North Staffordshire.

The making of pottery can be broken down into a multitude of stages, many requiring only a modicum of skill which can quickly be taught. The firing of a kiln requires altogether different muscular powers from the making of decorative flowers, the application of transfers to the sides of teapots or the throwing of a vase on a wheel. From about 1750 master potters began to bring together their employees, often in premises attached to their own homes, and to separate the different stages of manufacture. Ivy House, Burslem, a brick building roofed with tiles, built by Thomas and John Wedgwood in 1750, was perhaps the first pottery factory. It was used by Josiah Wedgwood from 1759 to 1762, when he moved to another site known as the Bell Works, named after the bell used to summon employees to work, a sign of the new discipline which he was attempting to create. In 1769 Wedgwood established an entirely new works at Etruria, in which the manufacturing processes were completely separated from his own home. The new factory was situated on the Ridge House estate, where the turnpike road from Leek to Newcastle under Lyme crossed the Trent and Mersey Canal, in which Wedgwood was a leading shareholder. The main fifteen-bay building faced the canal. A clock was set in its pediment and it was surmounted by a cupola with a bell in it, just like an Arkwright-style cotton mill. Workers' cottages lined the turnpike road, and the whole complex was overlooked by Etruria Hall, a mansion designed for Wedgwood in 1770 by Joseph Pickford.

The steam engine first appeared in the pottery trade in the late eighteenth century. In 1772, after a visit to Cornwall, John Turner of Lane End used a Newcomen engine to pump water back over a wheel, which he employed to power throwing engines and lathes. By 1782 the Spode factory was using a similar device. In 1784 Josiah Wedgwood installed a Boulton and Watt engine at Etruria; it drove clay and flint mills and colour grinding pans. Subsequently more engines were erected at Etruria, and at most of the principal potteries, and the engine house, with the tall chimney of its adjacent boiler house, became almost as common a feature of the North Staffordshire landscape as the bottle oven.

The expansion of the pottery industry was much remarked upon by visitors. John Wesley noted of Burslem in 1781 that 'since the Potteries

83

were introduced inhabitants have continually flowed in from every side. Hence the wilderness is literally become a fruitful field. Houses, villages and towns have sprung up.' Particularly attractive as sites for new works were the banks of canals, which could be used to deliver the increasing quantities and varieties of raw materials brought from a distance—china clay from Cornwall, flints from Kent and Sussex and spars from Derbyshire, as well as coal and fireclay from local mines. New settlements like Etruria, Longport and Middleport grew up where the main roads crossed the Trent and Mersey Canal. In the surrounding parts of Staffordshire the mills in the valleys of the Churnett, the Trent and the Maddershall were converted to grind flints for the potworks. During the 1780s paper mills began to manufacture tissue papers for making transfers. In the woodlands on the Staffordshire hills hearths were set up to make pliable the lengths of hazel used in the manufacture of the crates in which pottery was dispatched from North Staffordshire to the markets of the world.

Approaching the region from the south in 1792 Lord Torrington noted that the Potteries commenced at Lane End (now Longton), where the roads were repaired with fragments of broken pots. It continued as:

> a street of many miles; the men whiten'd with the powder are supplied with coals to keep alive the everlasting ovens, from every adjacent field hundreds of horses and asses with panniers are incessantly taking in their lading ... here I crossed the Trent; and soon, many branches of navigation. These intersecting canals with their passing boats, their bridges, the population, the pottery ovens, and the bustle of business, remind me of a Chinese picture, where the angler is momentarily interrupted by a boat.

Torrington went to Etruria and, while waiting for the employees to return to work from their lunch, 'saunter'd about Mr W's grounds; which are green and pleasant, with some pretty plantations, views of the navigation, &c.&c.'. However unwholesome the work on the potbanks, the landscape of the Potteries in the 1790s was neither bleak nor devoid of charms; but much of what was new about that landscape—the canals, the steam engines, the large, integrated pottery factories— had only appeared in the previous forty years.

The expansion of the pottery trade affected the English landscape in places other than North Staffordshire. The new types of ware being manufactured increased the demand for flints from the Downs, for spars from the Pennines and for clay from the West of England. Just after 1800 a visitor to the South-West observed steatite quarries near the Lizard producing materials for the works of Flight and Barr of Worcester, and near St Austell noted convoys of carts carrying china clay to the coast for shipment to North Staffordshire.

By 1790 most of the principal English towns were beginning to outgrow their ancient limits, and to expand into the surrounding countryside. Some, like Liverpool, Manchester, Birmingham, Sheffield, Bristol and the dockyard towns, had begun to grow quite early in the century. Others, like Leeds, Hull and Leicester, had been able to accommodate an increasing population within their ancient limits until the 1770s or 1780s.[15] While some of the largest industrial enterprises were well away from towns, in areas like the Coalbrookdale coalfield, the Derwent Valley or the North Staffordshire Potteries, very large numbers of smaller concerns grew up in and around the towns, often along the valleys of rivers and streams, which provided power for such industries as the metal trades of Birmingham and Sheffield, and water for textile finishing processes in places like Manchester and Leeds. The pattern of urban growth depended upon the pattern of landholding. Where there were large estates, there was often an element of formal planning in the growth of provincial towns. In Birmingham three landowning families combined to provide the church of St Paul's, Hockley, in 1777–9, which stood in a square entered by six streets, only three of which were at all built up by the time that Thomas Hanson's map of Birmingham was published in 1781. Often the pressures for growth were such that the planners' concepts were beyond realization. In Liverpool in the 1770s plans were prepared for a new town called Harrington, on the estate of the Earl of Sefton in Toxteth Park:

> the streets being regular, spacious and airy, the lots deep enough for gardens and other conveniences would induce gentlemen not obliged by business to reside in the centre and bustle of the town of Liverpool to resort thither.

The scheme was a failure. Only five or six houses were built on the wide streets, and before the end of the century the whole area was engulfed in housing of a very inferior standard. The areas intended for gardens had been quarried for stone and sand, and for clay for brick kilns, and some had been used as pasture by cow keepers. In most towns the creation of spacious estates for the middle class was a slow process, and only a wealthy landowner meticulous in enforcing the

85

terms of developers' contracts could afford to resist the pressures to allow the building of dwellings of an inferior class.

During the four decades after 1750 some entirely new elements appeared within the English landscape—the navigable canal, the iron railway, the water-powered cotton factory, the coal-fired, steam-powered integrated ironworks, the cupola lead smelter, the working class suburb. The landscapes of districts like the Greenfield Valley, Parys Mountain, the Swansea Valley, the parish of Gwennap, the Coalbrookdale coalfield, the western foothills of the Pennines, the North Staffordshire Potteries and the Derwent Valley had been completely transformed by new forms of mines and manufactures. The scale of industrial change was subsequently to increase, and ways of looking at it were to undergo many changes, but by 1790 the nature of the Industrial Revolution's impact upon the English landscape had been firmly established.

References

1   J. Freeth, *Inland Navigation: An Ode* (1769).
2   J.D. Porteous, *Canal Ports: the Urban Achievement of the Canal Age* (1977).
3   The Arkwright Society, *Canal-Shardlow* (1976).
4   John Kanefsky, *Devon Tollhouses* (1976).
5   C. Charlton, D. Hool and P. Strange, *Arkwright and the Mills at Cromford* (1971). Richard Hills, *Richard Arkwright and Cotton Spinning* (1973).
6   Jennifer Tann, *The Development of the Factory* (1970).
7   J.G. Timmins, *Handloom Weavers' Cottages in Central Lancashire* (1977).
8   J.R. Harris, 'The Employment of Steam Power in the Eighteenth Century', *History*, LII (1967).
9   D.B. Barton, *A History of Copper Mining in Cornwall and Devon* (1961).
10 T.C. Barker and J.R. Harris, *A Merseyside Town in the Industrial Revolution: St Helens 1750–1900* (1959).
11 J.R. Harris, *The Copper King* (1964).
12 K. Davies and C.J. Williams, *The Greenfield Valley* (1977).
13 Fred Brook and Martin Allbutt, *The Shropshire Lead Mines* (1973).
14 Jean Lindsey, *The History of the North Wales Slate Industry* (1974).
15 Christopher Chalklin, *The Provincial Towns of Georgian England* (1974).

4 The Heroic Age, 1790–1810

The essence of the industrial landscape is ambiguity, and at no time were the contradictions of industrial development more obvious than in the last decade of the eighteenth century and the opening years of the nineteenth. This was the period of the wars with revolutionary France, and of political repression and social crisis in Great Britain. It was also an age of spectacular achievements—of bridge building, of technological advances in textiles and ironmaking, in the use of the steam engine and the construction of fireproof factories, the completion of long-distance canals and the construction of docks for seagoing ships. It was a period, too, when the social costs of industrial development came to be appreciated, when the patterns of slums were set in many great cities, and when the first of the mushroom settlements of the Industrial Revolution began to wither away. It ceased to be possible to assume that any activity which provided employment was of necessity to the ultimate benefit of the poor.

The essentials of the landscape of the Industrial Revolution had all appeared by 1790. The coke-using blast furnace, the cotton mill, the canal, the steam engine house, the primitive iron railway, the turnpike road were already familiar features of the landscape in certain parts of Britain. After 1790 the pace of economic activity quickened and the rate of population growth increased. The industrial element in the landscape increased in scale and in its power to create feelings of horror. Increasingly the landscape of the industrial districts became one which was both heroic and tragic, and this was unfamiliar and disturbing to polite society.

The Iron Bridge in Shropshire, although completed as early as 1779, was one of the heroic symbols of the age. The idea of building a bridge in iron was first propounded by Thomas Farnolls Pritchard, a Shrewsbury architect. He had trained as a carpenter and, as the co-ordinator of a group of skilled craftsmen, had specialized in refurbishing town houses and country mansions in the West Midlands. He had been concerned with the construction of stone bridges in Shrewsbury and at Bringewood Forge, and had many contacts with the ironmasters of the Shropshire coalfield. Pritchard suggested the building of an iron bridge over the Severn to the ironmaster John Wilkinson, who had furnaces on both sides of the river. Wilkinson vigorously supported the idea, and a series of meetings led to a petition for an Act of Parliament, which was obtained in 1776. After much altercation between the proprietors, construction began late in 1777. The iron ribs were hauled into place in the summer of 1779 and the bridge was opened to traffic on New Year's Day 1781. The completion of the project was due largely to the energy and determination of Abraham Darby III, grandson of the inventor of the coke-smelting process. He was treasurer to the trustees and manager of the construction force, and may well have personally borne a large proportion of the costs.[1]

From the first the Iron Bridge was vigorously promoted as a spectacle. The artists William Williams and Michael Angelo Rooker were commissioned by the proprietors to paint the structure, and engravings of the paintings were printed and widely sold.[2] Thomas Jefferson purchased a print of the Rooker when he was in London in 1786, and subsequently hung it in the White House. In 1788 George Robertson published a series of six engravings of the Iron Bridge and its surroundings, including views of a coal mine, the pig bed of a blast furnace and an ironworks where cannon were manufactured. By 1790 the Ironbridge Gorge was attracting artists and seekers after the spectacular as much as it was drawing curious ironmasters and industrial spies. J.S. Cotman, J.M.W. Turner and Joseph Farrington were among those who depicted the area's furnaces, mines, lime kilns and, above all, the Iron Bridge itself. A regular tourist itinerary became established.[3] A visitor would admire the bridge, and perhaps cross over it to see a seventy-foot waterwheel at a corn mill within a few yards of the southern end. He would go to see the tapping of a blast furnace, probably at the Coalbrookdale ironworks. He would climb a nearby hill to look down into a vast hollow filled with lime kilns, from which radiated drifts running into pillar and stall workings in the limestone. He might inspect the Calcutts ironworks, where the chief attraction was the boring mill where cannon were completed. He could admire a new industrial village laid out by the ironmaster William Reynolds at Coalport, viewing its spectacular canal inclined plane, and buying porcelain from the newly established chinaworks. He might enter an underground level dug under Reynold's direction, where a spectacular

88

spring of natural bitumen had been discovered; this always stimulated visitors with a classical education to make comparisons with Virgil's Hades. The landscape of the Ironbridge Gorge was horrendous and, at the same time, compulsively fascinating. Its sides were honeycombed with the shallow burrowings of miners and littered with their spoil tips, horse gins and winding drums. The slopes were scattered with crudely built cottages and criss-crossed by cumbersome wooden railways and meandering lanes. By 1800 some sixteen groups of blast furnaces, permanently flame-topped and crowned with palls of reddish-grey smoke, were scattered across the Shropshire coalfield. From them radiated railways along which horses hauled waggons loaded with coal, iron ore and limestone from the mines and quarries in one direction, and with pig iron in the other. The furnaces were surrounded by glowing heaps of coal being coked, ore being calcined and piles of limestone which the least skilled labourers were paid about seven shillings a week to break. They were flanked with lofty engine houses from which steam engines, working like giant pairs of bellows, pumped air into them. Twice daily each furnace was tapped, the vivid, quivering, terrifying light which came from the escaping molten iron throwing puny labourers starkly into silhouette and disturbing the equanimity of even the most work-hardened horses. The landscape was both repulsive and attractive. By 1802 innkeepers found it worthwhile to advertise facilities for 'families that wish to stop and see the manufactories in Coalbrookdale'.

Many travellers described the Ironbridge Gorge in terms of classical landscapes. John Wesley compared the Iron Bridge to the Colossus at Rhodes. An Italian traveller found the approach to the Gorge in 1787:

> a veritable descent to the infernal regions. A dense column of smoke arose from the earth; volumes of steam were ejected from the fire engines; a blacker cloud issued from a tower in which was a forge; and smoke arose from a mountain of burning coals which burst out into turbid flames. In the midst of this gloom I descended towards the Severn, which runs slowly between two high mountains, and after leaving which, passes under a bridge constructed entirely of iron. It appears as a gate of mystery, and night already falling added to the impressiveness of the scene, which could only be compared to the regions so powerfully described by Virgil.

In 1805 Robert Parker of Bath passed through Ketley, some four miles north of the Iron Bridge, and noted:

89

you are at once surrounded with Coal Pits and Iron Stone Pits, Steam Engines, Furnaces and Forges, innumerable, immense beds of Coal blazing around, burning into Coke for the Furnaces, and Chimneys pouring out thick volumes of smoke in all directions as far as the eye can reach; this appearance, with the black faces of all the Men I saw, gave me an Idea of the Regions of Pluto.

Henry Skrine wrote of a visit to Coalbrookdale in 1798:

by night the numerous fires arising from the works on the opposite hills, and along the several channels of the two valleys, aided by the clangour of the forges in every direction, affect the mind of one unpractised in such scenes with an indescribable sensation of wonder, and transport in fancy the classic observer to the workshop of Vulcan, or an epitome of infernal regions.

Charles Dibdin, the actor, was stimulated to similar thoughts:

Coalbrookdale wants nothing but Cerberus to give you an idea of the heathen hell. The Severn may pass for the Styx, with this difference that Charon, turned turnpike man, ushers you over the bridge instead of rowing in his crazy boat; the men and women might easily be mistaken for devils and fairies, and the entrance of any one of those blazing caverns where they polish the cylinders, for Tartarus; and, really, if an atheist, who had never heard of Coalbrookdale, could be transported there in a dream, and left to awake at the mouth of one of those furnaces, surrounded on all sides by such a number of infernal objects, though he had been all his life the most profligate unbeliever that ever added blasphemy to incredulity, he would infallibly tremble at the last judgement that in imagination would appear to him.

Dibdin was one of the few visitors whose writings convey an impression of what living close to the ironworks must have meant for those employed there:

It was our intention to stay all the night, but this was impossible, for the day was insufferably hot, and the prodigious piles of coal burning to coke, the furnaces, the forges, and the other tremendous objects emitting fire and smoke to an immense extent, together with the intolerable stench of the sulphur, approached very nearly to an idea of being placed in an air pump. We were glad enough to get away and sleep at Shifnal.

The iron bridge across the Wear at Sunderland was regarded with the same awe as that over the Severn at Coalbrookdale. It marked a significant change in the technology of bridge building. The ribs were not cast in solid halves, but each of the six was made up of 105 wedge-shaped iron boxes, which fitted together like the voussoirs of a stone arch. The bridge spanned 236 feet and was 32 feet wide, and was designed by Rowland Burdon, a banker and member of an old Durham landed family. It completed a route round the coast from Newcastle to Tees-side by linking the two communities of Bishop's and Monks' Wearmouth, carrying traffic high above the tideway, and offering no obstacle to shipping at any state of the tide. The bridge was opened with elaborate ceremonial by Prince William of Gloucester in August 1796. It became the subject of numerous engravings, and its image appeared on plates, tankards, jugs and glass beakers. A popular verse about it declared:

> Ye sons of Sunderland with shouts
> That rival Ocean's War,
> Hail Burdon in his iron boots
> Who strides from shore to shore.

Like the Coalbrookdale bridge, the iron bridge at Sunderland was the focus of a busy and varied industrial landscape which was described by a visitor in the 1820s:

> Beneath Sunderland Bridge the Wear flows between reinforced banks. It is lined with docks and shipbuilding yards, and the tall brick cones of the glassworks. Curling clouds of black smoke issue from these furnaces, even blacker than the whirlwinds which rise above the coal drops when the coal waggons discharge their loads. Clouds of white dust circle upwards when the limestone waggons are unloaded. Noises like thunder echo around the bridge each time a waggon is emptied. All of this forms a spectacle which you must see before you can have any idea of how imposing it is.

Thomas Telford's great aqueduct which carried the Ellesmere Canal over the River Dee at Pontcysyllte was likewise regarded from the first as one of the wonders of the world. Over 1000 feet long and 127 feet above the Dee at its highest point, a cast iron trough carried on cast iron arches between slender stone pillars, it excited the imagination of all who saw it. It was opened with much ceremony: a flotilla of six boats carrying the proprietors, the workmen and a military band ventured out across the trough on 26 November 1805, to be greeted by a fifteen-gun salute and the cheers of thousands of spectators. A visitor the following year remarked that it was 'one of the most stupendous works of art that ever was accomplished by man. . . . Mr Telford was the engineer, and if this were the only work he had ever produced, it would deservedly give immortality to his name.' The great aqueduct crossed a valley which was increasingly industrialized. On its northern slopes were the iron and coal works of Plas Kynaston, while between the aqueduct and Llangollen were the great limestone quarries of Trevor Rocks. Perhaps the most eloquent impression of the landscape was that written by a French engineer in 1816:

> A sky-born canal, whose iron trough is held up by piers which are both sturdy and elegant. Heavily laden boats and the horses which haul them may safely cross this passage over an abyss, and carry away towards Ellesmere the coal, limestone and iron from the mines, quarries and foundries of the Vale of Llangollen. . . . After a long and exhausting walk, I came into the valley on a fine autumn evening, just as the sun was setting. Never had I seen such an imposing sight. In the midst of the luxuriant woodlands, still flourishing with all their natural freshness, arose whirlwinds of flame and smoke, continual eruptions from the craters of industry. There were blast furnaces, forges, limekilns, piles of coal being coked, workshops, fine mansions, villages built in an amphitheatre around the flanks of the valley. At the bottom was a foaming torrent, while above it the canal, enclosed in its iron envelope, hung, like something enchanted, on its high, slender pillars, a supreme work of architecture, elegant and unadorned, and this magnificent achievement was the outcome of the boldness and daring of one of my friends!

It is not difficult to understand how travellers could be impressed by structures like bridges, in which new technologies were employed to achieve what could not have been done previously. When dazzled by the innovative daring of the Iron Bridge, the Sunderland Bridge or Pontcysyllte, visitors could easily have regarded the smoke of blast furnaces or glass cones, the clouds of coal and limestone dust in Sunderland harbour, merely as backcloths against which spectacular inventions were displayed. However, the imaginations of writers and artists in this period were fired by other spectacular industrial scenes, in which there were no obvious heroic elements.

Foremost among these was the Parys Mountain copper mine in Anglesey. While countless seekers after the curious went to North

Wales, it was no easy matter to visit the mines. They were in an obscure corner of the island, which itself could only be reached, in the period before the bridging of the Menai Straits, by using a dangerous ferry. The mine was nevertheless much visited. William Bingley described it in much the same classical terms used by others to portray the Ironbridge Gorge:

> Having ascended to the top, I found myself standing on the very edge of a vast and tremendous chasm. I stepped on one of the stages suspended over the edges of the steep, and the prospect was dreadful. The number of caverns at different heights along the sides; the broken and irregular masses of rock which everywhere present themselves; the multitudes of men at work in different parts, and apparently in the most perilous situations; the motions of the Whimsies, and the raising and lowering of the buckets, to draw out the ores and the rubbish; the noise of picking the ore from the rock, and of hammering the wadding, when it was about to be blasted, with, at intervals, the roar of the blast in distant parts of the mines, altogether excited the most sublime ideas, intermixt, however, with sensations of terror. . . . The roofs of the work, having in many places fallen in, have left some of the rudest scenes that imagination can paint; these, with the sulphureous fumes from the kilns in which the ore is roasted, rendered it to me a perfect counterpart of Virgil's entrance into Tartarus.

Henry Skrine who climbed Parys Mountain in 1798 found it:

> by far the great curiosity Anglesey can boast, and its most considerable source of wealth . . . as a spectacle it is not a little striking to behold a large arid mountain, entirely stripped of its herbage by the steam of the sulphur works and perforated with numberless caverns, which, opening under lofty arches, one below the other, seem to disclose the deepest arcena of the earth. The various positions of the crowds of men employed, the ascent and descent of innumerable baskets to bring up the ore, and the perpetual echo of the blasts of gunpowder introduced to dislodge it from the rock, produce an effect on the mind which I have seldom known to arise from the complicated and difficult investigation of mines otherwise circumstanced.

Richard Fenton observed in 1810 that:

> from the base of the mountain to its summit there are no signs of vegetation owing to the vapour from the mines, but all is bare earth as if it had been peeled. The excavations formed by

the working of the mines exhibit scenes of the grandest and most picturesque kinds. Everything seems to be thrown about as if it had been done by a painter to produce effect, and the tints are inexpressibly fine.

The landscape of the Cornish mining districts could appear equally dramatic. Richard Warner noted at Dolcoath that he was 'in a country whose very entrails have been torn out by the industry of man. . . . Here everything is upon a grand scale', and that the Dolcoath mine had five winding and three pumping engines, and 1600 men were employed there. The first half of the nineteenth century was a period of great prosperity in the Cornish copper industry, during which the traditional Cornish steam pumping engine house became a familiar feature of the landscape, and the first horse-drawn railways were built in the mining districts. The granite monument to Francis Basset, Baron de Dunstanville, erected on Carn Brea hill in 1836, was an acknowledgment of the heroic qualities of the landscape around Redruth.

The Greenfield Valley evoked similar feelings of shocked admiration. The first decade of the nineteenth century marked the peak of the district's prosperity; the town of Holywell had a population of over five-and-a-half thousand by 1801. Visitors were amazed by both the variety and the scale of the water-powered industries in the Greenfield Valley, in the mile between Holywell and the sea, and also by the curious association between large-scale manufacturing industry and the medieval shrine of St Winifred. Henry Skrine wrote in 1798 that the works were:

carried on in a deep hollow beneath the town, where the little stream flowing from the celebrated well of St Winifred rushes with incredible impetuosity through the narrow valley between two well-wooded hills to the sea, and in the course of a mile turns an incredible number of cotton, brass and copper mills.

Richard Warner noted in the same year that:

in the short course of little more than a mile from its first appearance out of the rock to its blending with the Chester Channel, this torrent works one large corn mill, four cotton manufactories under the firm of the Holywell Cotton-Twist Company, a copper and brass work, one under the firm of the Mona Mine Company, the other under that of the Parys Mine Company, hammer mills, where copper, brewing and other vessels are manufactured, a mill for drawing off copper wire, a calcinary of calamine and a building for making brass.

At the Holywell Level Lead Mine, which was entered by an adit about a hundred yards from the Upper Cotton Mill, a navigable level was used to bring out ore and to transport miners to the workings. In the 1790s it became an object of interest to tourists, who could enter it on passenger boats and take refreshments in one of the caverns, where tables and chairs were set out.[4]

The Wye Valley was another area where travellers could contrast Romantic scenery with mines and ironworks. Wealthy travellers often hired a covered boat well-stocked with provisions to take them from Wilton Bridge or Ross through Monmouth to Chepstow. William Mavor on such a voyage in 1805 noted pig iron from Bishops Wood furnace waiting to be loaded on barges, and saw a wharf, a railway and coal barges at Lidbrook. In 1788 Stebbing Shaw observed woodland on the banks of the river which was cropped every twelve years for charcoal, lime kilns on the hillside below Goodrich and impressively large coal workings at Lidbrook. He was acutely conscious of the sylvan setting in which the industries of Dean flourished:

> We entered a profound dell for several miles, a gurgling brook
> winding through the umbrageous cavity, which supplies a
> number of large Ironworks above the village of Abbey Tintern.

He noted the use of iron ore from Dalton in Furness in the ironworks, observed cast iron cylindrical bellows supplying the furnaces with air and noted that crushed slag was sold to glass manufacturers. Near Lydney he saw another blast furnace, where 'a long spout supported by pillars across the road, conveys water from the opposite hill to move the great wheel of these works'. Another visitor to the Wye Valley in 1798 wrote:

> . . . when the fretful stir
> Unprofitable, and the fever of the world,
> Have hung upon the beatings of my heart –
> How oft, in spirit, have I turned to thee,
> O sylvan Wye, thou wanderer thro' the wood,
> How often has my spirit turned to thee!

Wordsworth's senses were obviously not offended by the clamour of industry as he made his four- or five-day ramble from Tintern Abbey to Bristol in 1798. The mines and manufactories of Dean could impress those who looked for them, but the Wye Valley, unlike Coalbrookdale or Parys Mountain, was a place where it was still possible to ignore the impact of industry upon the landscape.

95

There were still many places in the early nineteenth century where it was possible to take delight in the achievements of industry. At Cromford in 1801 the artist Joseph Farington observed groups of children 'very healthy and many with fine healthy complexions' coming from Arkwright's mills, and he praised the educational provision made for them. The Duke of Bridgewater's passenger boats on the canal between Manchester and Runcorn were a common source of wonder and amazement. Several travellers sailed with delight through the navigable levels of the mine at Worsley. In Scotland the great mills constructed by David Dale at New Lanark vied for the attention of the curious with the nearby waterfall at Cora Lynn, and became more famous when Robert Owen succeeded to the management of the enterprise after 1799. It was still possible to see the landscapes of mining and manufacturing districts in heroic terms, to view the spectacular constructions of industry in the same way as rugged outcrops of rock or thickly wooded hillsides. The paintings of the Ironbridge Gorge by Philip De Loutherbourg or J.S. Cotman bear a close resemblance to the representations of the eruption of Vesuvius by Joseph Wright of Derby. Artists decorated their industrial landscapes with ruined buildings, blasted trees or rugged crags, just as they adorned their representations of classical landscapes.

If industrial structures could be seen as examples of the spectacular, like volcanoes or deep rocky clefts, they could also be viewed as means of taming hostile natural environments. While to some people in the late eighteenth century the wildness of a landscape was itself attractive and satisfying, to others it posed a challenge to reduce chaos to order. The quest for improvement, for the subjection of nature to ordered ornamentation or to profitable enterprise, was one of the most profound influences on the English landscape of the late eighteenth and early nineteenth centuries. Such improvement could be concerned with agricultural change, with the ordered enclosure of open fields or the cultivation of sparsely grazed commons. In the upland regions, especially, it was equally likely to be concerned with the creation of mines or manufactures. This was particularly so in North Wales, one of the regions most frequented by seekers after the curious and the spectacular.

During the years from 1790 until his death in 1801 the first Lord Penrhyn transformed the Ogwen Valley between Lake Ogwen at the foot of Tryfan and the sea near Bangor.[5] The principal slate quarry at Bethesda had been opened in 1785, rationalizing the old haphazard methods of extracting slate on the open commons. By 1790 the new harbour of Port Penrhyn was capable of taking vessels of up to three hundred tons. The following year a new road up the west side of the pass of Nant Ffrancon was completed; in 1800 it was extended to Capel Curig on the far side of the summit, where Penrhyn built an inn. This road was replaced by a new turnpike road from Pentrefoelas to Bangor Ferry, authorized by an Act of Parliament in 1802 and completed in the autumn of 1804. In addition to Penrhyn, the promoters of the new road included Robert Lawrence, a Shrewsbury innkeeper, who had been operating coaches between Shrewsbury and Holyhead since 1779. By 1798 Penrhyn had established a slate 'factory', with a saw mill, where writing slates, gravestones and chimney pieces were manufactured. Large areas of land in the valley were enclosed, most of the fences being constructed of blue slate, and sixty-three dwellings for workmen were built during the 1790s. At a cottage called Ogwen Bank, about half a mile from the main quarry, refreshments were offered to visitors. A model dairy was established which, similarly, was open for inspection by respectable travellers. In 1801 a railway, including three inclined planes, was completed between the quarry and Port Penrhyn. Trains of twenty-four waggons were each drawn by two horses, cutting the cost of carrying slate to the coast from five shillings to one shilling a ton.

Richard Fenton wrote in 1810 that the Ogwen Valley was:

> enlivened by the course of the Rail Road carriages laden with slates, a load that would be more perhaps than 20 horses could draw, drawn by two; neat cottages, mills for the different manufactories, cottages for the workmen employed in the mines, and a chapel adjoining for their use.

He saw the cottage *ornée* and its model dairy with milk pans of Queensware, the factory where slates were cut for chimney pieces, and a water-powered saw mill making frames for schoolchildren's slates. The enterprises were rapidly diversifying. Pencils were being manufactured as well as slates, using materials brought in from the North of England. Near to Llandegai was a mill grinding flints brought by sea from Southampton and the 'downey' counties, the powder from which was sent to the Herculaneum Potteries at Liverpool. In 1808 Penrhyn's obituarist wrote that 'by the creation of an active and extensive traffic, the materials of which were drawn from his own estates, employment and food have been given to thousands'.

Nevertheless, much of the workers' housing in the area was totally unplanned. John Street, Bethesda, which grew up in the 1820s, is 'not so much a street as a network of linked footpaths and alleyways', with houses of different types laid out in an irregular fashion, unfenced plots of land, meandering, unpaved passageways, awkward junctions and changes of ground level.

There were similar developments in slate quarrying elsewhere in Snowdonia. At Dinorwic the old workings on the commons were taken over in 1787 by three entrepreneurs. They were themselves displaced when the landlord, Thomas Assheton Smith, took the quarries in hand in 1809. New roads were built and a quarry at Port Dinorwic, which had come into use in 1793, was linked to the quarries in 1824 by a six-mile tramway. Enclosure acts in 1806 and 1808 enforced the rights of the landlord against squatters. At Nanttle and Blaenau Ffestiniog similar rationalizations of quarrying were coupled with enclosures and the building of roads. Between 1786 and 1831 slate production expanded from 20,000 to 90,000 tons in Caernarvonshire, and from 500 to 12,000 tons in Merioneth.

Some of the most spectacular changes in the landscape of North Wales were concerned only indirectly with slate quarrying. In 1798 William Alexander Madocks, a member of a Denbighshire landed family, began to purchase land on the northern side of Traeth Mawr, the great sands, where the River Glaslyn flows into the sea to the south of the Snowdon range.[6] Like Lord Penrhyn he considered that economic vitality could be brought to the area by linking it effectively with other parts of Britain. He obtained an Act of Parliament in 1803 for a road running across the sands to Porth Dinllaen, which he saw as a potential packet station for Ireland. Under a crag which had once marked the northern shore of the estuary he created a new market and thoroughfare town called Tremadoc, whose main streets were named after London and Dublin. There was a town hall with a market space which could be used as a theatre, a shop, an inn called the Madocks Arms, a Gothic church, a dissenting chapel and a water-powered woollen manufactory. A canal linked Tremadoc with the river, through which access was gained to the sea. Markets, cattle fairs, theatrical performances and race meetings were sponsored. By 1806 Madocks had begun to build a vast embankment called the Cob to close off the sands from the sea, the stones for its construction being carried on an iron railway. The building operations were watched by a French visitor in 1810–11:

> From an elevated spot we were shewn at the extremity of the
> valley some miles distant, a great embankment undertaken by a
> Mr Madock, by which about 3000 acres of land, mostly sand
> and peat land, are to be reclaimed from the sea. The mountains
> on each side of the valley furnish stones, which are carried
> forward *en talus* by means of a railway. There are 300 men at
> work, and the two projections nearly meet in the middle where
> the tide is so violent as to carry away the stones before they
> reach the bottom.

The completion of the Cob in 1811 was marked by an ox-roasting, a
race meeting and an eisteddfod, but the following year it was breached
by the sea. Madocks built a new harbour, later called Portmadoc, at its
north-western end, the first quays being completed in 1824. At first
slate was carted to the new harbour by road, but he began to consider
the prospect of a railway to the Ffestiniog Quarries, utilizing the Cob.
This was eventually opened in 1836, eight years after Madocks's
death.[7] The Festiniog Railway belongs to a subsequent phase of
development but the Cob which it crosses, and the elegant buildings of
Tremadoc, are perhaps the most impressive memorials in North
Wales to the optimism of the early nineteenth century.

Further south, on the shores of Cardigan Bay, the Revd Alban Jones
Gwynne decided in 1805 to devote an inheritance to the creation of a
new port at Aberaeron. A harbour was completed in 1811, which was
soon carrying on a busy trade in slate, limestone, coal, timber and
grain. Streets and a square were laid out, and subsequently shipbuilding and the manufacture of agricultural tools flourished in the town.[8]

The same spirit of improvement could be observed in Cornwall.[9] In
1791 the landowner Charles Rashleigh commissioned John Smeaton
to create a harbour at West Polmear near St Austell, which was
subsequently known as Charlestown. Smeaton built a curved pier and
a wet dock in which ships could lie at all states of the tide. Warehouses,
cottages, a shipyard, a rope walk and fish cellars were constructed. At
first copper ore was exported, but Charlestown became concerned
principally with the shipping of china clay, brought by carts from St
Stephens, north of St Austell. It was taken to Liverpool by sea, and
subsequently to North Staffordshire. Charles Hatchett, who saw the
port in 1796, noted that it was part of an improved estate and thought
it 'a wonderful work for a private gentleman'. A subsequent visitor
was less favourably impressed:

> The smoke of its torment ascended in heavy clouds of black
> and white dust as we scrambled down the steep hill-side into

the gruesome pit, where a crowd of undistinguishable beings are for ever emptying and loading an inexhaustible fleet of schooners. What the natural features of Charlestown originally were it is impossible to say, for everything is coated with white or black dust, and sometimes with both together, the result being a most depressing grey, as of ashes. . . . At first we could see nothing, but gradually our eyes accustomed themselves to the murk, and we made out that on one side of the harbour vessels were being loaded with china clay, and their crews were as white as millers. On the other side coal was being discharged, and the crews were as black as Erebus. The villagers . . . were black or white, according to which side of the port they resided on, while some were both black and white, like magpies.

The idea that industry could tame nature, that it could actually improve a landscape, is found in Richard Ayton's description of the Cornish harbour of Portreath in 1813. A pier had been constructed at Portreath as early as 1760, but the narrow harbour was not built until 1800; nine years later it was served by the first Cornish railway, a horse-powered line to Poldice. Ayton found it a place of much bustle and busy-ness, with ships bringing coal from Neath and Swansea and loading copper ore. Yet it did not satisfy his thirst for improvement:

Portreath, in all its parts, in spite of the efforts of art, still preserves an appearance so savage and unhewn, that it furnishes a most satisfactory specimen of the wilds of Cornwall. A few chimneys and a little smoke give it a slight air of improvement, but nature has cast it in so uncouth a mould, that it can never be altogether tamed or chiselled and planed into forms of comfort or regularity.

Ayton was similarly impressed by the wildness of the mining country east of Portreath. 'The country about St Agnes', he wrote, 'is particularly rich in tin and copper mines and these furnish the only inducements that could have tempted any human beings to settle near it.' He saw mines and manufactures as means of civilizing a rugged landscape rather than as intrusions which defiled it.

Others, nevertheless, saw industrial activity as something which was destructive of the natural order, both in the landscape and in social relationships. Richard Warner wrote in 1808 of the approach through the mining districts to Penrhyn:

Nothing surely can be more hostile to the beauties of Nature than the processes of mining. Its first step is to level the little wood (if, indeed, any there be) with which she may have garnished the spot where she has concealed her ores. It then penetrates into the earth, and covers the neighbouring soil with unproductive rubbish. It proceeds to poison the brooks around with its mineral impregnations, spreads far and wide the sulphureous smoke of its smelting houses, blasting vegetation with their deleterious vapours, and obscuring the atmosphere with the infernal fumes of arsenic and sulphur.

It was difficult to be favourably impressed with the landscape created by those who built the copper smelthouses around Neath and Swansea. Ayton wrote in 1813:

there is always something interesting in the busy bustle of industry; but in copper works and ironworks it certainly presents itself to the eye under its most unfavourable appearances. . . . In the neighbourhood of Swansea, there are some very extensive copper works, which are situated in a hollow, and immediately above them is not a blade of grass, a green bush, nor any form of vegetation, volumes of smoke, thick and pestilential, are seen crawling up the sides of the hills, which are as bare as a turnpike road.

The working class population which lived in the new industrial landscapes was often disinclined to behave like the deferential peasantry in Romantic paintings, and the place accorded to women in the new social order was sometimes upsetting to bourgeois Romantic views of their role. New aspects of social behaviour could appear as horrifying to the genteel traveller as the most terrifying effects of pollution. During his visit to the Swansea Valley Ayton wrote:

women, in all parts of Wales are employed in offices of the hardest and dirtiest drudgery, like the men. On the banks of the canal I saw little companies of them chipping the large coals into small pieces for the furnaces without shoes or stockings, their clothes hanging about them, released for the sake of ease from pins and strings, and their faces as black as the coals except when channelled by the streams of perspiration that trickled down them. . . . I am particularly struck with the wretched, filthy, ragged appearance of the lower orders of people. The women are beyond all sufferance, dirty and slovenly, and as they unfortunately all dress alike, there is no competition among them, and they are equally unmoved by the love of cleanliness and the shame of dirt. Few of them ever wear shoes or stocks, though some do wear stocking legs, reaching down to the ankles and attached by a loop to the great toe; their outer garments are always of woollen, as coarse as a horse cloth, and of a dark colour that does not require washing; on their heads they wear a man's hat, sometimes without a brim, sometimes without a crown, and sometimes without a brim or a crown; and thus generally disguised, they present a form of more roughness and rudeness in the shape of women, than I ever saw in any other part of the kingdom. . . . But there is a far more serious subject for reproof. . . in the corruption of morals and manners which the increase of manufactories has occasioned among the people within the last half century . . . the streets of Swansea are almost as notorious for scenes of loud and shameless profligacy as the Point at Portsmouth. That this degeneracy results from the increase of manufactories, and the consequent attraction of a larger population to one point there can be no doubt.

Some years earlier Richard Warner had been similarly dismayed by the horrors of the industrial landscape of Neath and Swansea. He was able to interpret the area in the manner of an earlier generation, listing its various enterprises—the Neath Abbey ironworks, the copper works of Roe and Co. of Macclesfield, the Mines Royal, Bewick and Horne's chemical works, and the numerous collieries which gave 'an incalculable advantage to all its manufactories' as did the 'canal running up its beautiful valley'. Like Ayton he found the new working class offensive; and destructive of the picturesque elements within the landscape:

We . . . paid a visit to the remains of its abbey. . . . The ruins are of prodigious extent, but being in the immediate neighbourhood of the metal works, and inhabited by the squalid families of the workmen employed there, they do not produce the pleasing emotion that religious remains, under different circumstances, so naturally and generally do inspire.

In many parts of Britain the development of mines and manufactures was influenced by the spirit of improvement, of bringing rationality to an unkempt landscape or order to one which was wild, as was exemplified at Tremadoc, Aberaeron or Charlestown. In the West Midlands a series of five enclosure acts between 1776 and 1799 enabled the Earls of Dudley to promote large-scale mining, ironmaking and other enterprises on their estates around Stourbridge, Dudley and Kingswinford.[10] The preamble to one of the acts stated:

the said . . . Lands . . . afford very little profit or Advantage, but are capable of great Improvements and . . . would, if divided and inclosed, so as to be converted into Tillage, be of great

Advantage to the several Persons interested therein, and of public utility.

The Act proclaimed that nothing would be allowed to prejudice:

the Right of the Lord . . . of the Manor . . . or his . . . Lessees, in and to all Mines of Coal, Ironstone, Limestone, Glass House Pot Clay, Fire Brick Clay, and all other Mines whatsoever . . . in or under the said Commons . . . he and they . . . may . . . have, hold, enjoy, raise, get, take and carry away all such Mines and Minerals . . . as fully . . . as before the passing of this Act . . . to use all Pits already sunk . . . and all Gins, Engines and Buildings thereon erected.

The Lords Dudley energetically promoted the Stourbridge and Dudley Canals which gave access to the mines on their newly enclosed estates, and by 1800 they had been able to lease several tracts of land for the building of blast furnaces.

In the Shropshire coalfield the lands of the Leveson Gower family were similarly rationalized. Both industrial and agricultural parts of the estate were loosely administered in the eighteenth century. A company formed in 1764 by Earl Gower had built a canal and operated limeworks, but the iron ore mines and blast furnaces on the estate were built by other concerns. In 1802 a new company was formed into which the Bishton family, then agents to the estate, brought their shares in three ironworks. In 1812 the Leveson Gower estates came under the control of a new Scottish agent, James Loch, who rigorously reorganized both its agricultural and its industrial parts. The cottages of industrial squatters in Ketley, 'huts little better in their appearance or their construction than some of those in Sutherland', were demolished or rebuilt to a standard estate style, with dormer windows, herringbone lintels and square-sectioned yellow chimney pots. Middlemen were excluded from any role in the provision of housing, and all the cottages were brought under the direct control of the estate. There were mass executions of the cottagers' bulldogs. Plots of garden ground were granted to favoured tenants, and those considered undesirable were encouraged to leave. The drainage of the Weald Moors to the west of the coalfield, authorized by an enclosure act of 1801, were accelerated, and by 1820 Loch was able to claim:

No where have the united exertions of landlord and farmer done more, or is there more doing at this moment for the improvement and cultivation of the country. No where have

103

the wants, which of late years have, occasionally, so heavily pressed upon the labouring classes, been more the subject of consideration.

The period of the wars with France, between 1793 and 1815, was marked by alternating spells of elation and depression in the textile trade. The main movement on the spinning side of the industry was towards polarization, with such large concerns as the Peels', with twenty-three mills at Blackburn, Bury, Bolton, Burton on Trent and Tamworth, and William Douglas, with mills near Manchester and in the Greenfield Valley, Carlisle and Scotland, dominating the market. The majority of spinning works were small, often urban concerns. Between 1797 and 1834 the number of cotton spinning factories increased by about a third, while the consumption of raw materials increased tenfold, suggesting a substantial degree of concentration. Water power was still widely used in cotton spinning, and the majority of mills, whether urban or rural, were situated along valley floors. Some mills, like the worsted spinning concern of Davison and Hawksley at Arnold near Nottingham, built in the early 1790s, used water power on some days of the week and a steam engine when the water supply was inadequate.[11]

Much of the new cotton mill building in this period was in Lancashire, but in times of optimism mills were erected in the most unlikely places. Those in the remoter parts of the Pennines, where the distant influences of the two great centres of Nottingham and Manchester overlapped, faced considerable disadvantages; but some mills were built in places from which contact with the main centres must have been almost impossible. In 1812 Richard Ayton noted the remains of a failed cotton mill at Maryport in Cumberland. In the mid 1780s a worsted spinning mill was built at Louth in Lincolnshire, with the object of creating employment for the poor and reducing the poor rates. It was not well-managed and closed in 1793. In Shrewsbury a woollen manufactory with three five-storey buildings was established in 1790, and quickly failed. It housed French prisoners of war, for a while, but was taken over by a Mancunian entrepreneur in the period of excited optimism just after the Peace of Amiens in 1802. Linked with a spinning works at Llangollen and a print works at Oswestry, it was principally concerned with weaving cotton fabrics, but it did not prosper. The proprietor turned to wholesaling rather than manufacturing, letting out parts of the mill for accommodation and for workshops, and eventually selling it to make his living from writing and auctioneering. In 1805 William Mavor was told that the associated concern in Llangollen was proving 'injurious to Manchester', but like most such country mills it fell quickly into obscurity. An even more remote factory—a mill for carding and spinning cotton, erected in 1794 at a cost of about £4000—was on the River Rea in the parish of Stottesdon on the southern slopes of the Clee Hills. Access to the site even today is by a series of steep and narrow tracks, so it is not astonishing that by 1804 the mill was offered for sale under bankruptcy proceedings. It was demolished in the second half of the nineteenth century, its last recorded use being as a Primitive Methodist meeting house in 1851, but its pool and leets, and the slag from the ironworks which preceded it on the site, remain as features of the landscape.

Early textile mills were prone to destruction by fire since their floors, the joists on which they rested and the upright columns supporting the joists were normally of wood. In 1792 William Strutt, the Derbyshire cottonmaster, erected a mill in Derby and a warehouse at Milford which had cast iron uprights but wooden cross beams, and his West Mill of 1793–5 at Belper was of similar construction. Strutt corresponded regularly with Charles Bage, a Shrewsbury wine merchant of Derbyshire origins who, in 1796, went into partnership with the flax manufacturing concern of John Marshall and Thomas and Benjamin Bage. In 1793 Marshall, who lived in Leeds, perfected a series of processes for producing linen thread and yarn similar to that which Richard Arkwright had devised for processing cotton. He took into partnership the brothers Benyon who had experience of the linen industry as wholesalers in their native Shrewsbury. The partnership's second mill in Leeds was destroyed by fire in February 1796 and they decided to replace it with a new factory in Shrewsbury which, with the prospect of new canal communications, was becoming an attractive location for the linen industry. Bage was one of a group of men of unusual ability who flourished in Shrewsbury at that time; they included Samuel Butler, headmaster of Shrewsbury School, Joseph Plymley, archdeacon and agricultural improver, William Hazledine, the ironfounder, and Thomas Telford. Bage utilized experiments carried out at the Ketley ironworks during the designing of Telford's iron aqueduct at Longdon on Tern to design a mill 177 feet 3 inches long and 39 feet 6 inches wide, with five storeys and 31,000 square feet of floor space. No wood was used in the construction. The floors were carried on brick arches, springing from iron cross beams, cast in two pieces and supported by three lines of cruciform columns. The mill was wider than most textile factories because its dimensions were not restricted by the size of timber that was available for cross beams. It stood alongside the Shrewsbury Canal, from which its steam engines were supplied with coal, and was surrounded by fields filled with racks on which yarn from the bleaching vats was dried. Between the canal and the nearby main road stood several groups of houses for the most skilled workers. These cottages, in clusters of four, surrounded by large gardens, were of the same basic design as the houses for supervisors and skilled men in Strutt's village at Belper, or those at Darley Abbey near Derby, the home of Bage's father. The fireproof mill was rather more expensive than mills of conventional construction and was adopted only slowly, but many of the principles used by Bage eventually became commonplace in the building of textile factories. The mechanized linen industry pioneered by John Marshall flourished, particularly in Leeds, but Shrewsbury remained a centre of some importance and a second fireproof mill was built, within sight of the first, in 1804–5.[12]

The first mills housing power looms for weaving cotton were built during the first decade of the nineteenth century, but initially the range of fabrics which could be woven by machine was limited, and it was not until the 1820s and 1830s that such mills were generally adopted. It was estimated in 1818 that there were only fourteen powered weaving mills in the Manchester region. The ever-increasing quantities of yarn produced by mechanized factories were, for the most part, woven by handloom weavers, the majority working in their own homes, but increasing numbers in large buildings set aside for the purpose. The spinning of worsted thread was increasingly mechanized after the successful demonstration of the throstle in Bradford in 1794, but power weaving of woollen cloths remained difficult as late as the 1830s. There were nevertheless increasing numbers of woollen mills in which the scribbling and carding processes were mechanized, in which gig mills were used in finishing, and where space was provided for hand-operated looms and other machines. One of the most impressive was Benjamin Gott's Bean Ing factory in Leeds, built in 1792, where he 'designed to bring under one roof the whole process of manufacture from the first breaking of the wool to the finishing of the piece'.

The industry was increasingly concentrated in the West Riding of Yorkshire, as the steam engine was gradually applied in woollen mills, and the decline of the once-prosperous textile areas of East Anglia and

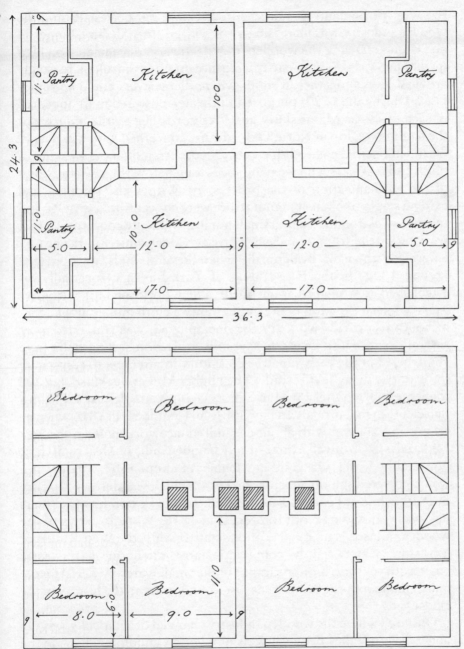

Figure 7 (*a*) and (*b*) Cluster houses. Plans for houses built for Messrs Marshall, Benyon and Bage during the winter of 1796–7, adjacent to their flax mill in Shrewsbury

the West of England was accelerated. Outside the West Riding the woollen industry was increasingly specialized. In Wiltshire, Somerset and Gloucestershire the woollen manufacturers concentrated on high quality fancy cloths and, partly to ensure quality control, increasingly grouped looms together in shops where the weavers could be supervised. During the 1790s purpose-built water-powered mills appeared in such places as Malmesbury and Freshford. The textile industry of the Banbury region in North Oxfordshire, concerned with a variety of fabrics in the mid eighteenth century, concentrated on the weaving of plush and masters set up weaving sheds long before there was any hint of the mechanization of the process. At Witney the spinning and carding stages of blanket manufacture were concentrated in mills, and the trade was dominated by a small number of family concerns. Carpet weaving spread from its ancient centre at Kidderminster to the nearby Severnside town of Bridgnorth, where several mills were erected around 1800. In the East Riding of Yorkshire a carpet mill was established at Wansford about 1790, which flourished for thirty-five years, while at Boynton in the same county a cloth mill, built like that at Louth to provide work for the unemployed, was converted after several decades into an estate saw mill. In Devon several mills were constructed in the early nineteenth century in attempts to resuscitate the county's dying textile trade. The Higher Mill at Buckfastleigh and the Serge Mill at Ottery St Mary are surviving examples. At Tiverton a failed cotton mill provided a base for John Heathcoat in 1816 when he moved to the town with about a hundred laceworkers from the East Midlands. In Cornwall a three-storey woollen mill, 120 feet by 50 feet, powered by water, was built at Menheniot about 1803. There was a water-powered spinning factory in Truro, which was destroyed by fire in 1820, while at Penrhyn a fulling mill, said to be two hundred years old, was still finding cloth to process in 1816. While in terms of the woollen industry's national economic history it is the West Riding of Yorkshire which rightly commands most attention in the early nineteenth century, the appearance of the small water-powered textile mill in many parts of Britain was just as significant in the history of the landscape.

One area where the woollen industry changed dramatically was the upper Severn Valley between Welshpool and Llanidloes where, in the closing years of the eighteenth century, there was an increasing concentration on flannel manufacture. Richard Fenton noted in 1804 that the great flannel manufactory of Newtown was increasing every day, and when passing from Plymlimmon to Llanidloes the following year William Mavor observed many long pieces of flannel stretched out on tenters. The first mill in the region was built at Meifod in 1789 and subsequently many more mills for carding and spinning were established. Some were in the countryside, but there were large concentrations in Llanidloes, and particularly in Newtown. In the suburb of Penygloddfa rows of cottages, sometimes back-to-backs, were erected, surmounted by through rooms on the third floors where weavers could work at their looms. One such row in Ladywell Street, constructed with a timber frame in 1810, contained six back-to-back cottages, with a room on each floor, a larder beneath the stairs and a work room above.[13]

The silk industry also changed considerably in the late eighteenth and early nineteenth centuries. Increasingly it moved from the Spitalfields district of east London to the provinces, especially to Macclesfield, Leek and Congleton on the Cheshire/Staffordshire border, and to Middleton in Lancashire. The appearance of Macclesfield, with its massively elegant spinning mills, almost every one as perfectly proportioned as a Georgian country house, and its many streets of three-storey cottages with long light windows on the top floors, has until recently been one of the most evocative reminders of this stage of the Industrial Revolution. Silk manufacture also expanded considerably in Hertfordshire in this period, with mills at Watford, Rickmansworth, St Albans, Hatfield, Hitchin, Tring and Redbourn. Some were converted corn mills and used water power, but those at Rickmansworth and Redbourn were new steam-powered concerns.

The 1790s saw a remarkable growth in the iron trade. Production of pig iron in Great Britain rose from less than 100,000 tons per year in 1790 to about 250,000 tons in 1805. The East Shropshire coalfield continued to be an area of major importance in terms of production as well as an attraction for seekers after spectacular scenery, but it was rapidly being overtaken by two other regions. In 1798 Richard Warner noted that Glamorgan and Monmouthshire were becoming the centre of the iron trade for the whole kingdom. There were only eight blast furnaces in South Wales in 1788, but the total rose to twelve in 1791, to twenty-eight in 1796, forty-seven in 1806 and ninety in 1812. Three of the six largest ironworks in Great Britain in 1806 were those at Cyfarthfa, Penydarren and Blaenavon. Most of the South Wales ironworks were built at the heads of the valleys, near to the outcrops of iron ore. Iron was taken to the coast by canals, which became a familiar feature of the South Wales landscape during the 1790s. The Glamorgan Canal was opened from Merthyr to Cardiff in 1794, the Monmouthshire Canal from Pontnewydd and Crumlin to Newport in 1799, the Neath Canal in 1795–9 and the Swansea Canal in 1798. Numerous iron railways were built to connect with the canals and to carry materials to the furnaces from mines and quarries inaccessible to water transport. Many such tramroads were themselves substantial works of engineering. The Sirhowy tramroad, a plateway with a gauge of four feet two inches, was opened in 1805 and with its associated Nine Mile Point tramroad, opened the following year, extended some twenty-five miles from Newport to Sirhowy, and included at Risca a viaduct between forty and fifty feet high with thirty-six arches.

Many of the South Wales ironworks were built in isolated areas to which workers had to be attracted by the provision of housing. (This has been the object of an exhaustive study by Jeremy Lowe.) At the Blaenavon works, established between 1789 and 1792, the houses nearest to the furnaces were of traditional Welsh construction and plan, with four rooms of quite generous size. Two parallel rows of dwellings were linked by a range which included a company shop, and perhaps some offices. They appear to have been designed for foremen or skilled workers. By contrast Bunkers Row, higher up the hillside, built at about the same time, was originally a terrace of twenty single storey back-to-back dwellings of remarkably mean dimensions, designed apparently for the lower paid unskilled workers. Before 1814 detached larders were constructed for each house, and about 1860 the row was rebuilt as ten through houses, with higher outside walls, a new roof and first floor, and new doors and windows. By the 1820s the

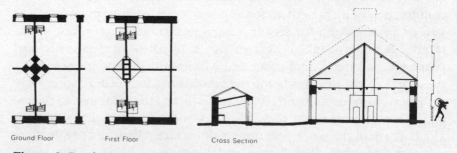

Ground Floor   First Floor   Cross Section

Figure 8 Bunkers Row, Blaenavon. Originally single-room back-to-back houses with detached pantries, but converted into four-room through-houses in the mid nineteenth century

110

Blaenavon Company was building houses to a standard design with a kitchen and small bedroom on the ground floor, and a larger sleeping room above. About 225 such houses were built at the Company's various works. Some of the other ironmaking companies in South Wales also built houses to standard patterns. The catslide house, with a kitchen and a bedroom above it, and an outshot containing another sleeping area and a larder is a familiar feature of the landscape around the ironworks of the Crawshay family, near Merthyr and at Hirwaun and Nant-y-glo. The design was used from about 1795 to 1830, and was probably introduced to the region by the Crawshays. Another type of house constructed at some ironworks was the 'dual' row, a terrace of two-storey houses on a hillside, erected above a basement row of dwellings opening in the opposite direction. Such houses were built at Nant-y-glo and Clydach, the lower rooms forming some of the most cramped and damp family accommodation imaginable.[14]

The landscape of the South Wales valleys in the early nineteenth century was one of the wildest and least ordered in Britain. Houses were rarely built to any set plan but followed the lines of tramroads or even the banks of canals. The streets of Hirwaun near Aberdare follow the lines of tramroads which conveyed raw materials to the blast furnaces whose ruins still stand. Merthyr, a bowl among the hills at the heads of the valleys, was in the process of becoming the largest town in Wales, and gaining a reputation as a spectacular place to visit.

The other new ironworking area was the Black Country of South Staffordshire and North Worcestershire. There were only six blast furnaces in the whole of Staffordshire in 1788, but three were under construction in the south of the county. By 1796 there were fourteen, by 1805 forty-two and by 1820 there were ninety. As in South Wales the growth of ironmaking depended heavily upon canals, and many extensions to the Stourbridge, Dudley and Birmingham Canals in the 1790s gave access to new ironworking sites. Many of the Staffordshire works, unlike those in Shropshire or South Wales, were built on fairly flat ground, and the inclined hoist to lift raw materials to the charging platforms of the blast furnaces became a familiar feature of the Black Country landscape. While the South Wales ironworks were built in almost empty valleys, the Black Country was already thickly populated by miners and iron-using craftsmen. The industrial landscape of the region was largely shaped by the pattern of landholding. In Shropshire and South Wales most land was leased from big landowners in large blocks by the ironworking company, and the companies

111

themselves were integrated concerns, mining raw materials, smelting iron, forging and rolling pig iron to make wrought iron, and in some cases making complex items like steam engines and bridges. There were some integrated ironworks in the Black Country like the Bradley works of John Wilkinson and the Hallen family's Monway Field works at Wednesbury, and the Earls of Dudley were large-scale landowners by any standards, but the majority of enterprises were small, operating a mine or working a furnace or rolling mill, on a site leased from a small proprietor. Gilbert Gilpin wrote in 1819:

> In Staffordshire landed property is very much divided; and naturally, all the proprietors desirous of turning their coal and iron mines to *immediate* account. Hence there is a colliery in almost every field. As there is not sale for such an immense quantity of coal and ironstone, several of these little proprietors unite together and build furnaces; clerks from the neighbouring manufactories are taken in as partners to direct the concern; the tradesmen of the towns in the vicinity who can raise a hundred or two hundred pounds form part of the firm; and it is in this way that the ironworks have been multiplied in that county.[15]

The blast furnace and the steam winding engine became familiar features of the landscape between Birmingham and Wolverhampton, but the various towns of the region maintained their speciality manufactures: saddlers' ironmongery at Walsall, hardware at Wolverhampton, locks in Willenhall and Sedgley, springs at West Bromwich. Nailmaking was widely practised in cottages on the heaths, and chain making was carried on at Cradley Heath. James Kerr in 1798 described the manufacture of nails:

> Executed at the workman's own house, to each of which houses a small nailing shop is annexed, where the man and his wife and children can work without going home; and thus an existence is given to an uncommon multitude of small houses and cottages, scattered all over the country, and to a great degree of population, independently of towns.[16]

The landscape of the Black Country has been totally transformed in the twentieth century with the spread of modern factories and suburban housing. A few groups of cottages still stand in enclosures once fenced off on open heaths, however, and at Mushroom Green something of the random nature of industrial settlement in the region is still preserved.

In the west of the Black Country the glass industry continued to prosper in the area north of Stourbridge. There were glassworks in the region by the 1790s, many of them on the banks of the recently constructed canals, their tall conical kilns giving to the landscape of the area a character unique within the region.

The long-established ironworks owned by the Walker family at Rotherham achieved great fame after the construction of the Sunderland Bridge and was much visited by tourists. In the East Midlands ironworking began in this period in the Moira area on the Leicestershire/Derbyshire border where, following the discovery of a salt-water spring while the pits were being sunk, a bathing establishment and an hotel were erected. After about twenty years the conjunction of spa and industry proved impossible to maintain, so the waters were shipped to Ashby de la Zouch where new bath buildings were constructed. While such areas were thriving, the iron industry of the Weald was quietly disappearing. The last blast furnace, at Ashburnham, was blown out in 1809–10, and the last forge, also at Ashburnham, ceased work in 1820.

The coal industry grew rapidly at the end of the eighteenth century, both in coalfields where there were many ironworks and in those where there were none. In the North-East the coal trade increased by about a third in the years between 1790 and 1815, when the total coastal and overseas exports from Newcastle and Sunderland went up from 704,000 to 1,048,000 chaldrons per year. In the same period imports to London increased from 753,000 to 1,148,000 chaldrons per year. The coalfields of the Midlands, Lancashire and Yorkshire benefited directly from the building of canals, and their production increased through sales in areas which were previously difficult of access.

The most significant change in the landscape of the coalfields followed the introduction of the pit winding engine in the late 1780s. The date of the first successful use of steam to wind pits is uncertain. In the Shropshire coalfield, William Reynolds began to work a winding engine at Wombridge in 1789, although discussion of it and of other winding engine projects had been carried on for some years. In the East Midlands Joseph Wilkes employed a Boulton and Watt engine to wind a pit at Oakthorpe in 1787. Wherever the first such engines were used, it was during the 1790s that the landscape of the coalfields was transformed by the erection of very large numbers of small, cheap steam engines, used for winding. They were of many kinds, only a

113

small proportion being built according to James Watt's patents, at least until after their expiry in 1800. In 1811 it was estimated that there were more than fifty winding engines in the Nottinghamshire and Derbyshire coalfield, the majority of them atmospherics. In Shropshire there were about a hundred such engines by 1800. A spectator in 1801 looking north from the hills above Coalbrookdale saw:

> several Steam Engines, erected for the purposes of raising Coals, Ironstone, &c. from the Pits, they being now in almost general use instead of horses, performing the business much quicker & at considerably less expense, the apparatus of which being so simple and yet so substantial that the person who has the management of it has so far at his command as to stop the machine in a moment.

In the North-East steam winding engines superseded the winders operated by waterwheels, supplied with water by pumping engines, which had become popular in the 1780s. In 1800 the characteristic North-Eastern vertical single cylinder engine was patented by Phineas Crowther of Newcastle upon Tyne and such engines, housed in tall buildings adjacent to the pit headstocks, became familiar features of the landscape of the region.

In the coal-shipping ports of the North-East the mighty staithes, whose origins dated back to the seventeenth century, were supplemented from about 1800 by coal drops, devices on which a chaldron or railway waggon could be lowered to the deck of a ship before its load was discharged, thereby avoiding the great breakage of coal caused when it was dropped from the tops of the staithes.[17]

In non-ferrous mining areas the greatest change of the period was the appearance of the distinctive Cornish mining engine. The first was erected by Richard Trevithick at Wheal Prosper mine in Cornwall in 1811. It was a single-acting condensing engine, on which the steam piston on its downstroke raised through the beam a heavy weight on the pump ram which, on its subsequent downstroke, pumped the water. The Cornish engine was by far the most efficient single cylinder pumping engine, and its efficiency was stimulated by the monthly reports of the duties performed by pumping engines in Cornwall which were regularly published. These engines became a speciality of the Cornish foundries, which installed them in all parts of the world during the nineteenth century, as well as in mining areas in Britain where fuel was scarce. The typical engine house—rectangular in plan, with a round chimney at one corner and, at the opposite end, a particularly massive bob wall on which the beam rocked—is still a characteristic feature of the mining districts of the West of England, and many isolated examples can be found in upland mining areas elsewhere. Over three hundred such houses, many of mid nineteenth-century date, survive in the western counties. The majority are derelict, but seven retain their engines and a few have been converted to dwelling houses. They now stand in largely empty landscapes, but when working would have been surrounded by pulleys, ropes, rods, wooden frames and trucks, and miners going to and from their work.

The increasing use of steam power was one of the most obvious developments of the closing years of the eighteenth century. By 1800 there may have been as many as two thousand steam engines in use in Britain. The majority were in mining areas, but they were being put to an ever-increasing variety of tasks. Nevertheless, older forms of power remained of considerable importance. Many of the larger textile mills were worked by waterwheels, while the smaller mills in urban areas were often horse-powered. Engineers continued to devote much time and attention to water power, and Thomas Telford wrote a treatise on the subject. The greatest innovator in this sphere was probably John Smeaton, who died in 1792. He had introduced cast iron waterwheel shafts in 1769 and wrought iron wheel buckets in 1780, and was responsible for many ingenious mills. The more spectacular examples of water power became objects to be visited. The circular tumbling weir constructed in 1790 to provide power for the serge mills at Ottery St Mary in Devon drew many visitors. In 1800 a waterwheel fifty feet in diameter and six feet wide was built to blow a blast furnace at Merthyr Tydfil. Near the Iron Bridge in Shropshire was a wheel about seventy feet in diameter which drove a corn mill; it attracted the attention of many visitors to the bridge who drew or described it. About two miles away at Coalport was a similar mill, built in 1805, so famous that it was mentioned in a 'Book of Trades' published in 1821 as 'proof of the extent to which machinery is arrived in this country'. Many water mills were put to new uses in this period. As charcoal blast furnaces, forges and fulling mills fell out of use, the pools and leets which had supplied them with water were adapted to drive corn or paper mills.

The English paper industry underwent considerable changes in this period, and the peak number of mills—564—was reached about 1821. Many of them used traditional technology, but some utilized innovations which were ultimately to transform the industry. In 1804 machines to make paper on an endless web, of a kind patented by John Gamble in 1801, were built by the London engineer Bryan Donkin, and installed by Henry and Sealy Fourdrinier in mills at Two Waters and Frogmore in Hertfordshire, and at St Neots in Huntingdonshire. In 1809 John Dickinson installed his own version of the Fourdrinier machine in a mill at Apsley, Hemel Hempstead, which was the beginning of the growth of a large-scale paper industry in the valley of the River Gade. Transport was provided by the Grand Junction Canal, and cottages for workers were erected at Apsley and Croxley. By 1834 water from the Gade was no longer suitable for drinking because, according to Thomas Telford, it was 'infected by the deleterious substances used for paper mills'. Fourdrinier machines were also installed in mills at Sawston in Cambridgeshire, which became a papermaking centre of considerable importance. The industry was first established in the parish at Dernford Mill in the 1660s. This mill had previously been used for fulling, and when given up by the papermakers in favour of another site about 1796, it was used for grinding grain and crushing oil seeds for the tanning industry. The first steam engine to work a paper mill was installed at Wilmington near Hull about 1786, and by 1815 there were several mills in various parts of Britain which were steam-powered.

There were great changes in the British canal system at the end of the eighteenth century, the period of so-called 'canal mania'. The 'Silver Cross' network of long-distance waterways was considerably improved. The Warwick and Birmingham, the Warwick and Napton and the Grand Junction all, with the exception of the section of the latter through Blisworth Tunnel in Northamptonshire, opened in 1800, giving a much-improved route from the North and Midlands to London which avoided the need to use the Thames. In 1814 the Grand Union linked this system with Leicester and ultimately with the Trent and Humber. The Worcester and Birmingham Canal opened in 1815, improving access to the lower Severn from Birmingham, while the Stratford upon Avon Canal linked the heart of the Midlands with the Avon, and gave new access from the western parts of the Black Country to the Warwick and Birmingham at Kingswood. The waterways across the Pennines were all completed in this period, the Rochdale Canal in 1804, the Huddersfield in 1811 and the Leeds and Liverpool in 1816. The Kennet and Avon Canal, linking London with Bristol, was opened in 1810.

The proprietors of other waterways had ambitions which they were unable to realize. The Ellesmere Canal, authorized in 1793, was intended to link the Mersey, the Dee and the Severn. It was distinguished by the two great aqueducts built by Thomas Telford across the Ceiriog at Chirk in 1801, and over the Dee at Pontcysyllte in 1805. A link across the base of the Wirral peninsula from Chester to a sparsely populated spot called Whiteby was opened in 1795, and at the Merseyside terminus, designated Ellesmere Port by the company, basins, locks and a small inn were erected, together with some gardens, bath houses and shooting butts. Like its fellow canal ports, Runcorn and Stourport, Ellesmere Port was for a time a resort town. Passenger services to Chester began soon after the canal opened, ferry connections being supplied across the Mersey to Liverpool. Far from following a direct line from the Mersey to the Severn, however, the Ellesmere became a rambling route linking Montgomeryshire, North Shropshire and Cheshire with Ellesmere Port. The line to the Severn near Shrewsbury was abandoned in a field near the village of Western Lullingfields in 1797. The line to Chester was never carried beyond the northern end of Pontcysyllte, from where there was only a short canal, extended by tramways, serving nearby mines and ironworks, and a water feeder line to Llangollen, which was also used to collect cargoes of limestone from quarries at Trevor Rocks. The main line of the canal ran in an easterly direction from Chirk, serving the company's namesake town of Ellesmere with a short branch, passing close to Whitchurch, and eventually near Nantwich joining the earlier and unprosperous Chester Canal, over which vessels could circuitously make their way to Chester and Ellesmere Port. At Welsh Frankton the line to Shrewsbury went off in a south-easterly direction, and towards the south-west was a branch which served the limestone rocks of Llanymynech, and made a junction with the Montgomeryshire Canal at Carreghofa. The canal distributed throughout the acid soils of the region limestone from Trevor and Llanymynech and coal from Chirk and Ruabon which was used to burn it to lime in the many canalside kilns. The opening of the canal led to the building on the great rock of Llanymynech of four remarkable inclined planes which brought the limestone from the quarries to the wharves. Over the flat peat mosses of North Shropshire the canal was crossed by numerous elegant lifting bridges. The Ellesmere, like many other canals, adorned the landscape of its region and provided it with useful services, but it never fulfilled the ambitions of its promoters.

There were several innovations in canal technology in this period. The tub-boat canals of the Shropshire coalfield included six inclined planes—double track railways on which boats were lifted up and down slopes—all built between 1788 and 1796. One of these, the Hay incline in the Ironbridge Gorge, was much visited by tourists. On the Somersetshire Coal Canal, which linked collieries in the Mendips with the Kennet and Avon, a change of level near Combe Hay was accomplished first by a caisson lock, completed in 1798 after much delay. It proved almost impossible to operate and was replaced by an inclined plane, completed in 1801, and then by a flight of nineteen pound locks. An iron aqueduct was built on the Shrewsbury Canal, an extension of the tub-boat network, carrying the waterway over the River Tern at Longdon. The aqueduct, a cast iron trough carried on cruciform section uprights, was designed by Thomas Telford and opened in 1796. A similar trough, though carried on iron arches springing from stone pillars, and with the towpath cantilevered over the water, was used on the vastly larger Pontcysyllte aqueduct. Iron aqueducts appeared only as the canal mania was drawing to a close, but one was constructed at Wolverton to carry the Grand Junction Canal over the River Ouse, and there were three on the Stratford Canal.

The canal became an established feature of the landscape in most parts of Britain during this period, except in the far West and the remoter regions of the highland zone. Canals at the end of the century showed considerably more engineering enterprise than those of the first generation. Engineers were less afraid to dig deep cuttings and create high embankments. Rivers were crossed in style, either on stone aqueducts—like the Dundas Aqueduct which carries the Kennet and Avon over the River Avon near Bath, or John Rennie's magnificent aqueduct which takes the Lancaster Canal over the Lune, or the structure designed by Robert Fulton lifting the Peak Forest Canal over the Goyt at Marple—or iron ones. From time to time they tunnelled under hills. Increasingly they used iron bridges, like those over the Kennet and Avon in Sydney Gardens, Bath, to carry towpaths or for the accommodation of light traffic. Several of Rennie's canals were distinguished by skew bridges. Many of the canals' features were standardized, but this often enhanced the qualities of the landscapes through which they passed. Rennie's perfectly proportioned stone bridges across the Lancaster Canal, the bowed brick accommodation bridges of the Leicester line of the Grand Union, and the curiously curved footbridges over the ends of the locks of the great staircase on the Peak Forest Canal at Marple, with steps like the rood stairs of a medieval church and carved heads on the key stones, are memorable features of the landscapes which they adorn.

Canal companies made increasing use of railways. For five years from 1800 to 1805 traffic on the Grand Junction Canal was conveyed around Blisworth Tunnel by a railway nearly two miles long, the construction of which was supervised by William Jessop. When the tunnel was completed, much of the track was used to form a line from the canal at Gayton to Northampton. Many of the South Wales canals had tramway extensions. A French visitor in 1810–11 commented:

> We crossed several iron railways leading from foundries and coal mines in the country to the sea. Four low cast iron wheels run in an iron groove lying along the road. It is now however the general custom to place the groove on the circumference of the wheel running upon the rail, which is a mere edge of iron upon which no stone or other impediment can lodge. Five small waggons and sometimes six, fastened together, each carrying two tons of coal, are drawn by three horses, that is four tons to each horse, besides the weight of the waggon – about five or six times as much as they could draw on a common road.

In 1802 limestone quarries at Ticknall and Breedon in the East Midlands were linked to the terminus of the Ashby Canal by iron plateways. There were many railways among the industrial concerns of Joseph Wilkes of Measham. In 1799 a steeply inclined iron railway was constructed to convey bags of salt from canal boats on the Trent and Mersey to barges on the River Weaver. At Purfleet in Essex railways were used in the chalk quarries by 1807. In the coalfields of the North-East and around Coalbrookdale the railway networks were steadily extended.

The growing trade of the late eighteenth century led to a transformation in the appearance of the larger seaports. At Hull the former town defences were replaced by docks which encircled the old part of the town with water. Work on the first began as early as 1774 and a second scheme commenced in 1809. In Liverpool there were fifty acres of docks by 1824. The greatest transformation, however, was in London. Before 1800 there were only two wet docks on the Thames, both small and both used for refitting rather than loading ships. London's trade had doubled between 1700 and 1770, and it doubled again in the following thirty years. By the 1790s the port was in crisis. There was intolerable congestion made worse by the seasonal nature

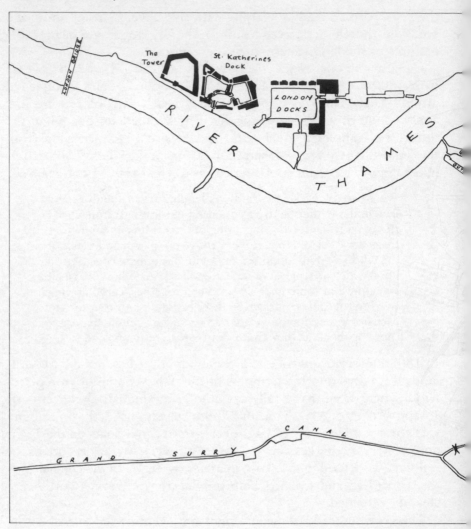

Figure 9 The docks in London in 1833

of many of the trades carried on from London. Goods were piled high on the quays, easily available to the least-practised of thieves and a satisfying source of income to many experienced criminals. One solution proposed in the years before 1800 was the creation of facilities in the Pool of London, between London and Blackfriars Bridges, for which the construction of a new London Bridge was necessary in order to allow larger ships to proceed upriver. It was as part of these plans that Thomas Telford's remarkable design for a new bridge with a

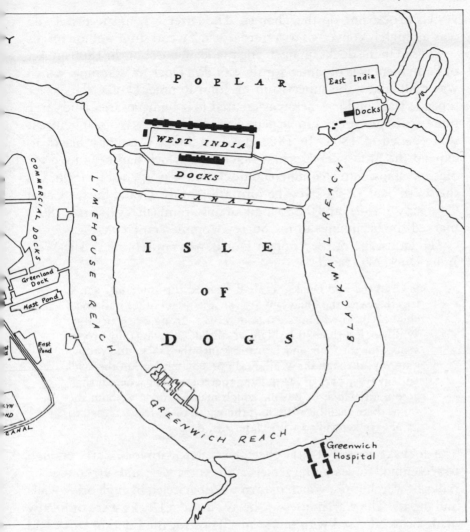

single 600-foot iron arch was put forward in 1800. The solution to London's problems proved to be the creation of wet docks downriver from the Tower. The first of these, the West India Dock on the Isle of Dogs, was authorized in an Act of Parliament of 1799 and opened in 1802. The engineer for the scheme was William Jessop, but the construction was supervised by Ralph Walker. There was a thirty-acre rectangular import dock, with a twenty-four-acre export dock parallel to it, and a 'canal' to the south, intended to provide a short cut for

121

vessels proceeding up the Thames. The latter was unsuccessful and was ultimately converted to a third dock. Twenty-four million bricks were used in the docks, many being made on the spot. In 1800 an Act of Parliament was obtained for the London Dock at Wapping, which was built under the supervision of John Rennie. Unlike the earlier scheme, the London Dock was created in a built-up area, and large numbers of houses had to be demolished to make way for it before it was opened in 1805. In 1803 the East India Company began to expand the Brunswick Dock at Blackwall, which had been used for masting ships, into a commercial dock that was opened in 1806. On the south bank of the river the formation of the Grand Surrey Canal Company in 1801, and the opening of the Grand Surrey Basin in 1807, marked the beginnings of the Surrey Commercial Docks.

The landscape of the London Docks was entirely new. The West India Dock Act stated:

> Such of the said Docks, as shall be used for unloading ships, together with the Quays, Warehouses and all other buildings, shall be inclosed and surrounded by a strong brick or stone Wall, not less than 30 ft. high, on all sides, leaving only proper spaces for the Cuts and Entrances into the Dock, and proper gateways through the Wall, and immediately within the Wall and on every part of the outside thereof, except where it shall adjoin any Dock or Bason, which may be made without the same, there shall be a Ditch of the width of 12 feet, at least, to be always kept filled with water 6ft. deep.

The docks consisted of large sheets of water, with locks large enough to accommodate sea-going vessels at the entrances, and surrounded by ranks of warehouses, which in turn were encircled by high brick walls and moats. The warehouses at the West India Docks were of locally made bricks dressed with limestone. Those at the London Dock had wide bases of rusticated stone, ornamented with patterns suggesting the sea. The high walls and limited entrances, together with the formation of a special police force, were intended to counter the endemic pilfering which had afflicted the port. By 1820 the development of the London Docks was incomplete, but the basic pattern of the landscape had been established.[18]

Most English towns of consequence grew rapidly in the decades after 1790. The character of urban development was profoundly influenced by patterns of landholding. In Manchester, Liverpool, Sheffield, Birmingham and Bath large areas were developed by great estates which attempted, not always with success, to create coherent patterns of building. In Birmingham there were booms in building in the early 1790s and between 1808 and 1816. Most building was to the west and north of the old town centre, although some important tracts to the south were made available for development by the Gooch family. To the north the Colmore family were, from the 1770s, the principal beneficiaries of the city's growth, while to the north-east over a hundred acres of land belonging to the Holte family of Aston Hall were sold for building between 1788 and 1820. Thomas Hanson's 1781 map of the city, and that by C. Pye published in 1795, both show streets laid out in advance of building on several sides of the centre.

In Manchester developers were more active than in Birmingham, and rather more land was acquired from the great estates well ahead of construction. In Liverpool much property was owned by the Corporation, and by three estates which closely controlled the supply of land for building. Attempts to create spacious middle class suburbs failed, and the typical pattern of development in the port was the court of three-storey back-to-back houses with cellars, approached by a 'tunnel' through a terrace of houses with frontages on to a main street, which was structurally integrated with the back-to-backs behind. Even when land was released by great estates it proved almost impossible to enforce covenants governing street widths and the size and quality of houses, and prohibiting the construction of cellars for habitation. In towns where most land was held in small lots development was controlled only by market forces.[19]

Until the 1780s Leeds remained within the bounds which it had reached in the early seventeenth century. Most new housing was crowded into the yards and gardens of the town centre and, especially between 1750 and 1780, on to the many small folds which lined the roads radiating outwards, the tiny fields used by milk sellers or by butchers keeping animals awaiting slaughter, as market gardens or bowling greens. Building on the folds followed no set pattern. Sometimes the outer extremities of a fold were lined with short blind-back terraces, while other houses were scattered at random across the space in the centre. These folds have long since disappeared from the fringes of the centre of Leeds, but they can still be recognized in other parts of the West Riding conurbation, particularly along the road from Halifax to Bradford through Queensbury and Great Horton. In 1787 the first block of streets deliberately intended for working class cottages was laid out at the east end of Leeds, adjacent to an area where infilling had already created a largely working class district. The development was undertaken by a building club, and one of the streets was consequently called Union Street. During the next twenty years streets of working class cottages filled many of the fields to the north, east and south of Leeds. Professor W.G. Rimmer has estimated that between 1774 and 1815 an average of 150 new houses a year was built in the town, but that between 1790 and 1795 the rate reached 200 a year, and between 1800 and 1805 900 a year. Almost all of these new working class dwellings were back-to-back terraces, a type of house which may have derived from the rows built on the edges of the burghage plots of central Leeds; these had, of necessity, to face inwards on to narrow courtyards and were in consequence usually blind-backed.[20]

In Nottingham, as in Leeds, the expanding population of the mid eighteenth century was largely accommodated by building on the open spaces and yards within the city centre. There was a boom in the city's housing after 1784 when the typical house was, in the words of Dr S.D. Chapman, three boxes placed on top of each other, used for living, sleeping and framework knitting, often with a cellar below and sometimes a cockloft above. Nottingham was surrounded by open fields, unavailable for building. After the passing of the Lenton Enclosure Act of 1796, which brought on to the market land no more than a mile from the market place but outside the town, a ring of suburbs grew up beyond the fields.

The growth of many towns was, to a large extent, shaped by the fields which encircled them. Coventry was, like Nottingham, constricted by common land and began to develop suburbs beyond on enclosed property. In Leicester, by contrast, the enclosure of the open fields preceded pressures for development. The East Field had been enclosed in 1764, and the South Field in 1804. In Cambridge the East or Barnwell Field was enclosed in 1807. The largest allotment was soon sold off. It passed through many hands in smaller and smaller lots, and was quickly covered in buildings. Nevertheless many of the colleges retained their land, and sold it later for high quality developments. The colleges were also slow to develop their land on the West Field, which had been enclosed five years earlier. To the north-east the growth of Cambridge was checked by the open fields of Chesterton parish, which were not enclosed until 1840. In Bath and Sunderland the direction of development was similarly affected by obstructions to building caused by common land but in these towns, as in Leicester and Cambridge, there is no evidence that the commons positively caused a shortage of land for building such as existed in Nottingham and Coventry.

The actual patterns of building were often shaped by fields as well. This was particularly so in Leeds, where the back-to-backs to the east of the town were erected on long narrow rectangular fields, created by the parcelling out of furlongs of the former open arable fields in the late Middle Ages. A typical field was between 120 and 200 feet wide and about 600 feet long. Most were simply filled with a self-contained group of back-to-backs, with no ways through to other developments and with access on only one frontage. The many lines of blockages in the streets of Leeds of this period were the relics of the old field boundaries. In Portsmouth building took place on land which was still open arable fields in the 1790s. Two or three adjacent strips would be amalgamated and a narrow street erected on the plot. From the 1790s onwards many of Liverpool's new streets were erected on rectangular closes which had once been the open strips of the common fields, and the shapes of the closes helped to determine the typical Liverpool court.

Many townspeople in the late eighteenth and early nineteenth centuries were dazzled by the fortunes which had been made in the development of Bath, and which were still being made in Cheltenham and Leamington. They hoped to create squares and terraces fronting on to wide streets which would attract the 'pseudo-gentry'—those who were wealthy but did not have large landed estates—who would transform a town into a place of resort. The editor of a Shrewsbury newspaper commented in 1795 that the building of various new terraces and a new church would 'attract strangers and add to the number of genteel families'. A pamphleteer in Ludlow in 1812 urged that salt should be brought from Cheshire and used with the cheap local coal to create hot saline baths like those of Bath, and that terraces should be erected on the common land of Whitecliff, so that the town might attract retired merchants and army officers. Such projects— outside Bath, Cheltenham and Leamington, and later a few other spas and resorts—rarely succeeded. Middle class suburbs were superficially attractive to developers and landowners, offering the long-term prospect of higher rents than could be obtained from working class dwellings. Several were started on the edges of the growing industrial cities, but typically they grew only slowly, the streets taking several decades to fill up. Often they were overtaken by industrial pollution or advancing tides of working class terraces. The ambitious schemes for creating

125

spacious developments at the west end of Leeds came to an end because of pollution caused by the concentration of offensive trades along the banks of the Aire. Successful towns contained the seeds of their own destruction. In the textile regions it was the finishing trades, the most offensive polluters of air and water, which were concentrated in the towns, as they had been for centuries. By the late eighteenth century a town of significant size in all parts of the country attracted iron foundries, tanneries and the like, trades which were tolerable on the edges of small market centres but which became serious dangers to health when they multiplied and were surrounded by houses.

Yet, however rapidly the towns of England were growing between 1790 and 1820, they remained very small by modern standards. The circumference of Manchester and Salford, the largest conurbation outside London, was between four and six miles. The streets of what were to be the enlarged town centres of Victorian England had been laid out and industries were growing up on their edges, but in the year of Waterloo industry was still not seen as something which was essentially urban. The growth of towns had been rapid, but not so spectacular as the transformation of parts of the South Wales valleys, the Black Country or Parys Mountain.

References

1 Neil Cossons and Barrie Trinder, *The Iron Bridge* (1979).
2 Stuart Smith, *A View from the Iron Bridge* (1979).
3 Barrie Trinder, *The Most Extraordinary District in the World* (1977).
4 K. Davies and C.J. Williams, *The Greenfield Valley* (1977).
5 Jean Lindsey, *The History of the North Wales Slate Industry* (1974).
6 Elisabeth Beazley, *Madocks and the Wonder of Wales* (1967).
7 M.J.T. Lewis, *How Ffestiniog got its Railway* (1968).
8 Aylwin Sampson, *Aberaeron* (1971).
9 Cyril Noall, *The Story of Cornwall's Ports and Harbours* (n.d.).
10 T.J. Raybould, *The Economic Emergence of the Black Country* (1973).
11 Stanley D. Chapman, *The Early Factory Masters* (1967); *The Cotton Industry in the Industrial Revolution* (1972).
12 A.W. Skempton and H.R. Johnson, 'The First Iron Frames', *Architectural Review*, CXXXI, No. 751 (1962).
   W.G. Rimmer, *Marshalls of Leeds: Flax Spinners 1788–1886* (1960).
13 J.B. Lowe, *Welsh Industrial Workers' Housing 1775–1875* (1977).

14   J.B. Lowe and D.N. Anderson, *Catslide Roofed Outshot Houses in Merthyr Tydfil and Related Areas*, Iron Industry Housing Papers No. 5 (1973).
15   Madeleine Elsas, *Iron in the Making: Dowlais Iron Company Letters 1782–1860* (1960).
16   Quoted in D.M. Palliser, *The Staffordshire Landscape* (1976).
17   Frank Atkinson, *The Great Northern Coalfield 1700–1900* (1968).
18   John Pudney, *London's Docks* (1975).
19   Christopher Chalklin, *The Provincial Towns of Georgian England* (1974).
20   M.W. Beresford, 'The Back-to-Back House in Leeds 1787–1937' in S.D. Chapman, ed., *The History of Working-Class Housing* (1971).

5 The Age of the Engineer, 1810–50

It is difficult to see the English industrial landscape in the early nineteenth century as a unity. In the early stages of the Industrial Revolution engineers had acquired the ability to build multi-storeyed factories and complex ironworks, to sink deep mines, to carry canals on the level through hills and across valleys, to excavate docks and surround them by high walls, to lift railway waggons and canal boats on inclined planes. A new confidence had been gained in the use of traditional materials like stone, bricks and timber, and cast iron had been successfully developed as a constructional material. The growing sophistication of the financial system provided the capital which allowed engineers to apply their ideas. Between 1810 and 1850 all these processes were carried further. Many of the most spectacular feats of road, canal and bridge building in English history took place during these years, and within the space of a quarter of a century a railway system of over six thousand route miles was created. Yet it was no longer possible to hail the achievements of engineers with unqualified praise. The effects in the great cities of the rapid rise in population which accompanied economic expansion made it impossible to regard industrialization as an unquestionable blessing for the poor. The decline of some of the areas which had boomed in earlier decades, either through exhaustion of raw materials or as the result of short-term depression of demand, revealed the precarious nature of the prosperity brought by the growth of mines and manufactures. As early as 1814 Richard Ayton found Amlwch, the town nearest to Parys Mountain, in a state of precipitate decline. Families were going away to seek work, but there was still insufficient employment for those who were left:

> This wretched town stands in the midst of a hideous scene of desolation; the country round looks as if it had been blasted by a horrid pestilence, and raises in the mind no images but of misery and famine.

128

Visitors to the ironworking region of Shropshire in the years after the Battle of Waterloo found the works quaintly old-fashioned, the machinery clumsy and the level of activity low. The Ketley ironworks, the second largest in Britain in 1804, was described in 1817 as 'an appendage to the Wellington workhouse'. Such scenes were foretastes of the desperate depths of depression to be experienced in many industrial areas before the middle of the century. There were to be many casualties of technological progress: handloom weavers, wool-combers, cotton spinners in areas away from the main centres of the textile industry, stage coach drivers and nailers. Even in prosperous industries workers were to experience spells of bitter depression. After 1810 it is necessary to observe the changes in the industrial landscape from two different angles—to perceive it as if through the eyes of an artist like John Cooke Bourne, observing the confidence with which engineers transformed the landscapes of even the remotest parts of the country with new structures, and also to appreciate it as it was seen by a foreign visitor like Leon Faucher, as he was shown by a policeman in 1844 around the common lodging houses of Liverpool.

The early nineteenth century was the age of the polymath virtuoso engineer, of Telford, Rennie, Fairbairn, the Jessops, the Brunels and the Stephensons. In no other period of English history were there so many engineers in practice whose names are still recognized. It was a time of confidence and optimism. A German visitor to Manchester Grammar School in 1844 remarked that the favourite subjects among the graffiti on the desks were 'canals, railroads and rivers with barges, ships and locomotives on them'.

The network of navigable waterways in England and Wales was considerably enlarged in the early nineteenth century, reaching many places remote from the main centres of population. The Montgomery-shire Canal was extended from Welshpool to Newtown in 1819–21, greatly benefitting the local flannel industry. In 1818 the Pocklington Canal was constructed in the East Riding of Yorkshire, from the River Derwent to the town of that name, where a typical canal head land-scape of warehouses, a wharf, a lock and a saw mill developed. There was much canal building in the West of England. The fifteen-mile Bridgwater and Taunton Canal was completed in 1827 and the thirteen-and-a-half-mile Chard Canal in 1842. Glastonbury was reached by a fourteen-mile cut from Highbridge in 1833. The six-mile Torridge Canal was completed in 1827 and the thirty-five miles of the Bude Canal in 1823. The Grand Western Canal, originally authorized in 1796 from Taunton to Topsham, was never completed but two sections which were built were opened in 1814 and 1838. Several novel means of changing levels were employed on the canals of the South-West peninsula. There were four inclined planes on the Chard Canal, one on the Torridge and six on the Bude, while the Grand Western had seven lifts as well as an incline.

Of more economic importance than the isolated canals of the South-West were the improvements made to the connected narrow waterways of the Midlands. The Black Country and Birmingham formed the heart of the English canal system. Between Birmingham, Stourbridge, Wolverhampton and the Tame Valley was a network of canals at three levels, approached on each side by long flights of locks. These were traversed by many vessels making their way from one part of England to another, and by many more carrying goods over short distances for the heavy industries of the locality. The canalscape of the region is unique. Flyovers, where a canal at one level crosses over a line at another, can be seen in several places. There were toll offices, signposts, tunnels with towpaths, numerous towpath bridges and an infinite variety of bankside installations. The system was steadily extended during the first half of the nineteenth century. Some extensions were simply branches to serve new ironworks or mines. Others were major feats of engineering which eased the operation of the whole system. The most important was Thomas Telford's new line through Smethwick, completed in 1829, a vast cutting some seventy feet deep on the main line of the Birmingham Canal, avoiding the six locks by which the original line climbed over a summit. The new canal was forty feet wide and had a broad towpath on either side. It was crossed by several bridges, among them the Galton Bridge with a single 150-foot span of iron. A new reservoir was built at Rotton Park, and nearer to Wolverhampton were a further cutting at Deepfield and a tunnel at Coseley wide enough for boats to pass within it. The extent to which the landscape was changed can be judged by Telford's own account:

> I found adjacent to this great flourishing town a canal little better than a crooked ditch, with scarcely the appearance of a hauling path, the horses frequently sliding and staggering in the water, the hauling lines sweeping the gravel into the canal, and the entanglement at the meeting of boats incessant; whilst at the locks at each end of the short summit crowds of boatmen were always quarrelling or offering premiums for a preference

of passage, and the mine owners, injured by the delay, were loud in their just complaints. . . . I found that it was absolutely necessary that the numerous bends should be cut off and the canal reduced to nearly a direct line from the town to Smethwick summit, that an entirely new cutting should be made through that summit, 70 ft. in depth, moreover that the straight line should be continued across the flat ground called the Island, and the ridge at Bloomfield, so that the general direction should become a straight and level line to Bilston and Wolverhampton. The length of the main line from Birmingham to Autherley would be reduced from 22 to 14 miles, and adapted to an unlimited increase in traffic.

The Birmingham system continued to flourish even after the coming of main line railways. Basins were established to which canal boats brought coal to be transhipped to railway waggons for long-distance carriage, and since the ironworks of the region had grown up around the canals, much of their traffic continued to travel by water. Extensions continued even after 1850. In 1858 the 3027-yard Netherton Tunnel was opened, the third canal tunnel to penetrate the central ridge of the Black Country, providing an alternative route to the spectacular Dudley Tunnel, which passed through a series of limestone caverns but was subject to severe delays. At the same time the flight of locks at Delph on the Dudley Canal was rebuilt, and the number of locks reduced from nine to eight. The Birmingham and Warwick Junction and the Tame Valley Canals were completed in 1844 and provided a bypass round Birmingham to the east, avoiding the congested flight of locks at Farmers Bridge. The Cannock Extension, finished in 1863, was built to link the Black Country with new coal workings to the north-east.

Thomas Telford was also responsible for clearing another of the major bottlenecks of the eighteenth-century canal system. The Harecastle Tunnel, through which the Grand Trunk Canal gained access to the Trent Valley, was nearly three thousand yards long and could be negotiated by only one boat at a time. Telford built a new tunnel parallel to the old one. Steam engines had to be employed to pump dry some of the saturated strata through which the new tunnel passed. Railways were used to carry away spoil. Bricks were fired on the spot. Work began in 1824 and the tunnel was opened in 1827.

By the mid 1820s the building of railways linking the major industrial regions was a real possibility, and one such line was proposed

131

from Birmingham to Merseyside. The reaction of the waterways' interests was to promote a new canal, the Birmingham and Liverpool Junction, linking the Staffordshire and Worcestershire and Birmingham Canals outside Wolverhampton with the Ellesmere and Chester at Nantwich, a distance of some forty miles. From Nantwich vessels could proceed through Chester to Ellesmere Port. The new line, authorized in 1826 and designed by Telford, was an exercise in virtuoso canal construction which has few equals in Britain. It passes through deep cuttings like those at Woodseaves and Grub Street, and across high embankments at Shebdon and Shelmore. The latter, built across unstable ground to avoid game coverts, posed many difficulties and delayed the opening of the canal until 1835. With one exception the locks were concentrated into flights at Audlem, Nantwich and on either side of Market Drayton. The bridges were confidently constructed of local stone. The so-called Rocket Bridge, over the deep cutting south of Tyrley Locks, was built with a style and panache which belies the insignificance of the farm track which crosses it. From Norbury Junction a branch of the Birmingham and Liverpool Junction Canal descended a flight of twenty-three locks to a junction with the Shrewsbury Canal at Wappenshall. The junction became the site of an interchange wharf to which coal, iron and bricks from the Coalbrookdale coalfield were transported by tub-boat and waggon, to be taken by narrow boat to other parts of Britain; and where shop goods were received and distributed in the locality. The wharf was the property of the Duke of Sutherland and was so profitable that a second warehouse was constructed in 1844, and another wharf for bulk cargoes was opened at the end of a short branch to Lubstree, about a mile away. The Wappenshall branch enabled narrow boats to reach Shrewsbury, an event which was celebrated by the construction of a magnificent classically styled butter and cheese market at the canal terminus.

Ellesmere Port gained new life from the vast traffic generated by the canal. During the first thirty years of its existence the basins where the Wirral line of the Ellesmere Canal reached the Mersey saw little hectic activity. Transhipment from narrow boats to broad-beamed flats took place at Chester, so that freight traffic simply passed through the locks to and from the Mersey. Like other canal ports, Ellesmere Port had pretensions to resort status and some provisions were made for bathers, but the population in 1831 was only 234. Construction of Telford's magnificent range of warehouses began in 1829. The old

19 Cotton mills in the Greenfield Valley, from an aquatint by J. White. The Upper Mill of 1783 is in the foreground with a clock in the pediment and a cupola with a bell on the roof, typical symbols of the work discipline which early factory masters attempted to instil into their employees. In the background is the Crescent Mill of 1790

20 The lower end of the Greenfield Valley in 1792 from a drawing by I. Ingleby engraved by W. Watts, entitled 'Cotton Works near Holywell, Flintshire'. The six-storey building in the centre is the Lower Cotton Mill of 1785, and to the left the buildings of a mill where brass and copper wire were drawn for nail- and pinmaking. On the extreme left a man appears to be emptying a sack into a lime kiln

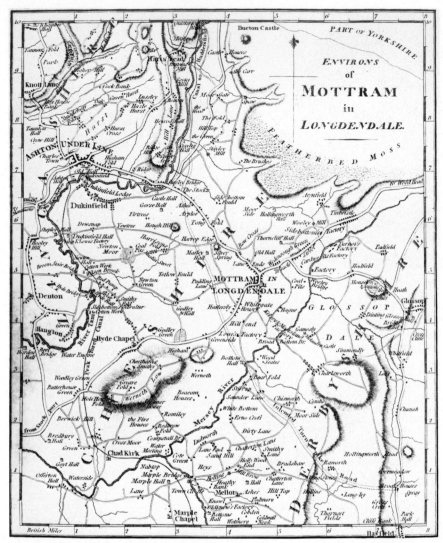

21 John Stockdale, 'The Environs of Mottram in Longendale', 1794, from J. Aikin, *The Country from 30 to 40 miles round Manchester*, 1795. Immediately to the south of Mottram is Broad Bottom Bridge on the River Mersey, on the upstream side of which is the cotton factory of Kelsey and Marsland. Numerous other cotton mills can be seen along the rivers, and the map conveys a vivid impression of the haphazard pattern of settlement in the period

22 A view of the Upper Works at Coalbrookdale, drawn by G. Perry and engraved by T. Vivares, published in 1758. The flame-topped furnace can be seen slightly to the left of centre, surrounded by a mass of other buildings, including two air furnaces, with tall stepped chimneys, and casting houses with ventilators on their roofs. In the right foreground heaps of coal are being coked on the banks of the pool, from which water flowed to power the wheels working the furnace bellows. A team of horses is hailing the cylinder for a steam engine. On the hill in the background the mansions of the Darby family stand in close proximity to the cottages of some of their workpeople

23 Curclaze Tin Mines, Cornwall, in 1813, from a drawing by L. Farrington engraved by S. Middiman. The mines were described in 1855 as 'a huge gap in the earth, a mile in circumference and all open to the light of day'

24 The facade of the Etruria factory built for Josiah Wedgwood by Joseph Pickford and opened on 13 June 1769. The waterway in the foreground is the Trent and Mersey Canal, of which Wedgwood was a prominent promoter. Its surface was originally level with the ground floor of the factory. The cupola containing a bell closely resembles those in contemporary cotton mills

25 'The Cast Iron Bridge near Coalbrookdale' by Michael Angelo Rooker, published in 1782. This view of the Iron Bridge was commissioned by the bridge proprietors and drawn by Rooker, scenery painter at the Haymarket Theatre, during a visit to Shropshire in 1782. It became the most popular of all the prints of the bridge

26 The Pontcysyllte Aqueduct, 1000 feet long and 127 feet above the River Dee at its highest point. Completed in 1805, it became one of the wonders of Wales, but the canal route from the Mersey to the Severn of which it was to form part was never completed

27 The western part of Parys Mountain, the portion of the mine controlled by the Parys Mountain Company. The windmill on the summit was not built until 1878, long after the peak of the mine's prosperity

28 Portmadoc, Caernarvonshire, with a rake of slate waggons descending towards the harbour, while the preceding train is hauled across the Cob by a pair of horses

29 'Coal Works. A view near Neath in Glamorgan', drawn by J. Hassel and published in 1798

30 Upper Colliers Row, Merthyr, a row of catslide outshot houses built between 1801 and 1805, probably for workers at the Ynysfach Ironworks, which was the property of the Crawshay family, who appear to have built the great majority of the houses of this type in South Wales

31 Glassworks alongside the Dudley Canal at Amblecote near Stourbridge

32 Locks on the staircase ascending from Fulton's aqueduct over the Goyt on the Peak Forest Canal at Marple

33 A coal drop at Wallsend, 1839, by T.H. Hair. A chaldron waggon can be seen on the platform of the coal drop waiting to be lowered to the ship

34 'Mr Whitbread's Chalk Quarry at Purfleet.' A view of one of the largest chalk quarries in Essex in 1807, by which time horse-drawn railways were in use

terminal buildings were swept away and the new warehouses, span-
ning arms of the docks on elliptical arches, were constructed in brick
and slate. There were facilities for handling grain, iron, flints and
timber, and new ranges of workshops and stables were erected.
Houses were built by the canal company for their employees in the
1830s, and during the following decade more housing was provided
by speculators. Traffic increased rapidly after the opening of the
Birmingham and Liverpool Junction Canal in 1835, and this phase of
the town's growth was completed by the ceremonial opening of a new
435 by 139-foot dock in 1843.[1]

Some other important new canal lines were built in the North-West
at this time. The Macclesfield Canal, completed in 1831, extended
twenty-six miles from Hall Green on the Trent and Mersey to the Peak
Forest Canal near Marple. The Ellesmere and Chester Company constructed a branch, completed in 1833, from Barbridge to Wardle near
Middlewich, where there was a junction with the Trent and Mersey.

River navigations were also improved in this period. In 1827 the
Gloucester and Berkeley Ship Canal was opened, enabling vessels to
avoid the treacherous waters of the lower Severn, and thus substantially improved the efficiency of operations downstream from
Gloucester. In 1842 an Act of Parliament was obtained for improving
the Severn itself between Gloucester and Stourport, and the locks over
that stretch of the river came into use in 1847.

In Yorkshire a new waterside town grew up at Goole, at the junction of the Ouse and the Dutch River; it had previously been an
insignificant hamlet, with a population of only 450 in 1821. In 1819,
in response to congestion on the routes between the mines and mills of
the West Riding and the North Sea coast, the Aire and Calder Navigation Company proposed to construct a new deep water channel from
the Aire at Knottingley to the Ouse at Goole, a line which opened in
1826. This channel necessitated the destruction of many buildings at
Goole, and a new town was created around two wet docks. The port
installations were impressive, the dominant building on the water-
front being a huge bonded warehouse. The first streets were laid out in
1823, one of them being wide enough to accommodate market stalls.
Much of Goole consisted of drab two-storey brick cottages but it was
emphatically a company town, with many ordered features derived
from the best Georgian architectural traditions relieving the mono-
tony. The low terraces were punctuated by taller buildings at the ends
of each street. Every corner in the new town was champfered, and the

133

bevelled corner has been aptly described as the leitmotif of the whole new town.[2] Sir George Head wrote of Goole in 1835:

> Ample space has been allotted to the streets, and the buildings, including spacious bonding warehouses, are of the finest red brick. Besides the extensive docks already completed, a new one, apparently by far the largest of any, is in a forward state, the cast iron gates of this dock and the lock, will, when finished, be, it is said, the largest in England.

Docks were also constructed at the established ports in the early nineteenth century. The principal development in London was St Katharine's Dock, downstream from the Tower, authorized in 1824 and designed by Thomas Telford. The project involved the demolition of 1250 houses and the disruption of over 11,000 people. The docks were designed with great skill, the warehouses being constructed close to the water's edge so that there was no need for separate transit sheds, and on the landward sides the warehouses extended to the extremities of the site, obviating the necessity to build high walls of the kind which had enclosed the earlier docks. Two Boulton and Watt steam pumping engines maintained the water level.

It was during this period that Liverpool became established as England's second port. There were only fifty acres of enclosed docks in 1824 when Jesse Hartley became engineer to the port, but the total had risen to over two hundred acres when he retired in 1860. The Albert Dock, completed in 1845, was the first in Liverpool where there were public enclosed warehouses. It is one of the most spectacular monuments of the Industrial Revolution. Four storeys of storage space are carried above open ground floors, supported on massive cast iron pillars. On the three upper storeys are taking-in doors, situated above elegant elliptical arches. The roofs are made up of wrought iron trusses covered with iron plates. The construction of the Albert Dock was described by a German visitor in 1844:

> the basin is almost finished and a number of the warehouses completed. These latter are built entirely without wood, being constructed of iron and stone. The foundation walls, as well as the walls of the basin, are of Scotch granite, the upper walls of brick; large columns of iron, a couple of feet in diameter support the gallery, which surrounds them entirely. Then come the several stories, one above the other, supported by smaller iron pillars and flattish arches of brick, and above all are the spacious floors immediately under the roof, which is entirely of

iron. The cellars are so arranged that casks can be rolled into them from the ships, through large portholes, and everything is simple, clean and regular, merely in the commonsense style.

The building of docks and warehouses went ahead at many other ports during this period, but on a less dramatic scale. The basic pattern of cargo handling, established in London at the very beginning of the century, was repeated by the engineers of this generation in most other British ports of consequence, and was to last for well over a century.

Until the end of the 1830s, and in some areas even later, passenger boats and the terminal and transfer facilities provided for them were features of the landscapes of many inland waterways. In 1835, some five years after the opening of the Liverpool and Manchester Railway, Sir George Head was able to sample three different routes between the two principal towns of Lancashire—by the Bridgewater and Leeds and Liverpool Canals through Wigan; by the Bridgewater Canal to Runcorn; and by the Mersey and Irwell Navigation or Old Quay Company through Runcorn. Such a mode of travel revealed the differences between rural and urban England. Head found it:

> far from disagreeable – without troubling himself with the world's concerns he sits basking in sunshine, and glides tranquilly onwards through a continuous panorama of cows, cottages and green fields, the latter gaily sparkling in the season with buttercups and daisies. . . . It is true that during a great part of the voyage there exists a very considerable drawback to the comfort of the travellers, for within a dozen miles of Manchester, the water of the canal is black as the Styx, and absolutely pestiferous from the gas and refuse of the manufactories.

Similar services could be enjoyed along the navigations of East Yorkshire, and on the Wirral line of the Ellesmere and Chester Canal.

There is much evidence to suggest that the first half of the nineteenth century was a period when new roads were built in many parts of England and Wales, and improvements on a considerable scale were carried out to existing routes. National surveys of turnpike roads have concentrated on the legislative and financial aspects of the system, but in areas where detailed studies have been carried out it is clear that, while in the eighteenth century turnpike trusts did little more than improve the surfaces of existing roads, in the nineteenth, with the help of many of the leading engineers of the time, they accomplished great changes in the landscape. Many of the turnpike trusts formed after

1810 were in industrial areas. There were fifty-nine new trusts in 1824–6, of which twenty-four were in Lancashire and Yorkshire. Some roads built at that time in these counties are recognizable on the ground as routes which strike boldly across the hills, and several are still known as 'new' roads. Research in Devon has shown that many new roads were built between 1815 and 1830, often taking easily graded routes through the valleys rather than ancient tracks over the hills. Roads like those from Combe Martin to South Molton, and from Barnstaple to Goodleigh, were completed as late as 1843–4. As new roads were built, so some of the old routes ceased to be turnpike roads. The tollhouses in Devon, the most characteristic relics of the turnpike roads in the modern landscape, nearly all date from after 1815.[3]

In the East Riding of Yorkshire a five-mile route from Hull to Hedon was completed in 1833 replacing an older circuitous road. In Derbyshire the direct route from Belper to Matlock through Arkwright's Cromford was finished in 1820. In North Staffordshire in the mid 1820s Thomas Telford was responsible for building a bypass around Talke, between Newcastle under Lyme and Alsager, the old and new routes being clearly recognizable on a modern map. A road from Hanford Bridge to Trentham was opened in 1836, and routes from Stoke to Milton and from Fenton to Shelton in 1846. The opening of main line railways sometimes stimulated road building. The route from Whitmore station on the Grand Junction Railway to Newcastle under Lyme was straightened in 1844, and a new route opened from Whitmore to Trentham in 1845. In Northamptonshire serious proposals were put forward in the late 1830s for a turnpike road from Weedon station on the London and Birmingham Railway to Banbury. The route was not built but substantial improvements were made to existing roads.

An examination of roads in Shropshire similarly shows that there were few radical alterations to the basic road pattern in the eighteenth century, but many new roads were built after 1810. Around Shrewsbury new straight sections were constructed in the 1820s, avoiding older circuitous lines on the roads to Church Stretton and Baschurch, and a deep cutting was dug on the turnpike road to Ellesmere where it climbed out of the Severn Valley at Cross Hill. A road was built from Coalbrookdale to Wellington in 1816, and linked to the existing turnpike system at Dawley by a line constructed in 1828, a year in which a new route was built from the south end of the Iron Bridge to the turnpike road to Bridgnorth. To the south of Ludlow, in the 1830s,

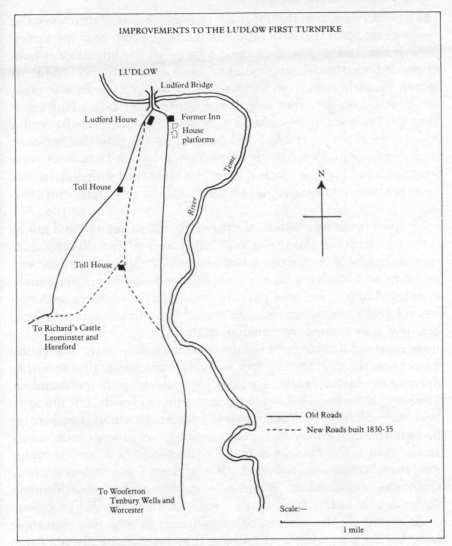

Figure 10 Roads south of Ludlow which were realigned in the 1830s

the routes of the Ludlow First Turnpike towards Worcester and Hereford were completely realigned between Ludford Bridge, Richard's Castle and Woofferton. New, straight and easily graded roads were built, with a tollhouse at the junction of the two routes. The old line to Hereford was preserved as a footpath, but public rights of way over the Worcester route were extinguished. A timber-framed inn in Ludford was left isolated by the new route, and the depression

137

which marks the line of the old road is lined by house platforms of the shrunken medieval village of Ludford. A new road up the Hope Valley through the lead mining area on the fringe of the Stiperstones was authorized as the Minsterley-Churchstoke turnpike in 1833. It became the main road from Shrewsbury to Bishop's Castle, superseding the route on the other side of the Stiperstones ridge. In 1843 a completely new seven-mile road was opened between Morville on the Bridgnorth–Shrewsbury road and Shipton on the turnpike between Much Wenlock and Ludlow. It formed a new lowland route between Bridgnorth and Ludlow, for it did not rise more than six hundred feet above sea level, while the summit of the old route was over a thousand feet.

Turnpike roads were often hampered by lack of capital, and many of the new trusts of the 1820s and 1830s were financially unstable. Even the busiest of the old roads often failed to yield in tolls the income necessary for borrowing on a scale to finance ambitious programmes of new building. This was particularly serious on important long-distance roads which ran through sparsely populated regions where there was only limited intermediate traffic.

The most usual route from London to Dublin in the early nineteenth century was through Shrewsbury and across the mountains of North Wales to the Menai Straits, by ferry to Anglesey, over the island to Holyhead, and then by packet to the Irish port of Howth. The shape of the route had largely been determined by Robert Lawrence, landlord of the Lion Hotel in Shrewsbury, who began to work stage coaches to Holyhead in 1779. He was one of the promoters of a new turnpike route from Pentrefoelas to Llandegai near Bangor across Snowdonia, which was completed in 1804, and had been active in establishing combines of innkeepers along the route. In 1800 the Act of Union amalgamated the Irish and British parliaments, and this increased traffic between London and Dublin, drawing the attention of the political nation to the poor state of communications between the two capitals, and particularly to the state of the roads across North Wales. Various engineers and committees inquired into the situation. In 1810 a committee summoned Thomas Telford as 'an engineer of great eminence' to advise them, and five years later when the Holyhead Road Commission was set up he became its engineer. The Commission was empowered to spend government money on the road, on a scale which could never have been matched by the revenue from tolls, particularly in the Welsh mountains when there was little traffic other than the long-distance mail, stage and posting coaches. A second Act of Parliament in 1819 set up another commission which acted as a 'new model' turnpike trust, completely taking over all the powers of the six existing trusts on the roads west of Shrewsbury. To the east of Shrewsbury, on the English section of the road, the original Commission of 1815 continued to work in conjunction with the existing turnpike authorities.[4]

The road between London and Shrewsbury was improved piecemeal. Through Hertfordshire, Bedfordshire and Northamptonshire hills on the ancient Roman Watling Street were eased with cuttings, embankments were built over valleys, corners were straightened, hedges set back and new drains installed. The same processes went on through Warwickshire, Staffordshire and Shropshire, parts of which were heavily industrialized. The superbly engineered descent from Hill Top, West Bromwich to Wednesbury, the deep cutting by which the road climbs from the crossing of the Staffordshire and Worcestershire Canal to Tettenhall Green west of Wolverhampton and the high embankment over the valley of the Ketley Brook near Wellington are but a few of the indications in the present-day landscape of the energy which was devoted to the improvement of the Holyhead Road. One of the most profound changes in the Black Country was the relocation of the centre of West Bromwich. The ancient medieval village had been clustered around the parish church on the western slopes of the Tame Valley but the construction of the new road, across what had previously been open heath to the west, led to the development of a shopping area, the building of a new church and ultimately the municipal offices. Finally, in the twentieth century, Telford's road became such a focus of commercial activity that it had to be bypassed.

West of Shrewsbury the changes were more dramatic. No other road in England or Wales before the age of the motor car was improved on such a scale and with so much government money as the 106-mile route from Shrewsbury to Holyhead. An itinerary of the road is a catalogue of major engineering works: Chirk embankment, the Glyn Diffwys pass, the Waterloo Bridge, the road through Nant Ffrancon, the Menai Bridge, the new road across Anglesey, the Stanley embankment. While in England improvements to the road were carried out gradually and continued until the railways drained it of traffic, most of the improvements in the highland zone were completed between 1815 and 1830.

139

Through the mountains the Holyhead Road was typically built on a shelf, with a retaining wall on the uphill side and a footpath and parapet on the opposite side. At close intervals were recesses or 'depots' in the walls for the storage of road metals. The surfaces of Telford's roads were unbonded and new broken stones had continually to be spread to keep the surface even. Footpaths were ideally placed on the south side so that the roadway could gain the full benefit of the sun's drying action. Walls were preferred to hedges for the sake of visibility, and because water dripping from trees could damage surfaces. Most of the walls were originally of dry stone, but they were mortared during the 1830s because the Welsh had pilfered building materials from them. The average width of the road was forty feet and it was never narrower than thirty feet, with an eighteen-foot minimum of gravelled surface in the centre. The whole of the road was lined with new milestones in 1826–8, for which stone was quarried near Red Wharf Bay on Anglesey, and cut and fitted with small cast iron plates containing the appropriate information in a yard near the Menai Bridge. Each stone weighed twenty-three hundredweight and cost five pounds to install. Fifteen tollhouses of standard patterns were built, four-room bungalows on the mainland and houses with three ground floor rooms and an octagonal tower bedroom on Anglesey. Telford thought that comfortable houses would enable the road authorities to employ respectable toll collectors, which maximized the income from tolls. Gates of standard patterns were also provided, sometimes of lattice construction in timber, sometimes in wrought iron with a rising sun design.

Several stretches of the route were completely new, including that from Gobowen to Chirk, the bypass around Cerrigydruidion, a section of about three miles to the east of Bangor around which the town of Bethesda grew up, and the whole route across Anglesey. From Anglesey proper to Holy Island, on which Holyhead stands, the road crosses the Stanley Embankment, sixteen feet high and 1300 yards long, completed in 1823. There are spectacular sections of the road through two passes—the Glyn Diffwys, through which the road ascends from the Dee Valley to the watershed between the Dee and the Conway, and the route on either side of Lake Ogwen, along which the road runs at its summit in Snowdonia. On the eastern side Telford took the Holyhead Road up the north side of the valley, while the old turnpike road went under the mountains on the southern side. West of the lake was the magnificent descent through the Nant Ffrancon pass, replacing what Telford had called 'the most dreadful horsepath in Wales'. After it was completed he described this section in terms which might apply to the Holyhead Road as a whole, 'an arduous and very expensive work . . . which may be expected, with reasonable attention, to endure for ages'.

Many of the bridges on the road were well-designed stone arches, but there were two iron bridges of especial quality. At the crossing of the Conway at Betws-y-coed Telford built an iron arch 105 feet in span, with the shamrock, the thistle, the leek and the rose cast in the spandrels. Proposals to cross the Menai Straits went back to the beginnings of the Holyhead project, for the ferry crossing was, in Telford's words, 'a disagreeable object of anticipation'. Several designs for cast iron arches were put forward but in 1818 Telford suggested a suspension bridge. This was not the first suspension bridge, but it was the first to be built on a large scale, and its 579-foot span taxed the limits of engineering knowledge at the time. The chains on the towers were lifted into position between April and June 1825, and the bridge was opened to traffic on 30 January 1826. Telford's own account of the day conveys a sense of the elation of the occasion:

> On Monday morning 30th January 1826, at 1.30 a.m. the London mail coach, occupied by W.A. Provis, W. Hazledine, the two junior Wilsons, Thomas Rhodes and the Mail Coach Superintendent, was the first that passed across the estuary at the level of a hundred feet above the tideway, which heretofore had presented a decisive obstruction to travellers. The Chester Mail passed at 3.30 a.m. and Sir Henry Parnell and I drove repeatedly over until about 9 a.m. and during the whole of the day there was an uninterrupted succession of passing carriages, horsemen and pedestrians who had assembled to witness and enjoy the novelty, and in the evening all the workmen were regaled with a joyous festival.

A German visitor in 1844 found the Menai Bridge awe-inspiring, a structure which seemed to defy credibility:

> When seen from the side, it is very difficult immediately to form a notion of the magnitude of the work; and besides, the simplicity of the outline gives at first an impression of very moderate extent. The feeling is very much the same as that with which strangers are impressed on the first view of St Peter's in Rome. They find it extremely difficult to believe that a structure of such magnitude is before them.

141

In sixteen years the improvements to the Holyhead Road reduced the time taken by the Royal Mail between London and Holyhead from forty-one to twenty-eight hours, a decrease of over thirty per cent. The road's improvement had many economic side effects. It was heavily used in the ironmaking areas of the Black Country and the Coalbrookdale coalfield. Between Oswestry and Llangollen it carried vast numbers of coal and lime carts. On Anglesey it stimulated production in the collieries on Maltreath Marsh in the middle of the island. Between Bethesda and Bangor it was used to take slate to the coast.

No other road in England or Wales was improved on the same scale, but new roads were built around the headlands of Penmaen Bach and Penmaen Mawr along the North Wales coast, and the Conway estuary was spanned with a 327-foot long suspension bridge opened a few months after the Menai Bridge. In the 1830s improvements began on the roads which led from the Holyhead Road in the West Midlands towards Liverpool and Manchester, but the building of railways prevented their development.

Menai was an outstanding achievement in a great age of bridge building. Many engineers employed cast iron in the early nineteenth century, and by 1815 Telford had perfected two basic designs of iron bridge. Many of the castings for his structures were made by the ironfounder William Hazledine, whose chief foundry was at Plas Kynaston near the Pontcysyllte aqueduct. The smaller bridges consisted of castings incorporating ribs, spandrel frames and deck-bearers in a grid pattern, erected in pairs joined in the centre. The larger bridges, the first of which was built across the Dornoch Firth at Bonar in 1811–12, had ribs made up from segments and the deck-bearers supported by vertical or inclined struts. One such bridge was cast by Hazledine for the Duke of Westminster's estate at Eaton near Chester. It amazed a German courtier who saw it:

> We were surprised at finding a good solid structure in iron over the river. Such a bridge for a place where no one comes, except, perhaps, now and then the owner himself! These very rich individuals must often find themselves in a state of singular embarrassment concerning means of disposing of all their wealth.

The iron bridge also appeared in London. James Walker's Vauxhall Bridge was completed in 1816, and John Rennie was responsible for the construction of Southwark Bridge, the widest arch of which spanned 240 feet, which was finished in 1819. J.U. Rastrick's bridge over the Wye at Chepstow, opened in 1816, and Joseph Potter's bridges at Alrewas and Mavesyn Ridware in Staffordshire were among the other notable iron bridges of the period.

Many of the best stone arched bridges in Britain were also built at this time. John Rennie is remembered as the designer of the stone Waterloo Bridge rather than the iron structure at Vauxhall. At Stoneleigh in Warwickshire he built the Sowe Bridge, eight segmental arches over the Avon, finished in 1818. London Bridge was completed by his sons in 1831. In Devon James Green designed the three-arched Cowley Bridge over the Exe which was opened in 1813, and Charles Fowler was responsible for the bridge over the Dart at Totnes, finished in 1828. The beautiful Grosvenor Bridge in Chester was designed by Thomas Harrison and opened in 1833, its single arch of two hundred feet making it the widest spanned stone bridge in Britain. Bridge builders turned away emphatically from the use of timber. The wooden bridges at and near London—those at Putney and Battersea especially—were visibly rotting in the early nineteenth century and there were many demands for their replacement. While some wooden bridges were built in the mid nineteenth century, that at Penmaenpool in Merioneth for example, they were few in number.

The work of engineers like Telford, MacAdam and Rennie greatly improved road travel in the early nineteenth century. 'The superiority of the English roads', wrote a French aristocrat in 1833, 'over those of the greater part of Europe, and more especially of France, cannot be contested.' He explained the various means of transport available. The fastest vehicles were the mail coaches which carried four inside and six outside passengers. The slightly slower stage coaches carried as many as eighteen passengers. Wealthier travellers went by post coach, a private vehicle hired at an inn specializing in the posting trade, hauled by two or four horses and driven by a postilion, a 'small man, with jacket, short breeches and half-boots'. Towns on main roads enjoyed a golden age of prosperity derived from the thoroughfare trade in the 1820s and 1830s. Places like Oxford, where the Mitre yard was one of the hubs of the stage coach system of southern England, Stone in Staffordshire and Towcester in Northamptonshire were full of inns alive with the business of posting or stage coaching. The same French commentator wrote:

> Among the wonders of English civilization the inns should be mentioned. In many of the larger towns they are magnificent and they are good and well-supplied in the smallest. In the

143

greater part of them the servants are in livery, and in all their attendance is prompt and respectful.

Coaching was a dramatic activity, abounding in legends of daring exploits and unusual happenings. On the day the Reform Bill became law the coachman of the *Mazeppa*, from London to Hereford, secured copies of *The Times* which he sold for successively higher prices as the coach journeyed westwards, the last one changing hands for five pounds in Hereford. In Shrewsbury in the 1830s it was traditional for all the coaches serving the town's principal inn to parade on the King's birthday. In 1836 sixteen vehicles took part, including the *Wonder* with six white horses in red harness, *L'Hirondelle* with four greys, the *Bristol Mail* with chestnuts and the *Young Prince* with piebalds. There was nevertheless an unglamorous side to coaching. The centres of coaching towns were crammed with stables and yards where horses were washed down. In some towns there were washing places on the banks of rivers where coach horses were cleaned after each day's work.

Railways in the eighteenth century were confined almost entirely to the coalfields and to a few other mineral working areas which copied coalfield practices. On the surface their function was to transport minerals to the nearest navigable water. From the beginning of the nineteenth century, however, railways began to supplement water transport in a more radical way, by crossing the watersheds between river valleys. During the first thirty years of the century there evolved what has been called the hybrid or composite railway, a line which was commercially more ambitious and in engineering terms more sophisticated than a mere mineral tramway worked by horses, but which was something less than a main line railway as the latter was understood after the opening of the Liverpool and Manchester Railway in 1830.

By 1800 newly built railways were usually laid with iron track, most commonly with the angled plate rails invented by John Curr in the 1770s. Contemporary illustrations of plate rails suggest that they could be obtained from ironworks in standard lengths, like the track of a model railway, and that they were relatively cheap and easy to lay. The sleepers on these railways were normally stone blocks, but sometimes timber cross ties or cast iron cross sleepers were employed. Most plateways were worked by horses, so it was necessary to build up a trotting path between the rails, sometimes of slag, stone or other waste products of the industry the line served, sometimes of brick. Plateways usually crossed ordinary roads by U-section channel rails, since upright flanges would have caused road vehicles crossing the track to overturn.

The typical hybrid railway had iron tracks. It was often planned like a canal, with level summit sections and inclined planes, instead of flights of locks, carrying traffic to them. Lines employed a variety of forms of locomotion—horses, self-acting inclined planes, locomotives and inclined planes worked by stationary engines. Substantial parts of the hybrid railways were on reserved tracks, but some sections often ran alongside public roads. These lines usually carried a variety of traffic and were often open to anyone who wished to take a waggon along them, subject to the payment of tolls. The majority were built across the properties of many different landowners, and so required authorization by an Act of Parliament. Leading engineers like Telford and Rennie were often consulted when they were being planned. Few lines of this type carried passengers regularly, but on festive occasions the conversion of mineral waggons for this purpose served to draw attention to the railways' potential for transporting people as well as goods.

Hybrid railways were built in many parts of Britain. The Surrey Iron Railway, which extended ten miles from a basin at Wandsworth to Mitcham and Croydon, was authorized in 1801. In 1810 a railway was projected linking the head of the Brecon and Abergavenny Canal at Brecon with the town of Hay in the Wye Valley. It was completed in 1816 and its opening was followed by the construction of further railways to Kington, so that goods could be carried over thirty-six miles by rail through some of the remotest parts of England and Wales.[5]

The Gloucester and Cheltenham Railway, authorized in 1809, ran from the basin of the Gloucester and Berkeley Canal, not then completed, to Cheltenham and the stone quarries on Leckhampton Hill owned by Charles Brandon Trye, one of the line's chief promoters. The section from the quarries to Cheltenham, opened in 1810, served a similar purpose to Ralph Allen's line to Bath in the 1730s. The 'main line' from Gloucester to Cheltenham was opened with some spirit in 1811:

> The important measure of a Railway or Tram Road from Gloucester to this town, having been completed on Monday evening last, the morning of Tuesday was ushered in by the ringing of bells; and about 11 o'clock a numerous assemblage of persons took place on the Railway Wharf, near the Turn-

pike, in order to celebrate the occasion. A train of carriages moved along the Railway, some of which were appropriately fitted up and occupied by Ladies and Gentlemen, preceded by an excellent band of music; others were laden with building-stone of a superior quality from Leckhampton Hill, and coals from Gloucester.

Parts of the line ran parallel to a new turnpike road. It was laid with plate rails to a gauge of 3 feet 6 inches with stone sleepers. There were several inclined planes on Leckhampton Hill, including one which ran between the famous Devil's Chimney and the hillside.[6]

The Stratford and Moreton Railway, authorized in 1821, ran from the basin where the Stratford upon Avon Canal joined the River Avon to Moreton in Marsh, with a branch to Shipston on Stour. The line crossed the Avon on a multi-arched bridge, and for much of its length followed the turnpike road to Oxford. It was laid with wrought iron edge rails of 4 feet 8½ inches gauge, following North-Eastern practice, and was envisaged by its projector, William James, as part of a trunk route from the Midlands to London.[7]

The first railway in Cornwall ran from the harbour at Portreath to Poldice and was built between 1812 and 1818. In the 1830s another line reached Portreath, descending to sea level by a spectacular inclined plane. This was a branch of the Hayle Railway, authorized in 1834 to run from Redruth to the sea at Hayle and completed in 1837. The Redruth and Chasewater Railway was built in 1824 from Redruth through the copper mining parish of Gwennap to a new harbour at Devoran on the Fal estuary. It had a 4-foot gauge with granite sleeper blocks, and was horse-worked until the 1850s. Sir Christopher Hawkins built a four-mile line of 2 feet 6 inches gauge from St Austell to his new harbour at Pentewan in 1826. The most ambitious of the Cornish lines was built by J.T. Austen, who later assumed the name Treffry, from his harbour at Par through the china clay district north of St Austell to the north coast at Newquay. The line was not authorized until 1843, and although in some respects it can be classed as a hybrid line, the scale of its major surviving monument, a viaduct which crosses the Luxylan Valley, is more in keeping with the age of main line railways.

The Severn and Wye Railway was projected in 1809 to extend thirteen-and-a-half miles from Lydney to Lidbrook across the Forest of Dean, with the intention of avoiding 'the tedious navigation of the Wye'. Sir John Rennie was consulted about its route, and its engineer for a time was Josiah, son of William Jessop. The line penetrated countryside which was inhospitable to railways, forming links with many mines and other industrial concerns. Eight branches were authorized in the Act and more were built. The Severn and Wye was an extended system of industrial sidings rather than a long-distance railway. It was laid with plate rails set on stone blocks, at a gauge of 3 feet 6 inches, and both blocks and rails can still be seen at Lydney harbour.[8]

The Pensnett or Kingswinford Railway ran from Ashwood Basin on the Staffordshire and Worcestershire Canal to several industrial concerns on the estates of Lord Dudley in the Brierley Hill area, on the western edge of the Black Country. One of its main instigators was James Foster, a prominent ironmaster of the time. The line was opened in 1829, with a gauge of 4 feet 8½ inches and edge rails. There were several self-acting inclined planes, including one five hundred yards long by which the line climbed away from its terminus in the Stour Valley. There were some quite considerable embankments, five level crossings and two bridges over public roads, and a bridge which carried a colliery tramroad over the line. Horses were the usual motive power but on a two-mile level section the locomotive *Agenoria*, built at James Foster's works in Stourbridge and now in the National Railway Museum, was employed.[9]

The Cromford and High Peak Railway, which was opened in 1831, linked a wharf on the Cromford Canal south of Cromford with the Peak Forest Canal on the western side of the Pennines at Whaley Bridge, a distance of thirty-three miles, with a summit 1264 feet above sea level. The engineer was Josiah Jessop. The line climbed out of the Derwent Valley by two inclined planes worked by winding engines at Sheep Pasture and Middleton Top, and there were four other inclines, between which motive power was provided by horses, supplemented by locomotives from the 1840s. Like the Stratford and Moreton Railway, the line was conceived as a long-distance route, in this case linking Derby, Nottingham and Leicester with Manchester and Liverpool. Its success in this sphere was limited, but it did prosper from traffic originating with the mines and quarries along the route.

The Leicester and Swannington Railway Company was formed in 1829 to carry coal from the ancient mining area around Coleorton in the west of Leicestershire to the county town some sixteen miles away. It had two inclined planes, one at Bagworth, which was self-acting, and another powered by a steam engine at its western terminus.

147

The most important hybrid railways were in the Northumberland–Durham coalfield. The North-East had been one of the two birthplaces of the English railway in the seventeenth century but in the eighteenth almost all the major innovations in railway technology—the iron wheel, the iron rail and the self-acting inclined plane—were first employed in Shropshire. Until the 1790s it was usual on Tyneside for a horse to pull only one waggon, but with the adoption of the iron rail the formation of trains of waggons became common practice. The first self-acting inclined plane in the North-East appears to have been built as late as 1798. After 1800 most of the principal innovations in the workings of railways took place in the North-East. In the years 1800 to 1810 the first inclined planes worked by steam engines were employed in the area. The North-East had not, except in a few isolated instances, taken up the plate rail and indeed had been slow to adopt iron rails. A visitor to Walker Colliery on Tyneside in 1807 observed:

> They are gradually giving up their wood road, and introducing iron, and they make them piece by piece keeping up the old waggons and running them partly on wood and partly iron.

The invention of the T-section wrought iron rail by James Birkinshaw of the Bedlington ironworks in 1820 was a decisive event in the evolution of railway technology, not only in the North-East but over the whole country, for it made possible the carriage of heavier loads at greater speeds than had ever been feasible on wooden or cast iron tracks.

Most of the hybrid railways in the North-East were built from west to east, direct to the coast rather than following the old waggonways in running north or south to the Tyne or Wear. The Hetton Colliery line, built by George Stephenson in 1823, linked the mines it served with Sunderland harbour. From the colliery the waggons were hauled up to a summit by a steam winding engine at Warden Law, and were then allowed to travel down a series of five self-acting inclined planes to the coast. The Bowes Railway from Mount Moor Colliery across the Team Valley to the Tyne at Jarrow, built by George Stephenson in 1826, incorporated stationary haulage engines, a self-acting inclined plane and sections worked by locomotives. The Clarence Railway, authorized in 1828, was intended to convey coal over the watershed between the Wear and the Tees, to the mouth of the former river. The Act of Parliament stipulated that on certain sections locomotives could only be used with the consent of the landowners.

The best known of the hybrid lines in the North-East was the Stockton and Darlington, built by George Stephenson for coalowners who sought an outlet from the pits of West Durham to the coast. The line was authorized in 1821 with a main line extending twenty-seven miles. It was essentially a hybrid line, with inclined planes worked by stationary engines and horses employed for haulage on some level sections, but it is best known as the first steam-hauled public railway, for on some sections Stephenson's locomotives were employed. The famous picture of the opening of the line in 1825 showing *Locomotion No. 1* hauling a train of vehicles filled with passengers, if hardly typical of Stockton and Darlington operations was an indication of future patterns of railway operation.

The most spectacular of the North-Eastern hybrid railways was the Stanhope and Tyne which climbed northwards from limestone quarries in Teesdale above the village of Stanhope, across the high moorlands around Consett and the coalfield near Chester-le-Street, to reach the mouth of the Tyne at South Shields. It was authorized in 1831, with a main line nearly thirty-eight miles long, over a third of it on inclined planes. There were horse-drawn sections between the inclines and locomotives were used on the flatter land near the coast. The inclines at Crawley and Weatherhill at the Stanhope end of the line remain spectacular features of the landscape, although it is many years since they carried traffic. The former rises at gradients as steep as 1 in 8, much of it in a deep rock cutting. The Weatherhill incline was not as steep but it was no less than 1 mile 128 yards long. Near Consett the deep ravine called Hownes Gill was crossed by raising and lowering waggons to and from the valley floor on lifts rather like a cliff tramway, with gradients of 1 in 2½ on the western and 1 in 3 on the eastern side.

The building of hybrid railways did not cease in the 1830s, in spite of the success of the new-style Liverpool and Manchester Railway. The Canterbury and Whitstable Railway, authorized in 1825, linked Canterbury with the coast some six miles away. The line included a tunnel with a particularly narrow bore and an inclined plane, but the locomotive *Invicta*, now preserved in Canterbury, was employed on it. The St Helens and Runcorn Gap Railway was authorized in 1830 from a colliery north of St Helens to Widnes, about eight miles away, on the Mersey. Although it crossed and made connection with the Liverpool and Manchester, it was essentially an industrial hybrid line, not unlike the Pensnett or the Severn and Wye. Somewhat grudgingly the company operated a passenger service. In 1835 Sir George Head described how he had travelled south from St Helens in a carriage drawn by a horse. There were long delays awaiting connections on the Liverpool and Manchester before the vehicle was drawn up an inclined plane by a stationary engine, and then attached to a rake of coalwaggons, which was drawn south by a locomotive.

After 1830 railways became a common feature of the landscape in most parts of England and Wales. Their birthplace, in the early nineteenth century, had been the North-East, where in many areas they dominated the landscape. J.G. Kohl wrote in 1844:

> Imagine these black roads, winding through verdant fields; the long trains of waggons heavily laden with their black treasures, rolling lightly over the railroads, the burning mounds of coal scattered over the plain, the black pit mouths, and here and there a simple unadorned Methodist chapel or school house, and you will have a tolerable idea of what the English delight to call their 'Black Indies'.... Durham ... of all counties in England is the one in which there have been constructed the greatest number of railroads of small extent. This gives to the country an aspect remarkably new and surprising in the eyes of a continentalist. In all directions he sees small trains in motion, small locomotives with two or three passenger carriages, for, as the intercourse is between places at no great distance from each other the trains can probably run frequently, but on that very account, perhaps, are obliged to content themselves with a small number of passengers at a time. If, however, the passenger trains are small, the trains of coal waggons are all the longer, and to one who could take a bird's eye view of the country, it would seem to swarm like an anthill with locomotives, hurrying trains and long lines of coal waggons.

The Liverpool and Manchester Railway was opened to traffic on 15 September 1830, and marked a decisive break with the hybrid railway of the previous generation. It was the first concern to fulfil all the conditions of a main line railway. It had entirely specialized and reserved track and did not, like many of the hybrid lines, run alongside public roads. It accommodated public traffic, not merely the minerals produced by one coalmaster's mines or the goods brought to one of its terminals by a canal company. It conveyed passengers in purpose-built carriages on a regularly timetabled basis, not just on special occasions in converted freight waggons. It employed mechanical traction in the form of a steam locomotive, not only on level sections between inclines, but throughout the length of the line, with the exception of an inclined plane from Edgehill to the terminus in Liverpool. It crossed the properties of numerous landowners, and was therefore subject to a measure of public control through Acts of Parliament. It did not merely follow a line of minimum resistance, but cut across the countryside, overcoming the obstacles in its path by engineering skills. At the Liverpool end was an immense cutting through the sandstone at Olive Mount, and a tunnel giving access to the terminal station. The Sankey Brook was crossed on a viaduct of nine fifty-foot arches. The bog of Chat Moss was crossed by floating the railway on a foundation of hurdles, brushwood and heather. It is some measure of the importance of the previous generation of hybrid railways that there was keen competition for the post of chief engineer. George Rennie, son of Sir John Rennie, and William James, builder of the Stratford and Moreton Railway, were among those in contention but the post was given to George Stephenson, a native of Killingworth, Northumberland. He had grown up with colliery railways, and brought to the Liverpool and Manchester the essentials of railway practice from the Northumberland–Durham coalfield. The form of traction was finally settled after a series of trials held at Rainhill near St Helens in October 1829, when Robert Stephenson's *Rocket*, incorporating the many improvements to the steam locomotive which had been made in the North-East during the previous decade, and many innovations as well, proved decisively better than its competitors. It is impossible to estimate accurately how many miles of composite railway there were in 1830. Within twenty years of the opening of the Liverpool and Manchester over six thousand miles of public railway had been built on the same principles, a total which was to double within the next two decades. The impact of the Liverpool and Manchester on the Lancashire landscape was vividly described by Alexander Somerville:

> at Manchester I saw a railway, locomotive engines, and railway trains for the first time. Upon the railway, not then out of the second year of its age, I proceeded to Liverpool. The opening of that railway is an epoch in the history of the world. In memory, I see my first whirl upon it, standing so prominently out among other recollections, that it seems like an epoch of my life. All sights which I had seen, in London or elsewhere, – the beautiful, the grand, the wonderful – shrunk into comparative nothingness, when, after reaching Liverpool, I went into the country a week, in the neighbourhood of Prescot, and saw (each day I sought to see it, each hour of the

151

day I could have stood to see it again) the white steam shooting
through the landscape of trees, meadows and villages, and the
long train, loaded with merchandise, men and women, and
human enterprise, rolling along under the steam. I had seen no
sight like that; I have seen nothing to excel it since. In beauty
and grandeur the world has nothing beyond it.

The growth of the railway system was uneven. There were fifty-four
Acts of Parliament for railway projects passed between 1825 and
1835, some for very minor lines, but the economic crisis of the late
1830s considerably reduced the pace of investment. The decade's most
important development was the completion of the two lines which
linked London with Lancashire. The Grand Junction Railway from
Birmingham to a junction with the Liverpool and Manchester near
Warrington was opened in 1837. The following year saw the completion of the London and Birmingham, a line which boldly demonstrated the abilities of engineers to cut across the grain of the
countryside. It passed through the Northamptonshire uplands with a
tunnel more than a mile long, at Kilsby near Rugby, and a deep cutting
at Roade. An embankment carried it over the broad valley of the Ouse
and Tring Cutting, and Watford Tunnel took it through the Chilterns.
The success of this group of main lines, together with the improving
economic situation after 1842, touched off 'railway mania', a period
of feverish speculation in the mid 1840s during which numerous
schemes with little prospect of realization were floated. Many lines
were built, nevertheless, and by 1850 it was possible to travel by rail
between most of the major English cities. One result of the mania was
the amalgamation of many of the first generation of companies. In
1846 the London and North-Western Railway incorporated the
Liverpool and Manchester, the Grand Junction, the London and
Birmingham and the Manchester and Birmingham. The Birmingham
and Derby Junction, the Midland Counties and the North Midland
came together in 1844 to form the Midland Railway, and within a year
took over the Birmingham and Gloucester. By the end of the decade
amalgamations had created the Lancashire and Yorkshire, the London, Brighton and South Coast, and the North-Eastern.

The majority of the lines built in the 1830s and 1840s adopted the
practices of Northumberland and Durham, and particularly the gauge
of 4 feet 8½ inches which had been common on Tyneside. The outstanding exception was the Great Western Railway which, together
with its associated companies, followed totally different principles. Its

engineer, Isambard Kingdom Brunel, rethought the whole technology of the railway. He proposed a gauge of 7 feet 0¼ inches, with the rails laid upon continuous longitudinal baulks of timber. The importance of interchange traffic was not foreseen when the gauge was adopted, and scenes of chaos ensued when the Great Western's lines joined those of narrow gauge, as happened at Gloucester in 1844. Throughout its length the Great Western was stamped with the originality of Brunel's thinking. Its major engineering works—the Wharncliffe Viaduct at Hanwell, the astonishingly flat arch which crosses the Thames at Maidenhead, Box Tunnel, the passage through Bath, the terminus at Temple Meads, Bristol—are all memorable as works of art, not simply as feats of functional engineering. Brunel's attention to detail was thorough. The signals, the wayside stations, the lesser bridges like that depicted in John Cooke Bourne's view of Chippenham, brought new features of distinction to the landscape.

In the West of England Brunel's railways were still more distinctive. The South Devon Railway from Exeter to Plymouth was authorized in 1844 and, because of doubts about the abilities of steam locomotives to climb the steep gradients on the southern fringes of Dartmoor, Brunel determined to employ the atmospheric principle which had been demonstrated with some success on a railway near Dublin. A cast iron pipe was laid between the tracks and the air was drawn out of it in advance of a train by a stationary steam pumping engine. The train was drawn along by a piston attached to the carriages by an arm which penetrated through a continuous hinged flap valve of leather, which was shut by rollers following the passage of the piston. Eight engine houses were constructed between Exeter and Newton Abbot, and the operation of atmospheric trains to Teignmouth began in September 1847, and to Newton Abbot in January 1848. By June 1848 it was evident that the system was unworkable, partly because the leather flap was rotting along the whole length of the line, but also because of operating difficulties inherent in the system. Atmospheric traction was immediately abandoned and the South Devon was worked by conventional locomotives, a legacy of the experiment being the severe gradients on the line from Newton Abbot to Plymouth. The atmospheric railway was lined with Italianate engine houses, two of which survive at Starcross and Torre; they created a landscape totally different from that of the conventional railway. The only other line of importance in England worked on the system was the London and Croydon, where William Cubitt built engine houses in the Gothic style and abandoned atmospheric traction with equal celerity.

It was the railway which took the landscape of the Industrial Revolution to the remotest corners of Britain. William Wordsworth, in opposing the building of the line from Kendal to Windermere on the grounds that an influx of pleasure-seekers to such an area would destroy the solitude they came to enjoy, insisted that he did not oppose railways but only the abuse of them. His lines written in 1844 beautifully depict the restless pressures of railway mania:

> Now, for your shame, a Power, the Thirst of Gold,
> That rules o'er Britain like a baneful star,
> Wills that your peace, your beauty, shall be sold,
> And clear way made for her triumphal car
> Through the beloved retreats your arms enfold!
> Heard YE that Whistle? As her long-linked Train
> Swept onwards, did the vision cross your view?

A German traveller on a journey from Wolverton to Chesterfield in 1844 described how he was 'dragged along backwards by the snorting engine with such rapidity, under thundering bridges, over lofty viaducts, and through long dark tunnels, filled with smoke and steam'. Cuttings and embankments on a scale which was commonplace even on the less ambitious railways had only been visible before 1830 on a few canals and roads. One of the most characteristic though ephemeral features of the landscape of the 1840s was the frail, temporary camp of canvas and timber from which gangs of navvies ventured daily to dig soil and rock with pick and shovel, to guide horses to tipping points on the ends of growing embankments and to wheel barrows up planked runs on the sides of deepening cuttings. Horses were employed in large numbers to pull barrows up such runs and to work trains of spoil on the lightly laid tracks which preceded the installation of the permanent way. When tunnels were dug through saturated strata, as at Kilsby on the London and Birmingham, horse gins and even steam engines were employed to pump away water. Thousands of bridges were constructed to take roads across the tracks, or to convey the rails over roads, streams or canals. The ventilating shafts of tunnels were topped with towers, which often arise, seemingly inexplicably in fields, like those at Kilsby in Northamptonshire or at Bramhope in the West Riding. In due course the linesides were flanked by masts carrying signals, huts used by permanent way men, and sidings leading to factories, mines or quarries. At intervals along

154

the lines were stations with platforms for passengers, water columns, signal boxes, docks for loading horses and road vehicles, goods sheds, warehouses, cranes, loading gauges and weighing machines. In the North-East most wayside stations had their own miniature staithes on which coal waggons discharged their loads through hopper doors, in the tradition established in the region in the seventeenth century. In most parts of the country, until the late twentieth century, coal waggons were emptied manually with the aid of a shovel.

Although railways, like canals, were sometimes diverted to avoid game coverts or so that they could not be seen from the drawing rooms of stately homes, they blended remarkably well with rural landscapes, like the enclosed fields, rationalized farmsteads and ornamental lakes of an earlier generation. In towns the impact of a railway could be dramatic, as at Stockport or Chippenham, but many lines took easy routes through river valleys and were often able to pass quite close to the centres of market towns, via riverside meadows, without destroying significant numbers of buildings. Sometimes engineers tried to harmonize the new railway structures with the venerable buildings along their route. Thomas Penson's Tudor Gothic station at Shrewsbury confronts the thirteenth-century towers of the castle on the other side of the station forecourt. At Conway the ends of Robert Stephenson's tubular bridge on the Chester and Holyhead were Gothicized in an attempt to harmonize with Edward I's castle, and the line passed beneath the town walls through Gothic arches. At Northampton and Berwick on Tweed castle ruins were destroyed by railway construction, but the line from Poole to Weymouth was diverted to the south of Dorchester station to avoid cutting through the Iron Age hill fort of Maumbury Rings. Sometimes railways made accidental additions to the landscape. At Kelsey Hill near Burstwick in the East Riding are several lakes which originated when gravel was removed for the construction of the railway from Hull to Withernsea. At Hinksey south of Oxford springs filled pits from which navvies dug ballast for the Great Western branch line from Didcot. Some of Oxford's drinking water was drawn from these pools for a time, and they are still used for boating, angling and swimming.

The early railway companies had only moderate expectations of passenger traffic and anticipated that most of their revenue would come from freight. The scale of demand for local passenger services surprised many managements and wayside accommodation was often improvised. The Leicester and Swannington used rooms in three different public houses which stood near its line for booking and sheltering passengers, while at Moreton on Lugg the Shrewsbury and Hereford took advantage of the fortuitous presence of a hollow tree at the lineside, and used it as a station. Some of the earliest wayside stations closely resembled turnpike tollhouses. The stations on the Leicester and Swannington at Glenfield (now demolished) and Bagworth had bay windows of a style found on many tollhouses and even spaces for toll boards. A station of similar appearance was built at Hampton in Arden, where the Birmingham and Derby Junction joined the London and Birmingham. Most companies adopted a distinctive architectural style for their wayside stations. At Beal, Belford, Christon Bank and other places on the Newcastle and Berwick, Benjamin Green designed stations like small Tudor Gothic manor houses. J.W. Livock used a similar late Gothic style on the Northampton–Peterborough line and on the Trent Valley route between Stafford and Rugby. Brunel's station buildings were constructed in local raw materials but were characterized by their all-round awnings. On the Great Northern Lewis Cubitt used yellow bricks to build stations in an Italianate style. The red brick Tudor of the North Staffordshire Railway is as memorable in the most insignificant village station as in the magnificent hub of that company's system at Stoke on Trent.

Many features of railway building expressed the optimism of the age with a style which is still impressive. The ornate portals of Brunel's tunnels between Swindon and Bristol—not just of Box Tunnel, 1 mile 1452 yards long and a major work of engineering by any standards, but of the shorter tunnels like Twerton Hill which are altogether lesser achievements—are striking expressions of confidence in the new mode of transport. Above all, the importance of railways was reflected in their principal stations. Few lines before 1850 were built without some fears that they might not prosper, so they rarely penetrated through the heavily built-up areas of towns for this would have incurred high land costs. Most termini, like those along the Euston Road in London, Curzon Street and Lawley Street in Birmingham, and Liverpool Road in Manchester, were built on the edges of the cities concerned and there was space for an element of display. Nowhere was this on a more opulent scale than at Euston, where Philip Hardwick's triumphal Doric arch, with lodges on either side, and his great hall, were a fitting entrance to 'the greatest railway port in England'. Euston was less welcoming beyond the frontage. One critic in 1851 said it reminded him of 'an architect's house, where a magnificent portico and hall leads to a dungeon-like dining room, and mean drawing room'. The starting point of the Great Western at Bristol was a terminus with a timber roof which has the appearance of hammer-beam construction. The long Italianate brick front of Chester station, built by Francis Thompson in 1847–8, the same architect's elegant work at Derby Midland, or J.P. Pritchett's 416-foot classical frontage at Huddersfield were works of distinction by any standards. Some wayside stations were similarly magnificent. Thompson's beautiful Regency-style buildings at Wingfield on the North Midland, the Newmarket terminus of the Newmarket and Chesterford with seven bays divided by pairs of Corinthian columns, or the stations built for the Dukes of Sutherland at Trentham or the Earls of Shrewsbury at Alton Towers were all buildings of unusual splendour. The most magnificent minor station was that built in 1848 at Monkwearmouth, Sunderland, for the Newcastle and Berwick Railway, at the time when George Hudson, the great railway spectacular, was MP for the borough. An iron-framed train shed was hidden behind a classical facade, producing perhaps the most balanced and harmonious of all early railway buildings. It was designed by Thomas Moore, a local architect.

Many early railway stations were quickly altered. Some were superseded when the lines on which they stood became through-routes, as at East Grinstead and Witney where the original buildings became goods sheds, or at Much Wenlock where the first station was moved a short distance to become a cricket pavilion. Others, originally conceived as through-stations, had to be altered when the ambitions of their builders were tempered and, as at Banbury (Merton Street), they became termini of minor lines. At Birmingham Philip Hardwick's Ionic Curzon Street terminus of the London and Birmingham lost its role with the opening of New Street station in 1854, and it is now an office in a goods yard.

The railways brought new standardized structures into the landscape of most parts of England. Signal boxes were usually of uniform pattern along any given line. The prefabricated timber structures of the Midland Railway survive on many minor lines, as do most of the boxes on the Shrewsbury and Hereford, with their low pitched roofs and stone walls. Goods sheds were similarly standardized. Along the Oxford, Worcester and Wolverhampton tarred wooden sheds were to be found at most stations up the Evenlode Valley from Oxford into the Cotswolds. The goods sheds at the larger centres were buildings of an altogether new kind. At places like Camden on the London and

157

Birmingham the demand for station room for merchandise was constantly increasing, and new warehouses, sidings, stables and other facilities were always under construction. Locomotives also required accommodation, and on every system sheds were built for their repair and maintenance. At Camden, Samuel Sidney noted in 1851:

> Twenty-four steam waggon horses, or engines for heavy loads are kept in a circular engine-house or stable, 160 feet in diameter, with an iron roof. This form renders every engine accessible at a moment's notice. The steam race-horses for the passenger work are kept in an oblong building opposite the carters. The demand being more regular there is no need for the expensive circular arrangement of stables for this class of engines.

A German visitor described the depot at Derby in 1844:

> Everything is on an immense scale. A great number of railways cross this colossal court, intended to accommodate several companies. About 100 engines are always ready, and in the middle of the court there is a large round building with a cupola into which the engines which have just been used are pushed, and placed concentrically on a large revolving metal plate, and easily turned round, so as to be readily replaced upon any of the converging radial lines on which they are next to be employed. Not less than sixteen engines were standing in this immense rotunda, and I compared the whole to a colossal stable for the reception of these snorting and roaring railway horses. Close by these is a hospital for the lamed or diseased cattle, to which they are sent in case of need.

At Stoke on Trent the mansion formerly occupied by Thomas Whieldon, one of the pioneers of the pottery industry and once a partner of Josiah Wedgwood, was incorporated into the roundhouse of the North Staffordshire Railway. Most early locomotive sheds, however, were small rectangular structures which were rapidly replaced as companies were amalgamated and traffic grew.

The bridges of the early main line railways were as much advertisements for the ambition and pride of the companies as their large stations. The Victoria Bridge over the Wear near Durham, completed in 1838, was modelled on a Roman bridge at Alcantara, built in honour of the Emperor Trajan. J.U. Rastrick's Ouse Viaduct on the London, Brighton and South Coast and Robert Stephenson's twenty-eight-arched Royal Border Bridge at Berwick on Tweed are magnificent examples of traditional forms of construction translated to serve new purposes. Stephenson's High Level Bridge between Newcastle upon Tyne and Gateshead, opened in 1849, was a structure of unusual daring. The only existing bridge over the river was the ancient low level Tyne Bridge, replaced in 1876 by the present swing bridge. Stephenson not only carried his railway over the river on a series of iron arches springing from stone pillars, but also suspended a roadway from the arches. Even more revolutionary was Stephenson's construction of the two tubular bridges which carried the Chester and Holyhead over the Conway estuary and the Menai Straits. The great wrought iron tubes were raised into place with hydraulic lifting tackle. There were housings in the tops of the three towers of the Britannia Bridge over the Menai Straits for suspension chains, but these were never installed, an indication of the extent to which this first application of the flat beam principle to a lengthy bridge was a venture into the unknown, just as the splendid lions which guard its portals reflect the optimism of the builders.

No bridge better typified the industrial landscape than the great twenty-two-arch 1786-foot viaduct designed by George Buck to carry the Manchester and Birmingham Railway over the Mersey at Stockport. This was completed in 1841, when a newspaper reported:

> It is impossible to convey to the reader by mere description any notion of the magnitude of this stupendous erection. Looking over the parapet the spectator gazes down upon the town of Stockport, which by the contrast looks comparatively insignificant. The houses and streets are seen far below enveloped in the intervening smoke which ascends from hundreds of chimneys. The old bridge over the river appears like a toy, so minute and so humble are its pretensions by the side of its mighty companion. . . . One of the arches near the river now far overtops a six-storey factory which stands close to the erection, and even the tall chimney of the building only surmounts the parapet of the viaduct by a few yards.

J.G. Kohl wrote in 1842:

> If England were not so rich in wonders of the same kind, the stranger might fancy the appearance of Stockport unique in the world. The houses of Stockport rise up the deep sides of a valley watered by the river on which the town stands. Over the whole gulf, right over the town and river, from height to height, stretches a gigantic viaduct, across which passes the railway to

159

London. . . . Even in England this is a striking and magnificent
work.

In the West Country, on the South Devon, the Cornwall and the
West Cornwall railways, Brunel's spindly but elegant viaducts in
Memel pine formed features of the landscape unmatched in any other
part of the country. There were five such viaducts between Totnes and
Plymouth on the South Devon, thirty-four between Plymouth and
Truro on the Cornwall Railway, ten on the twenty-six miles of the
West Cornwall and eight on the branch from Truro to Falmouth. The
designs were standardized, with sixty-six-foot spans on the main lines
and fifty-foot spans on the branches and the West Cornwall. Brunel
first used timber for a road bridge across the Great Western at Sonning
in Berkshire, and within a few years he became the greatest exponent
of timber in British engineering history. Any member of the viaducts
could be replaced without interrupting traffic. It proved impossible in
the twentieth century to obtain timber of sufficient quality to maintain
the viaducts and they have all been replaced, but in such places as
Devoran on the Falmouth branch the stubs of the piers remain alongside the steel viaducts which now carry the tracks.[10]

During the feverish activity of railway mania many lines were
projected but never built, some were begun but abandoned and others
were completed only to be superseded and rapidly closed. The Chesterton and Newmarket line was opened in 1848 but was subsequently
taken over by the Eastern Counties Railway and closed in 1851. Its
earthworks, together with some crossing-keepers' huts and station
buildings, are still features of the landscape east of Cambridge. The
Birmingham and Derby Junction Railway was opened on 12 August
1839 to a junction with the London and Birmingham at Hampton in
Arden. It provided the quickest route from the East Midlands and
many parts of the North to both London and Birmingham, and there
was heavy interchange traffic. In 1840 the Midland Counties Railway
reached a junction with the London and Birmingham at Rugby, and in
1842 the Birmingham and Derby opened a direct line into Birmingham from Whitacres. The line between Whitacre and Hampton,
which for a time had been a route of major importance, became an
inconsequential byway and, except for the station buildings at Hampton, its remains are hardly more substantial than those of a village
wiped out by the Black Death. Above the roofs of the inner Birmingham suburb of Duddeston tower the arches of a viaduct begun in the
late 1840s to enable trains from the Birmingham and Oxford Railway

to run on to the London and North-Western lines. When the former railway passed under the control of the Great Western the viaduct was abandoned, and it has never carried a train. At Tadcaster in the West Riding the River Wharfe is crossed by a handsome stone viaduct which has similarly never carried trains. It was part of a direct line from Leeds to York begun in the 1840s but never completed. South of the village of Bishop's Itchington in Warwickshire are earthworks adjoining the railway from Leamington to Banbury which appear to be the remains of a disused branch line. They have never carried rails but are the remnants of a junction planned between the Oxford, Fenny Compton and Rugby Railway and the Birmingham and Oxford, by which the Great Western hoped to carry the broad gauge to the north. The line to Rugby was abandoned, and the shallow cuttings and low embankments near Holmes House farm are monuments to the Gauge War and railway mania, just as the ridge and furrow in adjacent fields are a memorial to open field agriculture.

Some of the most poignant fossilized remains of the early years of railway development are at Fleetwood, at the mouth of the Wyre. Fleetwood was a seigniorial enterprise, planned by a landowner, Sir Peter Hesketh Fleetwood, who employed Decimus Burton to lay out spacious streets and terraces and to build the elegant North Euston Hotel around the terminus of a branch railway from Preston opened in 1840. Two lighthouses were erected to guide vessels into the estuary. The new town was intended to be a packet station at which travellers to Scotland could transfer from train to boat. Queen Victoria disembarked at Fleetwood on her way from Scotland to London in 1847, but the opening of the Lancaster and Carlisle Railway over Shap Fell undermined the whole basis of the venture. Fleetwood's prosperity revived under the aegis of the Lancashire and Yorkshire Railway in the 1870s as a fishing port and a packet station for Belfast and the Isle of Man, but Burton's hotel, terraces and spacious streets are strangely out of scale with the meaner buildings and narrow thoroughfares of a later generation.

The railways had to provide accommodation for many of their employees. At numerous wayside stations houses were built for station masters, and sometimes cottages for other employees. At isolated junctions it was sometimes necessary to build dwellings for signalmen or those employed at engine sheds. Some houses were built for railwaymen in the larger towns, like those in the streets adjacent to Francis Thompson's station in Derby. The most distinctive railway settlements were the towns created from insignificant beginnings for the accommodation of employees at locomotive and carriage works.

The Cheshire parishes of Monks Coppenhall and Church Coppenhall had a combined population of less than five hundred when the Grand Junction Railway passed through them in 1837, but by 1848 three other lines—from Chester, Manchester and Stoke on Trent—had joined the Grand Junction in the area. In 1840 the Grand Junction decided to move its works from Edgehill in Liverpool to Crewe, as the area was known, and the removal was actually carried out on 18 March 1843. By the end of the year a grid of streets had been laid out, a new parish church was under construction and schools were in operation. By 1851 Crewe's population was over five thousand. The houses built by the railway company were graded according to the class and status of occupants:

> first the villa-style lodges of the superior officers; next a kind of ornamental Gothic constitutes the houses of the next in authority; the engineers domiciled in detached mansions which accommodate four families with gardens and separate entrances (these are the famous 'blockhouses'); and last, the labourer delights in neat cottages of four apartments, the entrances with ancient porches. The first, second and third have all gardens and yards; the fourth has also gardens. . . . The rooms are all capacious; the ground-floors are tiled, and, as the back and front are open, ventilation is perfect.

Wolverton in Buckinghamshire was selected as the site for a locomotive repair depot by the London and Birmingham Railway because it was situated approximately midway between its two termini. The works opened in 1838 and employed four hundred. By 1845 an estate with over two hundred houses, a church and schools had been erected.[11]

In 1841 the Great Western Railway decided to build an 'engine establishment' at Swindon, where locomotives suitable for the flat line from London could be exchanged for those designed for the hilly route onwards to Bristol, where passengers could take refreshments and locomotives could be built and repaired. The station was more than a mile from the decayed market town of Swindon, and a village of three hundred houses was constructed, designed by Sir Matthew Digby Wyatt, the architect of Paddington Station. The grid of streets, all named after towns on the Great Western, is centred on Emlyn Square. The buildings on the ends of the terraces adjoining the square, mostly shops and public houses, are lofty structures of three storeys. In the square itself are the Great Western Mechanics' Institute and other communal buildings, including a hospital and a lodging house for locomotive men. The two-storey cottages were of local stone in several designs, many having unusual triangular porches shared by adjacent houses. Just outside the grid were villas for managers and a school; these were demolished later in the nineteenth century when the locomotive works was extended. St Mark's Church was constructed by the company in 1845, and a park was added at the edge of the village. Each house had a small front garden and a yard with a wash-house and privy at the back, but the cottages were not spacious and were considerably overcrowded at the time of the 1851 census.[12]

The South-Eastern Railway was responsible for a similar development on the edge of the market town of Ashford in Kent, where it purchased 185 acres for a locomotive works in February 1846. By the summer of 1847 seventy-two cottages had been built and a mechanics' institute inaugurated. Construction continued, and by 1850 the village had been named 'Alfred Town'. The cottages were built around a green and communal buildings included public baths, an inn, shops and schools. The earliest houses are two-storey flats, similar to those in Newcastle upon Tyne, but with entrances on opposite sides of the terraces.[13]

The subsequent histories of these towns, whose origins were so similar, varied considerably. Wolverton remained heavily dependent on the railway and, because land could not be obtained on its periphery, new houses later in the nineteenth century were built in the nearby village of Bradwell, which was linked by a branch line to Wolverton station. The expansion of the works led to the destruction of the earliest housing. At Swindon the original market town prospered with the increased trade brought by the railway. The Great Western abandoned its involvement in housing after 1854, and subsequent building was the work of speculators. Digby Wyatt's village was sufficiently distant from the original centre to be preserved. Ashford also grew, but the barriers formed by the railway tracks and the river prevented the integration of Alfred Town with the original settlement, and subsequent housing was provided by the company. Crewe, like Swindon, was a highly successful plantation. The LNWR, like the Great Western, found that the willingness of speculators to build houses meant that it no longer needed to be involved with such matters by the early 1850s. However it did, often ostentatiously, provide other

163

facilities, like Victoria Park, whose opening in 1887 marked both the Queen's Jubilee and the jubilee of the opening of the Grand Junction Railway. The lack of an original town centre at Crewe caused pressure on the LNWR-planned town which, from the 1870s, was increasingly turned over to shops, and only a few of the railway-built cottages now remain.

The railway towns epitomize both the achievements and the short-comings of the age of the engineer. They were well-built, sanitary, rational and well-provided with communal facilities. They were objects of great pride, something of which is reflected in F.B. Head's description of Wolverton in 1849:

> a little red-brick town, composed of 242 little red-brick houses – all running either this way or that way at right angles – three or four tall red-brick engine-chimneys, a number of very large red-brick workshops, six red houses for offices, one red beer-shop, two red public-houses, and, we are glad to add, a sub-stantial red school-room, and a neat stone church, the whole lately built by order of a Railway Board, at a railway station, by a railway contractor, for railway men, railway women, and railway children; in short, the round cast iron plate over the door of every house, bearing the letters LNWR is the generic symbol of the town.

Wolverton could appear a perfect example of rational planning. Samuel Sidney wrote in 1851:

> We have here a body of mechanics of intelligence above aver-age, regularly employed for ten and a half hours during five days, and for eight hours during the sixth day of the week, well-paid, well-housed, with schools for their children, a reading-room and mechanics' institution at their disposal, gar-dens for their leisure hours, and a church and a clergyman devoted to them.

Nevertheless he complained:

> It must be confessed that dullness and monotony exercise a very unfavourable influence on this comfortable colony. The people, not being Quakers, are not content without amuse-ment. They receive their appointed wages regularly, so that they have not even the amusement of making and losing money. It would be an excellent thing for the world if the kind, charitable, cold-blooded people of middle age, or with middle-aged heads and hearts, who think that a population

35 The northern portals of the Harecastle Tunnels on the Trent and Mersey Canal. The tunnel on the right is that constructed when the canal was built to the design of James Brindley in the 1770s. That on the left is Telford's relief tunnel built between 1824 and 1827

36 Delph Locks on the Dudley Canal, rebuilt in the 1850s, when the number of locks was reduced from nine to eight. The old line of locks ran up the track to the right

37 The Albert Dock, Liverpool, completed in 1845 to the designs of Jesse Hartley. The columns carrying the four upper storeys are of cast iron

38 A tollhouse at Richard's Castle, Shropshire, at the junction of the new roads from Ludlow to Worcester and Leominster, following realignment of routes south of Ludford Bridge during the 1830s

39 The inclined plane past the Devil's Chimney on the Leckhampton Quarry Tramroads, an extension of the Gloucester and Cheltenham Railway, c. 1830

40 'A hundred feet above the tideway.' A drawing by N. Beardmore depicting a coach crossing the Menai Suspension Bridge

41 J.C. Bourne's view of the bridge by which Isambard Kingdom Brunel carried the Great Western Railway through the Wiltshire market town of Chippenham

42 Dorchester South station. The railway from Poole to Weymouth curves sharply to avoid the destruction of the Iron Age hill fort of Maumbury Rings, whose ramparts can be seen behind the lamp standards beyond the passenger shelter

43 A railway viaduct under construction at Durham in 1855, with the centring already erected for a series of masonry arches

44 The surviving piers of Brunel's timber viaduct at Devoran on the branch railway from Truro to Falmouth, seen beneath the arches of the present masonry viaduct. The Redruth and Chasewater Railway passed along the shores of the estuary between the two pillars on the extreme left

45 Taunton Street, Swindon. In the centre is the Great Western hospital. The four-storey building with towers beyond it was first a lodging house, then a Methodist chapel and is now the railway museum

46 The 217-foot-long fireproof mill erected at Upper Tean, North Staffordshire, in 1823, for the manufacture of tapes. In the foreground is a range of late nineteenth-century top light weaving sheds

47 Steam-powered cotton mills on the canal bank: the image of Manchester by the 1830s. Cotton factories, Union Street, Manchester, from *Lancashire Illustrated*, published in 1829

48 The most celebrated ironworking centre in Britain, and the largest town in Wales, about 1840. Thomas Hornor's impression of the rolling mills at Merthyr, *c.* 1817

49 Price's National Teapot Works at Longport. A good example of a nineteenth-century pottery, with a faintly classical street frontage

50 A nineteenth-century view of bottle ovens at Etruria

51 Back Salisbury View, one of the terraces off Armley Lodge Road, Leeds

52 Bayliss Row, Nantyglo, a terrace in a cramped position on a South Wales hillside. Built in the 1820s, all the windows were on the uphill side, so that the house of the ironmaster Crawshay Bailey in the valley below would not be overlooked

53 A relic of the landscape of the pre-twentieth-century Black Country. The hamlet of Mushroom Green, a scattered group of much-extended squatter cottages near Brierley Hill

may be ruled into an everyday life of alternate work, study and constitutional walks, without anything warmer than a weak simper from year's end to year's end, would consult the residents of Wolverton and Crewe before planning their next parallelogram. We commend to amateur actors, who often need an audience, the idea of an occasional trip to Wolverton. The audience would be found indulgent of very indifferent performances.

The engineers of the early nineteenth century rarely articulated their wider objectives. They were capable of great flamboyance and ostentation, but much of what they did can be interpreted as the pursuit of rationality. It was, in a sense, more rational to convey goods through a cutting in waggons running on iron rails drawn by a steam locomotive, rather than over a steep hill in a cart hauled by overworked horses. It was rational to cross the Menai Straits on a bridge which was both beautiful and safe rather than to endure the dangers and discomforts of a ferry. Such pursuit of rationality, and such pride in the achievements of technology, can be observed in many other aspects of British society in the early nineteenth century.

In several parts of Britain waste lands were made productive and marshy places drained using the same kinds of expertise which were employed in the building of railways. The Fens were the subject of a succession of enclosure acts. The first steam pumping engine on the Cambridgeshire Fens was constructed in 1821 and at least fourteen similar engines were built in the next three decades. The typical Fenland pump was worked by a rotative beam engine in a tall brick engine house, with a long low building on one side for the boilers and a smaller one on the other containing a scoop wheel. These engines have long since been replaced by electric pumps, but the Stretham Old Engine, built in 1831 for the Waterbeach Level Drainage Commission, still survives. In the East Riding there was draining on a considerable scale of the carrs in the Hull Valley and the Vale of York, and in the West Riding the Humberhead Moors were brought into cultivation by allowing flood water from the Ouse and Trent to cover the land and deposit silt, thus building up the ground level. In Shropshire the Weald Moors were enclosed and drained in the early nineteenth century by engineers who had considerable interests in the iron trade. The straight roads of the area were constructed on embankments of blast furnace slag, much of which was transported by unemployed miners and ironworkers in the depression of 1815–18. An Act of Parliament for enclosing Exmoor was obtained in 1815, the largest tract, the King's Allotment of over three thousand acres, being purchased by John Knight of the Worcestershire ironworking family, who built new roads, farms and cottages, enclosed his property with a wall thirty miles long and began working a copper mine at Wheal Eliza.

The beginnings of a similar quest for rationality in the urban environment can also be observed in the early nineteenth century. About three hundred towns were the subject of Acts of Parliament establishing Paving and Lighting or Improvement Commissions. The authority of such bodies was often pitifully weak when confronted with the entrenched interests of property. They often lacked powers to drain the areas for which they were responsible and were thus unable significantly to improve standards of health. Even where they had such powers they were often restricted to thoroughfares, and they could do nothing about dung heaps and stagnant pools in enclosed courts. The surveyors they employed often lacked even such basic knowledge as what types of stone were suitable for paving streets. Nevertheless, in many towns building lines were straightened, corners were rounded and encroachments like porches, steps, bow windows and the hatches of coal cellars removed or rendered safe.

Engineers were also concerned with public utilities in the early nineteenth century. There had been public water supplies in some towns since Tudor times, but they were often grossly defective. In Shrewsbury and Bridgnorth waterwheels on the Severn pumped what was little better than diluted sewage into the upper parts of the towns. Often people drew their water in pitchers from rivers, or obtained it from wells which were polluted by burial grounds. Some water supply companies were set up in this period which used steam pumping engines and constructed new reservoirs, like the Sheffield company established in 1830. In wealthy districts more than one company might have pipes in the same street, but to provide water for the poor offered less chance of profit, and few companies ventured into the areas where they lived. After the practicalities of gas lighting had been demonstrated by William Murdoch in the early nineteenth century, systems to illuminate factories were supplied by his employers, Boulton and Watt. Many Improvement Commissions were closely associated with companies which provided gas street lighting, and ultimately supplies for private houses. The problems of public health remained terrifying in 1850, but they were being defined and a growing body of engineers was gaining experience in tackling them. The

Improvement Commission stone yard, the gas works and the water-works steam engine were becoming familiar sights alongside canal banks and railways.

Another means of creating rational living conditions was by founding 'new towns', separated from the pollution and disorderly populations of established town centres. Sometimes such developments were simply exclusive areas on the edges of towns, like the Bloomsbury squares whose residents alone had access to the gardens in the centre. Robin Chaplin has identified several new developments where villas and churches were built at a distance from existing town centres. Hillfields, Coventry, a mile from the old city across the valley of the River Sherbourne, began with the construction of villas in 1828. A church was built in 1840, but the development was overtaken by the pressure of expansion from the town centre, and workshops, pubs and cheap terraced housing were crammed on to plots intended for spacious middle class residences. Sometime in the 1830s the building of 'Aston New Town' commenced on the edge of Birmingham. Villas were built which were sold with the assurance that they had 'a close and interesting view of the old parish church'. As at Hillfields, the development attracted residents only slowly and was engulfed in the spread of industrial premises and working class housing from central Birmingham.[14]

The canals and railways enabled mechanical engineering to flourish in many parts of the country which had previously lacked the necessary raw materials. The cheap carriage of pig iron and coke enabled market town ironmongers and millwrights to set up their own foundries, and ultimately to make their own agricultural implements and steam engines. To estimate the number of steam engines in use becomes an impossibility after 1800. They were used for more and more purposes, as there were more local manufacturers able to construct small engines for particular needs. At the same time, the larger, more famous concerns like Boulton and Watt, Harveys of Hayle or the Coalbrookdale Company continued to meet demands for the larger engines.

As steam power was increasingly employed, so the sources of water power which in earlier generations sustained iron forges and fulling mills were set to new uses. Engineers like Telford and Rennie were as likely to be consulted about mills as about roads. While the work of the Fourdriniers in the early nineteenth century marked the beginnings of the Industrial Revolution in the paper industry, the number of

167

small, traditional mills multiplied. Many were on sites previously used for other purposes. At Bouldon in South Shropshire a paper mill was established about 1800 using the water power which previously worked a blast furnace. Like many other such mills it had a relatively short life, production ceasing in the 1840s. There were many skilled and ingenious new applications of water power. At a court case in Cornwall in 1830 a description was given of how J.T. Austen had cut a water course three miles long in the parish of Luxylan to work 'very expensive and powerful machinery' at one of his mines. The sixty-two-foot diameter waterwheel at Egerton Mill near Bolton was one of the sights of Lancashire and a visitors' book was kept to record the names of those who went to see it. New water or wind mills were no novelty. In 1826 a fifty-foot high wind mill was erected at Boverton Place in Glamorgan at a cost of £400. At Duxford in Cambridgeshire a new bone mill worked by water power was set up near the village corn mill in 1836.

The quest for rationality was not restricted to problems which were entirely within the scope of the engineers. New attitudes to time and work discipline led to the setting up of factories where processes could take place in a disciplined atmosphere, whether or not they depended on a centralized source of power. At Upper Tean in Staffordshire one of the most interesting sequences of factory buildings in Britain includes an immense, fireproof, steam-powered mill, 217 feet and twenty-seven bays long, fifty-one feet and five bays wide, with four storeys and three pediments, where tape weaving which had previously been put out to domestic workers was concentrated after 1823. Such a structure was in architectural or engineering terms a magnificent achievement, something which would have been beyond the technological capabilities of previous generations. For the employees it represented a complete change of lifestyle.

Sir George Head wrote in 1835:

> There can be no spectacle more grateful to the heart of an Englishman than viewing the interior of a manufactory of machinery, to observe the features of each hard-working mechanic blackened by smoke, yet radiant with the light of intelligence – to contrast with his humble station the lines of fervid thought that mark his countenance and direct his sinewy arm, and to reflect that to such combination of the powers of mind and body England owes her present state of commercial greatness.

Head was a paternalist, who appreciated the economic benefits which the achievements of engineers and the establishment of factories were bringing about, but it was difficult by 1840 to make such statements without agonies of guilt.

References

1 J.D. Porteous, *Canal Ports: the Urban Achievement of the Canal Age* (1977).
2 *Ibid.*
3 John Kanefsky, *Devon Tollhouses* (1976).
4 Barrie Trinder, 'The Holyhead Road: an Engineering Project in its Social Context' in Alistair Penfold, ed., *Thomas Telford: Engineer* (1980).
5 C.R. Clinker, *The Hay Railway* (1960).
6 D.E. Bick, *The Gloucester and Cheltenham Railway* (1968).
7 Charles Hadfield and John Norris, *Waterways to Stratford* (1962).
8 H.W. Paar, *The Severn and Wye Railway* (1963).
9 W.K.V. Gale and T.M. Hoskison, *A History of the Pensnett Railway* (1969).
10 L.G. Booth, 'Timber Works' in Sir Alfred Pugsley, ed., *The Works of Isambard Kingdom Brunel: an Engineering Appreciation* (1976).
11 W.H. Chaloner, *The Social and Economic Development of Crewe, 1780–1923* (1950).
12 Articles by David Eversley in *Victoria History of Wiltshire*, IV and IX.
13 Southern Railway, *Ashford Works Centenary 1847–1947* (1947).
14 Robin Chaplin, 'Discovering Lost New Towns of the Nineteenth Century' in *The Local Historian*, X, 4 (1972).

6 The Condition of the English Landscape, 1810–50

The social and economic history of England in the late 1830s and early 1840s can be viewed as a period of class warfare with three belligerents: the landed interest, the commercial and industrial middle class represented by the Anti-Corn Law League, and the organized working class, augmented for a time by many workers, in the Chartist movement, who were unorganized but desperate. It was a war which rarely flared into large-scale conflict. There were some open outbreaks of violence, as at Llanidloes in 1839 when Chartists stormed a public house in which magistrates were holding some of their number. There were many more occasions when Anti-Corn Law League lecturers were manhandled, or policemen trodden down by crowds, or when only the well-judged restraint of a lord lieutenant avoided a pitched battle. There was a prolonged debate about the nature of English society during the period of economic depression and Chartist agitation between 1838 and 1842, the consequences of which were remarkably similar to those of a war. Those in authority came to appreciate the conditions in which many of the people they ruled had to live, and the outcome was profound and lasting. After the early 1840s it was never again possible to regard the industrial landscape with the confidence and optimism of earlier generations.

One reason for the increasing awareness of the unhealthy conditions in which much of the population lived and worked was the growth of what was often called the 'sanitary idea' among civil servants and doctors, who know either from statistical sources or from practical experience something of the conditions which needed to be remedied. Concern was stimulated in the early 1830s by the first epidemic of Asiatic cholera, a horrifying disease, previously unknown in Europe, which was popularly believed to attack those whose way of life was dissolute. Edwin Chadwick, Southwood Smith and other pioneers of the sanitary movement strove to educate public opinion with facts about how the poor lived. They looked earnestly for practi-

170

cal ways of improving conditions, but continually encountered problems no one had previously attempted to solve, about which there was no accumulated body of knowledge. Chadwick's *Report on the Sanitary Condition of the Labouring Classes*, published on 9 July 1842, documented the squalor which was to be found in and around the abodes of the poor in all parts of the country. The following year the Health of Towns Commission began its deliberations, and in 1848 the Public Health Act was passed, providing the administrative machinery which enabled the problems of foul living conditions to be defined and tackled.

Unhealthy living conditions, overcrowded accommodation, polluted water supplies and lack of drainage were not just the consequence of the growth of mines and manufactures. Utterly foul areas could be found in market towns unaffected by industry and in villages devoted entirely to agriculture. Nevertheless the growth of towns, which was a consequence of industrial expansion, created new problems of scale. A cheap terrace of a dozen two-room cottages erected on an ill-drained meadow on the edge of a town like Dorchester, Totnes or Ludlow, with only two privies, a water supply polluted by a nearby graveyard and an average of eight inhabitants to a house was a blot on the landscape which might trouble the conscience of a few local doctors or ministers. Many acres of such housing on the edges of Manchester and Leeds became blots on the conscience of the nation.

Of more immediate impact than the sustained and serious lobbying of Chadwick was the explosion of interest in what was commonly called the 'Condition of England Question'. A sudden and to some extent temporary concern with the state of the labouring population—relating not just to the environments in which they lived but to their working conditions, their incomes and their morals—preoccupied educated society in the late 1830s and early 1840s. This concern was largely anti-rational, a hurried taking-up of a problem for pressing short-term reasons, an expression of disgust against the worst urban living conditions. Thomas Carlyle bluntly asserted that statistics were incapable of measuring the Condition of England Question. The examination of the industrial environment at this period was neither balanced nor rational. Anyone of moderately humane sensitivity who saw Little Ireland in Manchester, or the east end of Leeds, or the overcrowded cellars in Liverpool was unlikely to be concerned that housing elsewhere was not quite so bad. The natural reaction was one of outrage and anger. Similarly, when knowledge of child labour became widespread, when it became evident that in some cotton mills children under ten not only worked long hours but were sometimes savagely beaten, that in the narrow seams of some coal mines boys of seven or eight pulled 'dans' of coal with chains attached to their waists by leather girdles, the instinctive reaction was humanitarian outrage, a determination to eliminate such conditions whether or not they were typical.

There were a variety of reasons for this 'discovery' of the squalor of the industrial cities in the late 1830s and 1840s. Firstly, foreign visitors were dazzled, as they had been since the late eighteenth century, by Britain's overall economic success and were concerned to discover the sources from which that success had sprung. While in the 1780s and 1790s they had marvelled at Cromford, Etruria or the Iron Bridge, they were now appalled by the slums of Manchester or Liverpool. Manufacturing industry was well-established in several European countries by the 1830s, and visitors looked to Lancashire to discover their own futures in the same way that Englishmen in the 1930s looked to California or Soviet Russia. Secondly, the period of acute depression in the late 1830s and early 1840s caused massive short-term unemployment on the largely mechanized spinning side of the textile industry, and bleak prospects of perpetual unemployment for tens of thousands of handloom weavers. The towns of the North-West underwent a period of acute social tension, particularly in the summer of 1842. 'The haggard despair of Cotton-factory, Coal mine operatives, Chandos farm labourers in these days is painful to behold,' wrote Carlyle in 1843. Thirdly, concern with the manufacturing districts was intensified by the rise of the Chartist movement. On the surface Chartism was a political movement, specifically for the extension of the franchise. It had its roots in metropolitan agitation, with a programme whose pedigree went back to the 1790s. Yet from 1838 until the mid 1840s Chartism was far more than that. During those years it incorporated an enormous diversity of working class aspirations. As Carlyle correctly but pompously asserted:

> Chartism means the bitter discontent grown fierce and made, the wrong condition therefore or the wrong disposition of the Working Classes of England. It is a new name for a thing which has many names, which will yet have many. The matter of Chartism is weighty, deep-rooted, far-extending; did not begin yesterday; will by no means end this day or tomorrow.

Chartism was almost ubiquitous. There were Chartists in quiet market towns and in resorts like Torquay or Cheltenham. The movement's greatest strength was in manufacturing districts, particularly where there were concentrations of handloom weavers, as in parts of Lancashire or the upland townships of the West Riding, but also in such textile towns as Llanidloes, Newtown, Wotton under Edge, Frome and Trowbridge. The huge gatherings of demonstrators on such places as Kersall Moor outside Manchester or Peep Green in the West Riding were deeply impressive, and were perhaps the most significant ephemeral features of the industrial landscape of this period. R.G. Gammage, the Chartist historian, explained that there were no rooms capable of accommodating the numbers who wished to attend Chartist meetings in the autumn of 1838, and that the use of town halls was usually forbidden:

> a project speedily suggested itself to the minds of the leading men which would make them independent of all halls and places for indoor meetings. They suggested the holding of meetings by torch-light, as being better suited to the people's convenience both as regards time and expense. The expedient was but little sooner suggested than adopted, and for a short period the factory districts presented a series of such imposing popular demonstrations, as were perhaps never witnessed in any previous agitation. Bolton, Stockport, Ashton, Hyde, Staleybridge, Leigh, and various other places, large and small, were the scenes of these magnificent gatherings. At the whole of them the working people met in their thousands and tens of thousands to swear devotion to the common cause. . . . The people did not go singly to the place of meeting, but met in a body at a starting point, from whence, at a given time, they issued in huge numbers, formed into procession, traversing the principal streets, making the heavens echo with the thunder of their cheers on recognizing the idols of their worship in the men who were to address them, and sending forth volleys of the most hideous groans on passing the office of some hostile newspaper, or the house of some obnoxious magistrate or employer. The banners containing the more formidable devices, viewed by the red light of the glaring torches, presented a scene of awful grandeur. The death's heads, represented on some of them grinned like ghostly spectres, and served to remind many a mammon worshipper of his expected doom. The uncouth appearance of thousands of artisans who had not time from leaving the factory to go home and attend to the ordinary duties of cleanliness, and whose faces were there-

fore begrimed with sweat and dirt, added to the strange aspect of the scene. The processions were frequently of immense length, sometimes containing as many as fifty thousand people; and along the whole line there blazed a stream of light, illuminating the lofty sky, like the reflection from a large city in a general conflagration.

Philanthropic agitators of the period, like Lord Ashley and the leaders of the Ten Hours Movement, sought to ameliorate the condition of the working class by shortening the hours of work and improving working conditions. The struggle for such changes became deeply intertwined with another agitation, the demand of manufacturers for Free Trade in grain, expressed through the Anti-Corn Law League. The consequence of hostilities in this particular theatre of the class war was much 'inspection' of the industrial landscape. Leaders of the movement for shorter hours attempted to find factories where employees were treated especially badly, or where their living conditions were particularly squalid. The Free Traders drew attention to the best factories, usually in rural settings, where management was benevolent, cottages spacious and spotless and where it was possible to claim that workers preferred factory labour to other types of employment.

The period of the debate on the Condition of England Question was a time of acute class consciousness. It was a period of critical importance in the history of the English landscape, not so much for the changes which took place on the ground, but for changes in the ways people perceived what they saw. It was a time when the typical was less important than the horrific, when people were so incensed with the worst that it shaped their attitudes to the landscape as a whole—and these attitudes, formed in the 1830s and 1840s, were to affect how the industrial landscape was seen for a century and more.

Manchester was the town where the stock images of the industrial landscape were formed.[1] Carlyle wrote in 1843 of 'Ever toiling Manchester, its smoke and soot all burnt.' The commercial centre of the Lancashire cotton trade, as well as a substantial manufacturing town in its own right, Manchester's population, with that of Salford its neighbour, rose from 89,000 in 1801 to 288,000 in 1841, although it was only incorporated as a borough in 1838. Manchester had grown vigorously and without control. If some of its mills and warehouses were structures of monumental distinction, their surroundings were tawdry beyond belief. Writers like Dickens, Carlyle and Disraeli were fascinated alike by the town's vigour and its decrepitude. 'The age of ruins is past' said Sidonia in Disraeli's *Coningsby*, published in 1844. 'Have you seen Manchester?' replied his companion. J.G. Kohl wrote in 1844, 'Never since the world began was there a town like it, in its outward appearance, its wonderful activity, its mercantile and manufacturing prosperity, and its remarkable moral and political phenomena.' The place of Manchester in the popular thought of the time was perhaps best summarized by the French writer, Leon Faucher, who commented in 1844:

> Manchester, which gives direction to and almost holds in its hand all these industrial agglomerations, is, itself, the most extraordinary settlement, the most interesting, and in some respects the most monstrous that social progress had yet produced.

One of the most familiar images of Manchester in this period is the description of Little Ireland by Friedrich Engels:

> the most horrible spot . . . lies . . . immediately south-west of Oxford Road, and is known as Little Ireland. In a rather deep hole, in a curve of the Medlock and surrounded on all four sides by tall factories and high embankments, covered with buildings, stand two groups of about two hundred cottages built chiefly back to back, in which live about four thousand human beings, most of them Irish. The cottages are old, dirty, and of the smallest sort, the streets uneven, fallen into ruts, and in part without drains or pavement; masses of refuse, offal and sickening filth lie among standing pools in all directions; the atmosphere is poisoned by the effluvia from these, and laden and darked by the smoke of a dozen tall factory chimneys. A horde of ragged women and children swarm about here, as filthy as the swine that thrive upon the garbage heaps and in the puddles. . . . The race that lives in these ruinous cottages, behind broken windows, mended with oilskin, sprung doors, and rotten door-posts, or in dark, wet cellars, in measureless filth and stench, in this atmosphere penned in as if with a purpose, this race must really have reached the lowest stages of humanity.

Engels was born in 1820 at Barmen in the Wupper valley in Germany, the son of a cotton manufacturer. He already had radical views when he travelled to Manchester in 1842, but what he saw in Lancashire stimulated a burning hatred of the factory system and the evils which he considered it had engendered. Much of the information in his account of the English working class is drawn from secondary sources,

175

but he was well-acquainted with Manchester and the vigour of his language is itself evidence of how the town could move the emotions of visitors.

Little Ireland lay on what had once been meadowland within a bend on the Manchester side of the River Medlock (now culverted), not far from Oxford Road station.[2] It was notoriously unhealthy, its defective drainage, the pollution from the river and the smoke from surrounding factories being compounded by excessive overcrowding. On the opposite side of the river, in the township of Chorlton on Medlock, was one of the densest concentrations of mills in Lancashire. Development had started in the 1790s, along the axis of a turnpike road, and by the turn of the century several large mills had been established between the Medlock and Chester Street. In 1802–3 the vast Oxford Road mills were erected for H.H. Birley, leader of the Yeomanry at Peterloo in 1819; he used them for mule spinning and lit them with gas. By 1820 the last vacant factory plot in the area was filled. In the late 1820s the Birley family went into partnership with Charles Macintosh who had patented a waterproof double-layered fabric in which the layers were bonded by rubber dissolved by naptha. The factory became one of the sights of Manchester. It was visited in 1844 by the King of Saxony, one of whose aides described it as:

> a manufactory of the waterproof stuff called Macintosh . . . for which enormous quantities of indian rubber are used. We saw the way in which it is cut, melted and then in the form of a thick tough mass, passed between rollers; and finally, by means of polished steel rollers, laid upon the thin stuff, and covered with a still thinner covering of the cloth.

Only a few yards from the Birleys' mill stood Little Ireland, and the factory where the waterproof fabrics were made had but one of the thirteen tall chimneys whose soot poured down upon the slum.

Engels was collecting information for a biting indictment of the English middle classes, and he sought to expose the worst conditions in Manchester. Other writers, lacking his motives, formed similar conclusions about the town. Alexis de Tocqueville who, like Engels, foresaw the collapse of bourgeois society, but regarded its demise with regret rather than with relish, was impressed by the unkempt appearance of the town in 1835:

> An undulating plain, or rather a collection of little hills. Below the hills a narrow river (the Irwell) which flows slowly to the

Irish Sea. Two streams (the Medlock and the Irk) wind through uneven ground, and after a thousand bends flow into the river. Three canals made by man unite their tranquil lazy waters at the same point. On this watery land which nature and art have contributed to keep damp, are scattered palaces and hovels. Everything in the exterior appearance of the city attests the individual powers of man; nothing the directing power of society. At every turn human liberty shows its capricious creative force. There is no trace of the slow continuous action of government. . . . Thirty or forty factories rise on the tops of the hills. Their six storeys tower up; their huge enclosures give notice from afar of the centralization of industry. The wretched dwellings of the poor are scattered haphazard around them. Round them stretches land uncultivated but without the charm of rustic nature, and still without the amenities of a town. The soil has been taken away, scratched and torn up in a thousand places, but it is not yet covered with the habitations of men. The roads which connect the still-disjointed limbs of the great city, show, like the rest, every sign of hurried and unfinished work.

J.G. Kohl gained a similar impression of Manchester from the Irwell in 1844:

Standing upon one of these bridges, let us look around a little. What an extraordinary spectacle! There stand rows and groups of huge manufactories, each consisting of numerous buildings which are sometimes bound together by one surrounding wall. Sometimes these walls are fortified and guarded like fortresses, by vigilant sentinels who allow none to pass but such as have a right to enter. See how eagerly these manufactories suck up through pumps and buckets the river water, which dirty as it is, is invaluable to them, and which they pour back into the river, in black, brown and yellow currents after it has served their purposes. The river pours on its thick muddy current through the streets of the city to satisfy other thirsty manufactories further on. The blue heavens above are hidden from us by the thick smoke of the huge factory chimneys which weave a close impenetrable veil of brown fog between the city and the sky. . . . Between the great factories which each employ 500 or 1000 people, are scattered those of the smaller millowners which often consist merely of the owner's dwelling house, somewhat enlarged and extended. The great establishments are built in various ways; some piled up storey on storey, others on the straight line system in long successive rows; others like huge greenhouses, all on one floor lighted from the top. From these huge and oddly shaped buildings rise immense chimneys of all heights and diameters, many as tall as the steeples of St Paul's and St Stephen's, and sometimes architecturally ornamented with stone garlands, bas-reliefs and pedestals. As in former times, the huts of the vassals surrounded the castles of their lords; so now in the neighbourhood of the great manufactories, are seen the dwelling places of the workpeople, mean looking little buildings, huddled in rows and clusters. Sometimes the workpeople of each manufactory form a little community by themselves, living together in its neighbourhood in a little town of their own, but in general they occupy particular quarters of the town which contain nothing but long unbroken rows of small, low, dirty houses, each exactly like the other. These quarters are the most melancholy and disagreeable parts of the town, squalid, filthy and miserable to a deplorable degree. Here stand the abominable beerhouses, dram shops and gin palaces which are never without customers. Here the streets are filled with ragged women and naked children.

Manchester was an artless, unadorned town—overcrowded because of its fame as a magnet to the rural poor and the Irish, and because it offered in its warehouses and on its wharves unskilled employment on a scale not available in towns which concentrated on manufacturing.

Liverpool also attracted foreign visitors in the years around 1840. Those who sought the spectacular were impressed by its docks, the railway to Manchester and the wealth of goods in its warehouses. Those who sought a deeper understanding of social change looked to its slums, for it had the reputation of being the most unhealthy town in England. Leon Faucher was amazed by what he saw and by the demeanour of the poor. He toured the most squalid lodging houses near the docks in the company of the superintendent of police and was astonished that, although traditionally the Englishman considered his house as his castle, every door was opened to the policeman's knock and he was always received politely. He found the cellar lodging houses overcrowded and filthy beyond what he had previously regarded as possible:

Imagine a sort of hole dug in the ground, between ten and twelve feet square, and often less than six feet high, so that it is difficult for a grown man to stand upright. These holes do not have windows; air and light come in only through the door, the top part of which is generally at street level. You go down as if into a pit, by a ladder or an almost vertical staircase. Water,

dust and mud accumulate at the bottom. Since the floor is
rarely paved, and since no form of ventilation is possible, it is
perpetually dank and humid. In some places the cellar has two
compartments, the second of which, normally used as a bedroom, only gets light through the first. Every cellar is lived in by
three, four or five people.

Faucher remarked upon the two distinctive features of working class
housing in Liverpool—the prevalence of cellars and the construction
of back-to-back houses in enclosed courts. About half the city's working class population lived in courts and cellars for most of the
nineteenth century.[3] Land prices in Liverpool had been high in the late
eighteenth century, for three great estates tightly controlled the supply
of building land. Most workers in the city were unskilled and unable to
afford economic rents for well-constructed dwellings. The practice of
building enclosed courts was established by the 1780s, although it had
some earlier precedents. The three-storey back-to-back houses in
groups of six or eight which formed a court were usually integrated
structurally with houses which fronted on to a main street, through
which tunnels gave access to the courts. While the court layout could
be explained by economic factors, the prevalence of the cellar dwelling
could not. By about 1790 there were some 1728 occupied cellars in
Liverpool, most of them near to the docks. It is possible to link the
practice of building cellars with the custom of Liverpool merchants in
the early eighteenth century of using the cellars of their houses for
storage; but essentially the occupied cellar was a fashion. Dr Iain
Taylor has shown that cellar dwellings were not cheap; indeed they
were probably more expensive than the same amount of space for
accommodation above ground. Faucher noted that the weekly rent of
a cellar was as much as that of a first floor room, and that a tenant who
could pay by the year could have a whole house for the same price. The
father of a family told him that he preferred living in a cellar because he
was nearer the street for his children. Faucher observed something
which was true in all the great industrial cities—that the unorganized,
unrecorded street life was a dominant factor in the lives of many of the
population, particularly children. 'Without this customary outdoor
life', he wrote, 'the children, in any case very pale and disagreeable in
appearance in Liverpool, would get even worse.'

The landscapes of Birmingham and Manchester differed as much as
the economic structures of the two cities. Birmingham was essentially
a city of small concerns, a workshop-based rather than a factory-based

economy. Faucher compared its industrial structure with that of Paris. There were factories where a single source of power was shared by several users, but the impression gained by many visitors was of a small town on a hill, with several quite distinguished buildings, surrounded by a vast sprawl of uniform suburbs. Faucher observed that the allotment gardens cultivated by Birmingham artisans in the eighteenth century had largely been built upon, and that the city lacked public open spaces. The traditional working class house in early nineteenth-century Birmingham was the back-to-back court, not unlike that in Liverpool, although overcrowding was rarely as severe. J.G. Kohl described the differences between Manchester and Birmingham in 1844:

> In Manchester you see large manufacturing establishments and colossal warehouses . . . (but in Birmingham). . . . We beheld the principal churches, the Town Hall, the schools, the chief hotels &c. all comprised within the space of less than half an English square mile; in the great suburban wilderness that has grown up round the inner nucleus of the town, the only thing to interrupt the general uniformity is here and there a Methodist, an Independent or an Unitarian chapel.

Visitors like Kohl and Faucher missed many of the subtleties of the Birmingham landscape. Samuel Sidney, who knew Birmingham well, said that the city was far from picturesque, its few modern stone buildings being as much out of place as the odd idle dandy to be found among its busy mechanics and anxious manufacturers. The suburban sprawl was anything but uniform. Sidney described the controlled development of the suburb of Edgbaston on the Calthorpe estate:

> a crop of snug villas, either stucco or polished red brick; many of them surrounded by gardens and shrubberies and a few of considerable pretension. Of this suburb the Birmingham people think a great deal.

Some allotment gardens remained in cultivation and were noted by a Public Health Commission in the late 1840s, but they were probably too far from the centre for Faucher to have seen them. Nonconformity was certainly a powerful force in Birmingham and its chapels were among the most imposing buildings in the city, but there were also railway stations, mills and other structures which rose high among the workers' terraces. Yet the overall impression Birmingham made upon visitors was correct. It was very different from other industrial cities. It lacked very large manufactories. It was less of a town of passage and less crowded with unskilled immigrants. Its skilled working population was generally better paid and less prone to cyclical unemployment than that of Manchester or Liverpool.

Leeds seemed to some travellers a less disordered place than Manchester perhaps because, as a medieval planned town, its central streets remained wide and spacious. It had some industrial buildings of distinction, among them the flax mills of John Marshall and Co., built in 1838–40 by Ignatious Bonomi, in an Egyptian style, with lodges, a facade like that of a temple and a chimney in the shape of an obelisk. Internally it was a fireproof structure like the same company's Ditherington mill in Shrewsbury, with iron columns and brick floors carried on shallow brick arches, which formed the ceilings of the storeys below. Originally the mill had a roof garden on which sheep are said to have grazed. It was a magnificently exuberant structure, built at a period when mills generally were becoming less ornate. Much of the rest of Leeds presented a grim contrast. The fashion for building back-to-back terraces having been established in the late eighteenth century, it continued until well into the twentieth.[4] The areas being built up in the mid nineteenth century were mostly divided into small holdings, and development was mostly piecemeal, with short streets, blocked off by other streets built on fields purchased by other developers. Kohl wrote in 1844 that Leeds was:

> like all the great manufacturing cities in England . . . a dirty, smoky, disagreeable town . . . there are few neat rows of houses to be seen, because the factories take up a great deal of room and do not submit to any regular arrangement. The streets are not all paved, and no provision has been made for the regular carrying off of mud and rain water. . . . Leeds is perhaps the ugliest and least attractive town in England.

A.B. Reach found Leeds in 1849 less crowded than other industrial cities partly, he thought, because it was protected by the Pennines from sudden influxes of Irish immigrants. Throughout the West Riding he found that working class accommodation was almost always in back-to-back terraces. He was told by one man in Leeds that double houses (i.e. back-to-backs) were better than single ones because 'One heats the other like sleeping two in a bed'. The sheer scale of the squalor in the east end of Leeds, in little streets, built on small ill-drained fields, impressed even a reporter who had become hardened to industrial landscapes:

Conceive acre on acres of little streets, run up without attention to plan or health – acre on acres of closely-built and thickly-peopled ground, without a paving stone upon the surface, or an inch of sewer beneath, deep-trodden churned sloughs of mud forming the only thoroughfares – here and there an open space, used not exactly as the common cesspool, but as the common cess yard of the vicinity – in its centre, ashpits, employed for dirtier purposes than containing ashes – privies often ruinous, almost horribly foul – pig-sties very commonly left pro tempore untenanted because their usual inmates have been turned out to prey upon the garbage of the neighbourhood. Conceive streets and courts and yards which a scavenger never appears to have entered since King John incorporated Leeds, and which, in fact, give the idea of a town built in a slimy bog. Conceive such a surface drenched with the liquid slops which each family flings out daily and nightly before their own threshold, and further fouled by the malpractices of children, for which the parents and not the children deserve shame and punishment. Conceive, in short, a whole district to which the above description rigidly and truthfully applies, and you will, I am sorry to say, have a fair idea of what at present constitutes a large proportion of the operative part of Leeds. . . . I have plodded by the half hour through streets in which the undisturbed mud lay in wreaths from wall to wall; and across open spaces, overlooked by houses all around, in which the pigs, wandering from this central oasis, seemed to be roaming through what was only a large sty. Indeed pigs seem to be the natural inhabitants of such places. I think they are more common in some parts of Leeds than dogs and cats are in others; and wherever they abound, wherever the population is filthiest, there are the houses the smallest, the rooms the closest and the most overcrowded. One characteristic of such localities is a curious and significant one. Before almost every house door there lies, of course until the pig comes upon the deposit, a little heap of boiled out tea leaves. Although all the domestic refuse is thrown out, you hardly ever see bones; but the tea pot is evidently in operation at every meal. Here and there, I ought to add, the visitor will, even in the midst of such scenes as I have tried to sketch, come upon a cluster or row of houses better than ordinary, and through the almost invariably open doors he will see some indications of domestic comfort; but such buildings are the exceptions, and exceptions as they are, they rise out of the same slough of mud and filth and command the same ugly sights as their neighbours.

In the age of the railway the great cities were easily visited by foreigners and by English social scientists and men of letters. The debate on the Condition of England Question was thus dominated by urban images. The landscapes of the non-urban industrial districts were no more idyllic, but they were less noticed because they were less visited by the most widely read commentators.

Merthyr Tydfil, the largest town in Wales in the period, had a certain notoriety as having the greatest concentration of ironworks in Britain. It was visited by the King of Saxony and his doctor on 9 July 1844:

> We saw everywhere smelting houses and forges, little railways and canals for the conveyance of the iron from one place to another. In one valley we saw below a canal and a railway for locomotive engines; higher up, the road upon which we were, and still higher a tram road for the conveyance of materials and workmen belonging to the mines. We met on another occasion on such a tram road, a long train of black coal waggons, and others covered with workmen, black and brown with dust. And what mountains of dross were piled up!

Merthyr, like Coalbrookdale in the 1780s and 1790s, drew classical metaphors from the educated. The King insisted on remaining in the town to see the effects of the furnaces after dark. His companion wrote:

> We went out . . . to a height above the town, whence we had a view of five or six of these works where fires are constantly kept up by night as well as by day. One might imagine oneself in the land of the Cyclops. The effect was however, most impressive, when we descended into the nearest works, with their six blast furnaces and smithies filled with flames and sparks of fire. While viewing in the dark night behind these glowing works, the high volcanic looking cones of those mountains of dross, which I have noticed wonderfully illuminated by the red flames, one's fancy might easily represent at one time a blazing fortress, at another a burning castle, at another the fiery city of Pluto as represented by Dante.

A Welsh visitor a few years earlier noted the dense network of horse tramways conveying coal, iron ore and limestone, the plots granted by the Guest family to some of their employees for gardens and for building cottages, and the vast hayfields in the vicinity of Merthyr where fodder was grown for the one hundred and fifty horses employed in the Guests' works. One of the town's most impressive features was the way man-made mountains of slag, cinder, coal or ironstone mirrored the Welsh hills. Recent research has greatly enlarged what is known of housing at Merthyr and other ironmaking centres in South Wales.[5] In the 1840s the 'dual' row was still being built in the area, in which one range of houses formed the basement for an entirely separate terrace above. The lower row had doors at ground level on one side and extended back into the hillside in the form of a half-cellar. The upper range had its doors on the uphill side. Part of Merthyr known as 'The Cellars' was made up of houses of this type. They were described by a visitor in 1845:

> they are not cellars but a collection of small houses of two stories, situated in a depression between a line of road and a cinder heap. . . . The space between these houses is generally very limited; an open, stinking and nearly stagnant gutter, into which the house refuse is, as usual, flung, moves slowly before the doors. It is a labyrinth of miserable tenements and filth, filled with people, many of whom bear the worst characters.

One such row in Plymouth Street, Merthyr, was surveyed in 1970; the lower houses, having been empty for about sixty years, had water to a depth of several centimetres over the floors.

Not all housing in the region was of such a low standard. Cyfarthfa Row, Georgetown was built in 1840 by William Crawshay the Younger, of the Cyfarthfa Ironworks. It consisted of two parallel terraces comprising fifty houses in all, with short gardens in between, and the four-room dwellings were sufficiently well-constructed to justify modernization in the 1970s. Some South Wales ironworkers' housing had elements of ambitious planning about it. Chapel Row, Blaenavon was built in 1839 in the classical style, with an enormous chapel in the centre of symmetrical terraces of four-room houses. The Marquess of Bute built blast furnaces, in the same Egyptian style as displayed by Marshalls' mills in Leeds, in the Rhymney Valley in the

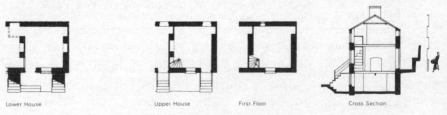

Lower House   Upper House   First Floor   Cross Section

Figure 11 Plan and section of dual houses, Plymouth Street, Merthyr

184

late 1820s. His furnacemen were housed in two-storey Palladian terraces of four-room dwellings, known as Butetown, which may have been modelled on the village of Lowther in Cumbria. At Abercarn on the east bank of a branch of the Monmouthshire Canal the local colliery company constructed a model colony of fifty-six houses between 1847 and 1850. However, much of the housing in South Wales was uncomfortably squeezed in on ill-drained tracts between plots of land used for industrial purposes. More typical than Abercarn or Butetown was Bayliss Row, Nantyglo, built in the 1820s by Crawshay Baily, an ironmaster with a reputation for autocracy and meanness. The terrace stands on a steep hillside above Baily's own house, which the cottages would have overlooked; but no windows were installed on the downhill side of the row.

In the Potteries the extension of turnpike roads and the building of the North Staffordshire Railway provided new sites suitable for ceramics works away from the banks of the canals. Groups of houses were constructed around the kilns, some in short terraces run up by speculators, others scattered almost at random around small folds. The larger potteries presented a formalized image to the outside world.[6] Most had imposing street frontages, consisting of a range of workshops and offices, usually with a waggon arch leading into a courtyard and a Venetian window above the arch. The ordered pattern disappeared in the yard to be replaced by a haphazard scatter of bottle ovens, workshops and piles of materials. The Potteries formed one of the most dramatic of British industrial landscapes. Kohl wrote in 1844:

> Burslem and Hanley are seen lying somewhat high. . . . A stranger might be tempted to believe he saw a vast line of fortifications rising before him. The surrounding hills are all crowned with the lofty columns and the huge pyramids of the chimneys and with the great rounded furnaces, of which dozens are often seen close together, looking like colossal bomb mortars. The high roofs of the drying houses, the magnificent warehouses and the many walls that enclose the whole great establishment or 'workhouse bank', with the piles of clay, flints, bones, cinders and other matters, serve rather to strengthen the illusion. Nor does the scene lose in interest as you pass through the district. Between the great workhouse banks lie scattered the small houses of the shopkeepers, the workmen, the painters, the engravers, the colourmen and others, while here and there the intervals are filled up by

185

churches and chapels, or by the stately houses of those who have grown rich by pottery.

Another visitor in 1849 described the landscape of the Potteries as:

> labyrinths of small, undistinguished, unpaved streets, the houses generally of two stories in height, and built of smoke-grimed brick. Here you will find a new row of cottages, the uniformity of the walls slightly broken by stone facings; hard by may be a cluster of old-fashioned houses with lead-latticed windows, and perhaps some attempt to cause ivy to train up the wall. Every few steps bring you in sight of a plain brown-brick chapel – Sion or Ebenezer or Bethesda, and numerous as are the Methodist places of worship, the public houses are more numerous still.

In the early nineteenth century the heathlands of the Black Country became the principal ironmaking region in England. The landscape of the region was remarkably varied. In the parish of Kingswinford in 1849 there remained numerous small agricultural holdings associated with the traditional domestic metal trades. There were still considerable areas of woodland, and the iron and glass furnaces were concentrated along the banks of the canals. Many of the Black Country mines were on a small scale, their winding drums powered by horse-operated gin rings. One visitor said that to go from Northumberland and Durham to South Staffordshire was to go back at least a century in the art of mining engineering. Samuel Sidney, who knew the Black Country well, described it in 1851:

> a perpetual twilight reigns during the day, and during the night fires on all sides light up the dark landscape with a fiery glow. The pleasant green of pastures is almost unknown, the streams, in which no fishes swim, are black and unwholesome; the natural dead flat is often broken by huge hills of cinders and spoil from the mines; the few trees are stunted and blasted; no birds are to be seen, except a few smoky sparrows; and for miles on miles a black waste spreads around, where furnaces continually smoke, steam engines thud and hiss, and long chains clank, while blind gin-horses walk their doleful round. From time to time you pass a cluster of deserted roofless cottages of dingiest brick, half-swallowed up in sinking pits, or inclining to every point of the compass, while the timbers point up like the ribs of a half-decayed corpse. . . . On working days few men are to be seen, they are in the pits or the ironworks, but women are met on the highroad clad in men's once white

linsey-woolsey coats and felt hats, driving and cursing strings of donkeys laden with coals or iron rods for the use of the nailers.

A visitor in 1843 thought the whole area an interminable village: the traveller was never out of sight of houses, not built in regular streets but in small groups among the furnaces, the heaps of coal being coked and ironstone being calcined, the spoil tips and the engine houses. It was remarked in 1849 that Bilston consisted of three or four suburbs but no town. Most of the cottages had been built by small speculators. A few fields of hay or corn survived among the heaps of clay and slag, so vast they made the experience of travelling along a road seem like that of going through a cutting. On every side could be seen buildings destroyed by subsidence. Other travellers were impressed by the paucity of vegetation caused by the quantities of sulphur in the air, which originated in the smoke of the blast furnaces and the coking and calcining heaps. Since the general topography of the region was flat the blast furnaces punctuated the landscape, being built on the level and charged by inclined ramps or vertical lifts; the furnaces in South Wales and Shropshire, by contrast, were usually constructed at the foot of a hill and charged from the hillside. In Willenhall Leon Faucher was impressed by the utter lack of any appearance of social order, and of links with the civilized world. It was a town made up entirely of workshops and pubs, with no magistrates, no police, no shopkeepers, no landed proprietors—only workers making locks by the gross to sell to factors in Wolverhampton. Friedrich von Raumer travelled from Manchester to Birmingham in 1835 and commented:

> about Wolverhampton, trees, grass and every trace of verdure disappear. As far as the eye can reach, all is black, with coal mines and ironworks, and from this gloomy desert rise countless slender pyramidical chimneys whose flames illumine the earth, while their smoke darkens the heavens; the whole is exceedingly striking, probably unique in its kind.

Colliery and ironworking settlements had the same raw, frontier-like qualities in most parts of Britain. J.G. Kohl was impressed by the close conjunction of coalmining and farming in the North-East in 1844:

> Along the Tyne the whole country is covered with collieries, lying like old smoky castles, among the green meadows and the teaming cornfields. . . . Close to the handsome farmhouses and the neat labourers' cottages lie the black dismal openings to

the pits. Here you see the seat of some wealthy landlord or capitalist, there a rural village peopled by agriculturalists, and a little further on, in a straight line, a regular uniform row of colliers' cottages. These dwellings are generally built for the colliers by the owners of the works and are all fashioned after nearly the same architectural model. The houses mostly stand in a long row all under one roof.

Another writer said of the North-East in 1849:

A pit-row is nothing whatever in the shape of a collocation of dwelling places that I know of in England. It is neither like a country village, nor a section of the meaner part of a manufacturing town; but it appears to possess more than the inconveniences of the one, and more than the ugliness of the other.

Frequently the cottages in such villages were of only one storey, although there was often a terrace of better dwellings for deputies or overmen which might have a name like 'Quality Row'. In the North-East, and sometimes in other mining districts, the first houses around the headstocks of a colliery were often built with the coal measure sandstones extracted when the shafts were being sunk and the main headings driven, and in consequence were often called the 'stone row'. Such a row might front a road, as at Grange Villas in Co. Durham, built in 1875, and have parallel ranks of later brick-built cottages laid out behind it. The pattern of cottages was broken by a few larger and smaller buildings, Methodist chapels, detached rows of pantries, and sometimes by communal bakehouses. Cottages rarely had gardens attached, but a field was often made available as garden plots where the miners might grow vegetables and flowers, and which might be dotted with pigeon crees, pig sties and hen houses. The drainage of such villages was no better than that of large towns:

some half dozen rows of perfectly uniform one-storied cottages, the intersecting lanes dotted with ash-heaps and middens, with, in rainy weather, perfect sloughs of mud formed round the hills of refuse. On the outskirts rise one or two modest looking dissenting chapels, as unadorned as though the line of beauty typified the path to destruction, and about as big as ordinary sized parlours. At one end probably rises the pit heap, at the other extends the garden field, and all around stretches a labyrinth of deep rutted mirey cross roads, through which in . . . wintry weather, the wayfarer wades rather than walks.

Several visitors found the cottages of the North-Eastern pitmen as well-furnished as those of working men in any other part of England. Cottages were kept spotlessly clean and great pride was taken in mahogany bedsteads and chests of drawers which reached to the ceiling. Samuel Sidney wrote that in the North-East:

> as you pass along the one street of a pitman's village, you will see the father reading a Chambers' Journal or a cheap religious magazine at the door of his cottage, while smoking a pipe and nursing a child or two on his knee; and through the open door a neat four-post bed and an oak or mahogany chest of drawers bears witness to his frugality.

He contrasted this impression of the North-East with the Black Country, where he thought the typical pattern was for the men to go to public houses and for the women to hang over the half-doors of their cottages gossipping or quarrelling. Another commentator in 1849 noted that the South Staffordshire miners' cottages had none of the handsome beds, ample and polished chests of drawers and burnished teapots and candlesticks of the North-East; the furniture was usually paltry and books were not to be seen.

Most colliery rows in the North-East were built by the companies which worked the mines. In other heavy industrial districts, where the prospects of success were less assured, speculators were left to provide housing or existing settlements on commons were enlarged piecemeal. A government commission visiting Tow Law in the hills of South Durham in 1846 noted that the construction of an ironworks would bring a population of about two thousand to moorland previously very sparsely inhabited. Houses would be built by speculators around the furnaces and the ore mines, shopkeepers and publicans would be drawn in by the prospects of trade, and Wesleyans and Primitive Methodists would follow, setting up meetings and then building chapels.[7] In the mining districts of Cornwall, where the uncertainties of mining along lodes of ore were greater than those of mining coal, many of the workings were remote from villages, and miners tended to walk long distances to their employment. In the remotest mining areas, in the Pennines and the Welsh mountains, barracks or lodging shops were built where men were accommodated during the working week and from which they returned to their homes at weekends. One such lodging shop, situated nine miles south of Stanhope in a remote part of the Pennines, was described in 1842 by a correspondent of

189

Edwin Chadwick. It was a plain sandstone building, about eighteen by fifteen feet, with a door and two windows on one side, and a large fireplace. Lockers and rows of hooks were provided for the forty-eight miners who stayed in the building, and there was a large box containing the clothes which the owners put on when visiting the mines. Beds were crammed in close beneath the roof of the first floor sleeping room. The miners slept in the lodging house on four nights of the week, bringing food in wallets on a Monday which would last until the following Friday.

The sudden expansion of iron ore mining in Cumberland transformed the scattered moorland townships in parishes like Cleator, where the population rose from 835 in 1841 to 17,651 in 1881; the number of miners increased from about 60 to over 6000 in the same period.[8] Some of the ore was exported to South Wales, some was sent for smelting to nearby Whitehaven, but in 1842 the construction of furnaces on Cleator Moor was begun. All the materials necessary for ironmaking were mined or quarried locally. Railways were built, linking mines and furnaces, and running through to the docks on the coast. Scattered groups of houses were constructed for the miners and ironworkers, some of them on the unenclosed moors. In 1857 six people died from sulphur dioxide poisoning caused by rain penetrating through the broken slag on which their new homes had been built. It was only later in the century that a coherent pattern of roads was imposed on a locality which had grown up along the lines of least resistance.

In the Shropshire coalfield there was a period of furnace building in the late 1820s, during which several new industrial villages were created. They were built in rows, like the pit villages of the North-East, but on a smaller scale. The standard of housing was in general lower than that built in the same area in the eighteenth century. However, in several villages housing of a higher standard was provided for skilled workers. At Horsehay the Coalbrookdale Company built cottages 'for the better class of workman' in the 1830s, with Gothic detailing and ceramic devices over the doors. Nearby cottages for the same company's brickmakers were less spacious and wholly without ornament. At Hinkshay another company built a village of three rows. One consisted of very cramped back-to-back houses, while another, of four-room houses, was known as 'New Row' or 'Ladies Row', and accommodated only skilled workers. At the same time the construction of houses on the pit mounts and on squatters' plots continued,

190

and a particularly crudely built cottage, which cannot have been constructed earlier than 1830, is now preserved in the Ironbridge Gorge Museum.

There were also untidy scattered settlements in the textile districts, particularly in handloom weaving areas. Thousands of cottages with loomshops were built in Lancashire in the early nineteenth century, although many, with the workrooms in cellars or on ground floors, are now scarcely distinguishable from other cottages. Handloom weaving severely declined in the 1830s and 1840s, but it survived in some woollen areas like Rochdale and Milnrow, and in silk working districts like Middleton in Lancashire and the towns of North Cheshire. Many of the most distinctive loomhouses were built in these areas in the first half of the nineteenth century, the last of them in Middleton as late as the mid 1860s.[9] Such houses generally have two, three and sometimes even four storeys, with loomshops lit by 'long light' windows on the upper floors. At one end of each working floor there was frequently a 'taking in' door, so that yarn and cloth could be lifted up without going through the house. Some of the loomshops of this period are buildings of considerable architectural distinction. At Chesham Fold, Bury, stood a terrace of ten three-storey loomhouses situated between a main road and a woollen mill. The workrooms on the first and second floors were lit by five-light sash windows at the front and by five-light mullion windows at the back.

Middleton, although only seven miles from the centre of Manchester, was a distinctive place within the region. The 'folk o' Middleton' wove silk on handlooms in their own houses, and the industrial landscape was quite different from that of the neighbouring cotton spinning towns. It was described by a visitor in 1849:

> I climbed a roughly paved lane, skirted by common-place mean houses, some of them little shops, and presently I heard on all sides the rattle of the shuttle. Still the aspect of the place was half rural. Trees here and there bowered the cottages and the noise of the flail mingled with that of the loom. The 'clubhouses' were a double row of two-storey cottages, constructed by an old club or building society. . . . They were reared upon the face of a steep hill, and the surface of the street between them being level, the ground floors on the lower side of the way are unavoidably underground floors. . . . I was met on the threshold by a decently dressed middle-aged woman who ushered me into the loom-shop where sat busy at his work her lord and master. The work-room boasted but an earthen floor,

191

scratched and scraped by half a dozen cocks and hens which were jerking their heads about beneath the mechanism of the four looms which the chamber contained.

In Milnrow, south of Rochdale, there survives what is probably now the greatest concentration of loomhouses in Lancashire. The present main street is lined with many two- and three-storey cottages, with long lights and taking-in doors. Some are grouped around a mill which bears the date 1863. Some have no 'long lights' visible on the street frontage, but they can be seen in the rear elevations. There are several groups of these cottages built in the side streets, one with an elegant classical porch. A close inspection of the town suggests that its superficially ordered appearance, with a straight main street, was probably imposed in the latter part of the nineteenth century by the Board of Health whose offices adorn one end of it. Milnrow appears to have consisted originally of untidily scattered clusters of cottages in folds and short terraces, and to have grown up in the same way that Hirwaun grew up around its tramways, Ketley among its pit mounds or Cleator Moor among its furnaces.

Until recently one of the most evocative of early nineteenth-century industrial landscapes was that of the Cheshire town of Macclesfield. Here, as at Middleton, the handloom weaving of silk flourished, and loomhouses were built until after the middle of the century. The town is dominated by massive buildings in the classical style, by silk spinning mills, among them some of the most elegant in Britain, Methodist chapels, and the four-storey, ten-bay Sunday School of 1813–14. Grouped around the mills are the weavers' cottages, mostly of three storeys with 'long light' windows on the top floors. All are built of brick and the older houses are roofed with thick stone slates. The terraces are staggered up the hills and follow the curves of the streets. In streets built in the mid nineteenth century the occasional three-storey loomhouse stands out among rows of two-storey cottages. Some streets are still surfaced with stone flags. In houses of all kinds, from the elegant dwellings of the middle class to the smallest cottages, are semi-circular headed brick arches over the doors. Some of the most attractive weavers' cottages have been preserved but many have been demolished, and it is now difficult to appreciate the close conjunction of the mills, where women worked to spin silk, and the cottages, where their menfolk worked at the trade of weaving.

One side in the debate about the Condition of England Question drew its evidence principally from the plentiful scenes of squalor to be

192

found in the cities. The evidence put forward by the apologists for the factory system, by contrast, was drawn largely from the rural mills and factory colonies, where it could be shown that cotton spinning was not inevitably associated with scenes like Little Ireland or the Liverpool cellars. The places most frequently drawn into the debate were no more typical of the conditions of the time than the worst examples of urban squalor, but they are important in the history of the English industrial landscape simply because they formed such a vital part of the debate.

In *The Manufacturing Population of England*, published in 1833, Peter Gaskell wrote that:

> An inspection of Belper, Cromford, Hyde, Duckenfield, Stayley Bridge, the villages and hamlets around Oldham, Bolton, Manchester, Stockport, Preston, Glasgow, &c. will show many magnificent factories surrounded by ranges of cottages, often exhibiting signs of comfort and cleanliness highly honourable to the proprietor and the occupants. These cottages are generally the property of the mill owner, and the occupants are universally his dependents. . . . Around many mills, a fixed population has arisen, which is as much a part and parcel of the property of the master as his machinery. The rapid improvement in the last has put an end to the necessity for new labourers, and thus little colonies are formed under the absolute government of the employer.

Andrew Ure, writing *The Philosophy of Manufactures* in 1835, drew attention to the successful plantations of the cotton masters in the Derwent Valley in Derbyshire, in particular to that built by the Strutts at Belper:

> The cotton factories of this eminent family have for half a century furnished steady employment and comfortable subsistence to a population of many thousands. . . . Under their auspices the handsome town of Belper has uprisen, built of hewn stone, with streets flagged with the same, in regular houses on the most commodious plans. . . . As no steam engines are employed, this manufacturing village has quite the picturesque air of an Italian scene, with its river, overhanging woods and distant range of hills.

Colonies like Belper were not recent creations in 1840, nor were their owners in the forefront of the political and economic controversies of the time. The most inspected rural industrial villages were the settlements of Turton, Egerton and Bank Top, which accommodated the employees of the brothers Ashworth to the north of Bolton.[10] The family first became concerned with cotton spinning when John Ashworth built the water-powered New Eagly mill in 1793. His sons Henry and Edmund subsequently transformed an insignificant concern into one which was internationally known for the quality of its yarns. New Eagly mill was doubled in size soon after 1818, and Egerton Mill, begun by others, was acquired when still unfinished in 1829. Its sixty-two-foot waterwheel became one of the sights of Lancashire. Henry Ashworth had a messianic belief in progress through unfettered private enterprise, and devoted himself to the cause of the Anti-Corn Law League. The League's aristocratic opponents sought diligently for evidence that the family's cotton spinning concerns had faults, while its propagandists lavished praise on conditions in the mills, on the villages and on the relationships between the Ashworths and their employees.

The Ashworths believed that there was a natural alliance between employers and workers, directed against the landlord class, and that any clash between masters and men arose purely from lack of education among the latter. They were strongly paternalistic and insisted on thrift, cleanliness at work, a change of shirt twice a week, attendance at a place of worship on Sundays, sobriety and sexual morality. Education was encouraged. Generous holidays were given, and wages for men were sufficiently high to ensure that their wives did not need to work. Cottages were inspected at regular intervals. Housing in the various settlements was built up gradually. Most of the cottages were exceptionally spacious with three or four bedrooms, a living room, a back kitchen and a pantry, with an outside lavatory in a walled backyard. By the fireplaces were water boilers and ovens, and there was piped water from 1835. Most of the cottages are built in small groups of neatly dressed local stone. They have low-pitched Regency-style roofs and face on to stone-flagged streets. There are few touches of architectural ostentation, although the central houses in Eleanor Street, Bank Top, are ornamented with a classical pediment. Names such as Cobden Street commemorate the political sympathies of the Ashworths. Lord Ashley, a determined opponent of the Anti-Corn Law League, thought the cottages the best dwellings for working men he had ever seen. Communal buildings included schools, a library, a newsroom, several chapels and a cook shop where bread and pies could be purchased. Public houses were rigorously excluded.

Almost every serious social investigator who visited Lancashire went to see the Ashworths' mills and villages. William Cooke Taylor, an apologist for the Anti-Corn Law League, wrote in 1842 that he preferred Turton to Egerton, since the waterwheel at the latter made it such a showplace. Few, he said, could 'fail to be attracted by the substantial neatness of the cottages in the village, and hence the families being used to inspection may be supposed in some cases to prepare for it'. Leon Faucher commended the superiority of rural industry, seeing such places as Turton as 'the germs of a better future for the working class which is already evident'. In his account of Turton he drew attention to the gardens, and to the evident tidiness and the abundance of books in the workers' houses, but his description has some linguistic similarities to that of Cooke Taylor, on which it may be based. Another visitor, in 1849, commented:

> The village of Egerton, although inhabited solely by a factory population, is as sweet, wholesome and smokeless as it could be were its denizens the most bucolic hinds of Devon. I wandered up and down its straggling streets. The houses are furnished in much the same fashion as those of the middling Manchester class; but every article of household use looks better, because cleaner and fresher. Here is no grime nor squalor. The people are hard-working labourers, but they live decently and fare wholesomely. There is no ragged wretchedness to be seen, no ruinous and squalid hovels. . . . Altogether the village of Egerton presents a gratifying spectacle of the manufacturing system working under favourable auspices.

Faucher also cited as evidence for the superiority of rural manufacturing another 'industrial republic', that of the Greg family at Quarry Bank near Wilmslow, where R.H. Greg had rebuilt the cottages in the 1830s, opened a Sunday School and provided a recreation ground. Cooke Taylor commended the colony of the Whitehead family at Hollymount near Rawtenstall, where he observed a flamboyant new mill in 1842, 'one of the most extraordinary architectural works in Lancashire', dwellings which he insisted were handsome houses rather than cottages, a school, a Methodist chapel in the Ionic order and the residences of the Whiteheads on a hilltop at a short distance from the factory.

These much-commended factory colonies were normally isolated, in locations where the owners had found it necessary to provide housing and where there was little other industry to encourage speculators to provide more. The lack of alternative sources of employment eased the imposition of work discipline. The factories were often water-powered, which freed the villages from smoke nuisance, universal in manufacturing towns. The proprietors normally lived on the spot and personally supervised their workers. There were schools, communal educational and recreational facilities, and gardens. The concerns often produced high quality yarns which sold at a premium. For those who could accept paternalistic discipline they were doubtless satisfying places in which to live.

Other industries also had their showplaces. A parliamentary commission drew attention in 1845 to Flockton near Wakefield in the West Riding, where Milnes Stansfeld had provided three- and four-room cottages for the miners employed at his collieries since 1839.[11] Gardens were attached to the cottages and additional garden plots were available for those who wanted them, in a field divided up by thorn hedges. A Cottagers' Horticultural Society had been formed to stimulate the love of gardening. A field equipped with gymnastic apparatus and another laid out for cricket were available for the miners' use. There was a school at which classes for adults were held, and it was claimed that 'collier boys can be heard in the street singing and whistling the beautiful airs from Handel, Haydn, Mozart and Spohr'. Between 1834 and 1860 the Butterley Company built a model village for workers at their Codnor Park furnaces and forges in Derbyshire, which they called Ironville.[12]

Some of the subtlest comments on the industrial landscape of the early nineteenth century were those provided by the Utopian settlements of the period. The visions of Robert Owen of New Lanark, propounded in many Owenite halls in the industrial areas, were essentially communitarian. At Tytherley in Hampshire Owen's adherents established a colony called Queenswood in 1839. The scheme was ill-judged, the poor land being unsuitable for the sustenance of large numbers of people, and there were frequent disagreements between craftsmen and farmers. Much of the money available for the project was spent on the lavish fittings of its main building, which was called Harmony Hall. G.J. Holyoake visited the colony when it was in its death throes in 1844:

> These half-developed rustics looked with bovine wonder on
> the colony of 'Zozialites' that had been planted amongst them.
> In that stately three-storied structure, with stained glass win-
> dows to its dining hall, a princely kitchen, a ball-room, and all

196

the rest, they were told to see the model of what every English worker's home would be like under an equitable system of industry; though their clergy disturbed them with suggestions of sulphur in its magic. . . . By this time, 1844, the shadow lay full upon it. Bravely the communists struggled and economized. Tea and sugar had already disappeared, but they still sang their cheerful music after the thin communal meal. Holyoake saw at a glance one reason for the terrible failure. The land was flinty and poor – better suited for a 'colony of gunsmiths'. In fact, one was impelled to the conclusion that it was chosen with an eye to insolvency, under the impression that the chalk pits in the neighbourhood would be convenient for white-washing. It was miles away from markets and so only possible as an agricultural colony; and for its success as such nature had done little and the directors less. Owen and his colleagues had built it in a panic of pride. It was squanderization not colonization. The most hidden material was of the costliest character. The ball room and the class rooms had richly furnished ceilings. A long vine wall was erected that probably cost a guinea a yard. . . .

Rather different aspirations were expressed in the villages laid out by Feargus O'Connor's Chartist Land Company.[13] As Chartism declined as a political movement in the mid 1840s, so the Land Company, founded in 1845, flourished. Subscriptions were raised through branches all over the country, and the plots on the estates distributed by ballot. Cottages were designed by O'Connor himself, and each one stood in a four-acre plot. Each village had a school, which was intended to be an educational centre for adults as well as children. The first estate at Heronsgate near Rickmansworth was acquired in March 1846, and the settlers moved in to the completed cottages on May Day 1847. Subsequent estates were built at Charterville, near Minster Lovell in Oxfordshire, Snigs End and Lowbands, both near Tewkesbury in Gloucestershire, and at Dodford near Bromsgrove in Worcestershire. The financial basis of the Land Company was unsound, however, and it eventually collapsed in 1851. Nevertheless, its dramatic success in attracting subscriptions shows how powerful was the appeal of the life of the rural smallholder to the town dwellers of industrial Britain, and how great the degree of dissatisfaction with the industrial environment. After the collapse of the Land Company the villages passed into other ownership, but they were deprived of their schools, the buildings being sold for other uses. They remain in the landscape as monuments to the appeal which individualism had for the generation which was most aware of the sufferings caused by industrial growth.

Neither Little Ireland, Egerton nor Charterville was in any way 'typical' of the industrial landscape of the 1840s, but each opens many insights into the understanding of that landscape and into the whole debate on the Condition of England Question. The debate was won by those who drew attention to the Little Irelands. The popular image of mining and manufacturing became one of smoke and squalor, of overcrowding, muddy streets, drunkenness and disorder. Nevertheless, during the 1840s commentators began to analyse the industrial landscape more objectively, and to appreciate some of the subtleties missed by the foreigners and novelists who travelled from London to Manchester by train, saw Little Ireland and returned with a pile of secondary accounts. The descriptions of the manufacturing districts, the rural districts and the metropolitan areas published in the *Morning Chronicle* from 1849 onwards, and written by Henry Mayhew, Angus Bethune Reach, Charles Mackay and others, represented a new mode of investigation.[14] Several of their accounts have been quoted earlier in this chapter, but Reach's description of Manchester deserves separate examination for the contrast it provides with impressions such as those of Engels, Kohl and de Tocqueville. It demonstrates that, while the city could at first sight appear horrifying and bewildering, and visitors could be overwhelmed by observing living conditions which were totally inhuman, it was nevertheless the centre of a prosperous industry, which paid high wages by the standards of the time, reflected in a considerable degree of domestic comfort for many of the workpeople. There were minute but observable differences between its various suburbs. The whole task of studying a great manufacturing city was transformed into something more demanding and at the same time more rewarding:

> The house of the Manchester operative, wherever it be – in the old district or in the new – in Ancoats or Cheetham or Hulme – is uniformly a two-storey dwelling. Sometimes it is of fair dimensions, sometimes a line fourteen feet long would reach from the eaves to the ground. In the old localities there is, in all probability a cellar beneath the house, sunk some four or five feet below the pavement, and occupied perhaps by a single poor old woman, or by a family, the heads of which are given to pretty regular alternation between their subterranean above and the neighbouring wine vaults. In the modern and improved *quartiers* the cellar retires modestly out of sight and is put to a

more legitimate use as a home for coals or lumber. Nothing struck me more while visiting and comparing notes in the different operative districts of Manchester, than in the regularity with which the better style of furniture went together with the better style of house; it always being kept in mind that, so far as wages are concerned, the inhabitants of one locality are almost, if not quite, on a par with those of another. But the superior class room seemed, by a sort of natural sequence, to attract the superior class furniture. A fair proportion of what was deal in Ancoats was mahogany in Hulme. Yet the people of Hulme get no higher wages than the people of Ancoats. The secret is that they live in better built houses and consequently take more pleasure and pride in their dwellings. . . . The worst class of houses, not being cellars, commonly inhabited by the mill hands, consist each of two rooms, not a 'but-and-a-ben', but an above and a below, the stair to the former leading directly up from the latter, and the door of the ground floor parlour being also the door of the street. In some cases the higher storey is divided into two small bedrooms, but in the superior class of houses, there are generally two small, but comfortable rooms on the ground floor, and two of corresponding size above. The street door in these tenements opens into a narrow passage from which the stairs of the bedrooms also ascend. The window of the ground floor room opening to the street, is always furnished with a pair of substantial outside shutters, and the threshold is elevated from the pavement, so as to admit of very emphatic stone doorsteps with flourishing scrapers, both of which are generally to be found in a very commendable state of purity.

Mayhew, Reach and their collaborators did not paint a rosier picture of manufacturing England than earlier writers, simply one which was more securely founded on fact and more acutely observed. They showed that there was more to the industrial landscape than Manchester, Leeds, Liverpool and Birmingham, that overall the industrial landscape was possibly far worse an environment in which to live than a superficial observation of some notorious black spots might suggest. They showed that there were still many manufacturing concerns which were not steam-powered, that there were mining settlements which had never been visited by previous observers.

The serious 'inspection effects' of the class war did not begin with the *Morning Chronicle*. The information collected by Chadwick for the *Report on the Sanitary Condition of the Labouring Classes* in 1842 was equally comprehensive, equally distant from sensationalism and equally horrifying in its total message, even if it lacked the subtle social observations of Mayhew and Reach. It showed that foul living and working conditions were not just to be found in the great cities. The shoemakers of Stafford, the tailors of Marlborough, the lead-miners of the Pennines lived and worked in conditions just as unhealthy as those of the Manchester cotton spinners. The 'inspection effect' was continued by a range of other government inquiries, some of a short-term nature, like those established to investigate the 'Plug Plot' riots of the summer of 1842, others, like the Poor Law Board and the Commission to inquire into the state of the population in the Mining Districts, bodies which were more or less permanent. In 1848 the Public Health Act was passed, which set in train a whole series of inquiries by Board of Health commissioners into the sanitary conditions of towns all over the country. The commissioners uncovered disturbing evidence of living and working conditions wherever they went, often caused not so much by major new industries as by ancient trades like butchery and tanning. The inspector who visited Shrewsbury found parts of the town engulfed in acrid fumes from a lead-works, established by two local plumbers. Cattle on nearby meadows sometimes died from lead poisoning, and an analysis of a piece of turf showed that it contained twelve grains of red lead to the square foot.

This was a time of debate about the industrial landscape, and while the landscape itself changed relatively little, opinions about it altered considerably. Typical of the more exaggerated opinions of England in this period was that of the Baron D'Haussez, ex-minister to the French Bourbon kings, who wrote in 1833:

> This feudality is the manufacturing power. Its dungeons are the workshops, where thousands of unfortunate beings find a precocious death, long preceded by diseases and infirmities, which are owing to the unwholesome air they breathe, and to the excessive labour and ill-treatment they undergo. The barons are the manufacturers, who, to gratify their cupidity, condemn those dependent upon them to the most oppressive and most deplorable slavery.

Apart from the main line railway, few wholly new features appeared in the industrial landscape between 1815 and 1850. There were no innovations like the textile mill, the canal and the steam engine to match the changes of the late eighteenth century, although substantial new areas were given over to mining and manufacturing. Nevertheless this period, and particularly the years around 1840, was a critical time

200

in the history of the English industrial landscape, for that landscape became a source of shame. It did so largely because of the various 'inspection effects' triggered off by the intensity of class warfare at the time, and by the debate on the Condition of England Question. In that controversy, debaters saw very largely what they wished to see. This did not mean that they were not generally alarmed, nor did it mean that the more comprehensive picture revealed by soberer investigators was, for all its qualifications, any less shocking or alarming.

References

1   Asa Briggs, *Victorian Cities* (1963).
2   Sylvia Clark, 'Chorlton Mills and their Neighbours', *Industrial Archaeology Review*, II, 3 (1978).
    Sylvia Clark and A.D. George, 'A note on "Little Ireland", Manchester', *Industrial Archaeology*, XIV, 1 (1979).
3   I.C. Taylor, 'The Court and Cellar Dwelling: the eighteenth-century origins of the Liverpool slum', *Transactions of the Historical Society of Lancashire and Cheshire* (1970–1).
4   M.W. Beresford, 'The Back-to-Back House in Leeds, 1787–1937' in S.D. Chapman, ed., *The History of Working Class Housing* (1971).
5   J.B. Lowe, *Welsh Industrial Workers' Housing 1775–1875* (1977).
6   D.M. Smith, 'Industrial Architecture in the Potteries', *North Staffordshire Journal of Field Studies*, V (1965).
7   *Report of the Commission into the State of the Population in the Mining Districts*, British Parliamentary Papers, 1846, XXIV.
8   Ross Barber, *Iron Ore and After: Boom Time, Depression and Survival in a West Cumbrian Town, Cleator Moor 1840–1960* (1976).
9   W.J. Smith, 'The Architecture of the Domestic System in South-east Lancashire and the Adjoining Pennines' in S.D. Chapman, ed., *The History of Working Class Housing* (1971).
10 Rhodes Boyson, *The Ashworth Cotton Enterprise: the rise and fall of a family firm 1818–1880* (1970).
11 *Report of the Commission into the State of the Population in the Mining Districts*, British Parliamentary Papers, 1845, XXVII.
12 The Arkwright Society, *Ironville* (1975).
13 A.M. Hadfield, *The Chartist Land Company* (1970).
    Peter Searby, 'Great Dodford and the later history of the Chartist Land Scheme', *Agricultural History Review*, I (1968).
14 P.E. Razzell and R.W. Wainwright, *The Victorian Working Class: selections from letters to the Morning Chronicle* (1973).

7 Palaces of Industry, 1850–90

On Thursday 1 May 1851 Thomas Babington Macaulay described the first day of the Great Exhibition in the Crystal Palace:

> there must have been near three hundred thousand people in Hyde Park at once. The sight among the green boughs was delightful. The boats and little frigates darting across the lake; the flags; the music; the guns; – everything was exhilarating, and the temper of the multitude the best possible. . . . I made my way into the building; a most gorgeous sight; vast; graceful; beyond the dreams of the Arabian romances; I cannot think that the Caesars ever exhibited a more splendid spectacle. I was quite dazzled, and I felt as I did on entering St Peter's.

The Crystal Palace was the most enduring image of the industrial landscape of the mid nineteenth century, and its significance can be interpreted in several ways. It demonstrated that new materials—cast iron and glass—could be used to create a structure ideal for its function, with a subtlety and novelty of style which itself gave an identity to the whole exhibition project. The Exhibition was also a triumph in the celebratory sense. If the late 1830s and 1840s was a period of bitter class warfare, the Exhibition can be seen as a celebration of peace. It was also a celebration in the longer term, an acknowledgment that the pains of industrialization the nation had suffered for a century had brought real material benefits. 'Lord' George Sanger remarked that the Exhibition:

> helped to mark the immense improvement that had taken place since the accession of Queen Victoria in the condition of the English nation and the people. It crystallized, as it were, these improvements under one vast roof for all to see; it brought home to the people the fact that they were living in times infinitely better than they could have imagined possible but a few short years before, and encouraged them to look and work for still better times to come.

The inspiration of the Exhibition was in part internationalist. Prince Albert spoke in 1850 of the 'realization of the unity of mankind' which was coming about through scientific, technological and economic progress. Joseph Paxton, designer of the Crystal Palace, was cheered by the mixture of races and classes at the Exhibition, and looked forward to a Brotherhood of Nations. Accounts of visits to the Exhibition emphasize the interest which people found in the products of India, China and the Near East, in the curiosities from Europe—a Gothic bookcase from Vienna or the stuffed frogs and cats from Wurtemburg—or the machines with interchangeable parts from the United States. Nevertheless, the exhibition remained overwhelmingly a festival commemorating decades of economic achievement in Britain. 'It would have been difficult', remarked one commentator, 'to select any department . . . which could compare with Class XXVI as an evidence of our national prosperity.' Class XXVI was the furniture section, in which most exhibits were provided by the cabinet makers and upholsterers of the metropolis, or by individual craftsmen of genius from provincial towns, and hardly any by factories, but the remark reveals clearly the pride in achievement accomplished that permeated the whole project.

The Crystal Palace itself symbolized the way in which industry could rapidly alter the landscape. Hyde Park was only transformed for a season, but the same energy, vigour and confidence were to be found in many of the rapidly expanding mining and manufacturing districts of the mid nineteenth century. The Exhibition derived from a series of displays of manufactures sponsored by the Royal Society of Arts in 1847, 1848 and 1849. A quinquennial international exhibition in London was planned by Prince Albert in collaboration with Henry Cole, a civil servant who was an active member of the society. A Royal Commission was set up in January 1850, but there was much opposition to the proposed erection of a large, durable building in Hyde Park. It was not until 11 June 1850 that Joseph Paxton, agent to the Duke of Devonshire and a director of the Midland Railway, doodling on blotting paper during a meeting for the disciplining of railway staff, produced a sketch of a building in cast iron and glass, an enlarged version of the conservatories which he had constructed at Chatsworth. The idea was publicized in the *Illustrated London News*, and on 15 July the Commission agreed that it should be built. A contract for the supply of the iron castings was given to Messrs Fox and Henderson of Smethwick, while Chance Bros of Birmingham supplied the glass. The concrete foundations were laid in August, and the first of the vertical columns raised into place on 26 September. Throughout the autumn visitors flocked to watch the work, paying five shillings apiece for the privilege. By December over 2000 men were employed. The castings which formed the frame were hauled to Hyde Park from railway sidings, tested and drawn up into place. The 'Paxton gutters', specially designed timber beams to hold the glass panes, each with three gutters to carry away exterior water and internal condensation, were shaped by purpose-built machines. The panes of glass, forty-nine by twelve inches, were installed by teams of glaziers, each of two men and two boys, who moved along the roof in glazing waggons running in the grooves of the Paxton gutters. The building was completed within twenty-two weeks and was ready for the reception of exhibits on 12 February 1851. It incorporated 4500 tons of iron, 600,000 cubic feet of timber and 293,655 panes of glass. Only a generation singularly free from self-doubt, the same generation which created the railway network, could have carried through the project, for less than eleven months elapsed between Joseph Paxton's first doodlings on blotting paper and the ceremonial opening of the Exhibition.

The Great Exhibition celebrated the success of those manufactures which had transformed the landscape of the industrial parts of Britain. Cotton fabrics from Lancashire, woollens from the West Riding, knives from Sheffield, guns from Birmingham, castings from Coalbrookdale, pottery from North Staffordshire, copper and tin ores from Cornwall, lead from the Pennines, hosiery from Nottingham, coal from Derbyshire and the North-East were displayed in abundance. The vitality of the London luxury trades—the carriage builders and silversmiths, the watchmakers and manufacturers of pianofortes —was amply demonstrated as well.

It was in the mid nineteenth century that the textile areas of Lancashire and Yorkshire were at their most prosperous and became largely urbanized. Up the valley of the Calder from Wakefield, through Horbury, Dewsbury, Mirfield, Brighouse, Elland, Halifax, Sowerby Bridge and Mytholmroyd to Hebden Bridge, up the Irwell from Manchester through Pendlebury, Farnworth, Radcliffe, Bury and Ramsbottom to Rawtenstall, Bacup and the Forest of Rossendale, and along the floors of most other valleys in the region grew up a landscape of steam-powered mills with towering chimneys, churches, chapels, mechanics' institutes, pubs and terraced housing, linked together by numerous railways and backed by the steep slopes of the Pennine moors. The present-day landscape of industrial Lancashire is still dominated by the housing of the latter part of the nineteenth century, by single-storey weaving sheds and, above all, by colossal mills built between 1880 and the First World War. These were of four, five or six storeys, with steel girder frames, generously fenestrated, with walls of shiny red brick dressed with terracotta or yellow bricks, water tanks on the roofs, relief panels in faience and often the name of the mill on the side.[1] Chimneys like that of the India Mill in Darwen are landmarks for miles around. Many extensions to the towns of Lancashire and Yorkshire were in effect factory colonies, built by millowners to house their employees. Freetown, to the north-east of Bury, was largely built by Thomas Greenhalgh for workers in his 'very large factory and steam loom sheds'. At Warthfold, between Bury and Radcliffe, the firm of J. and J. Mellor built cottages for over two hundred of their employees between 1863 and 1872, installing roads, drains and gas supplies.[2]

Two factory colonies in Yorkshire illuminate the history of the industrial landscape particularly well, not because they are typical of what was commonly built, but because they reveal so many of the contrasting assumptions of mid Victorian society.

Edward Akroyd, a Halifax worsted manufacturer, inherited £1,750,000 from his father in 1847.[3] Between 1849 and 1853 he built a 'model' village of two parallel terraces of back-to-backs with Gothic detailing, at Copley on the floor of the Calder Valley south of Halifax. In 1859 he began to construct a second village to the north of Halifax, adjacent to his Haley Hill mills. This village was designed by the architect George Gilbert Scott, although the cottages themselves were actually built to the designs of a local man, W.H. Crossland. Scott designed the magnificent church of All Souls, adjacent to the village, which he considered 'on the whole my best church'. Akroydon is laid out around a square, in imitation of what Akroyd and Scott believed was the layout of an old Pennine village. In the centre was a cross in the medieval style, inscribed:

> Erected as a monument of the Christian reverence for the emblem of the cross and of loyalty to Our Sovereign Lady Queen Victoria by Edward Akroyd, the founder of Akroydon. MDCCCLXX. Fear God. Honour the King.

It was remarked that:

> Mr Akroyd is very desirous of keeping up the old English

notion of a village – the squire and the parson as head, and then the tenant farmers and lastly the working population.

The stone cottages were built in the Gothic style, some with the initials of the first householders carved over the doors. The carved detailing on some of the larger dwellings along the old turnpike road to Bradford is magnificent, one house having the word 'Akroydon' carved in elongated letters within the Gothic arch above a first floor window. The Gothic style was not universally welcomed, either by the residents or by the investors whose money, lodged with the Halifax Building Society, had built the cottages. Dormer windows, said to have given the dwellings the appearance of almshouses, were in due course removed.

Akroyd's aims were twofold. He hoped that by providing good housing he would improve the moral condition of his workforce. He said in 1861:

> a clean, fresh, well-ordered house exercises on its inmates a moral no less than a physical influence, and has the direct tendency to make the members of a family sober, peaceable and considerate of the feelings and happiness of each other, whereas a filthy, squalid and unwholesome dwelling . . . tends directly to make every dweller in such a house selfish and sensual, and the connection is obvious between the constant indulgence of appetite of this class and the formation of habits of dishonesty and violence.

He also believed that the rural village of mythology was a better place in which to live than the industrial town, and that the world which had produced the Gothic style was a better world than that of the mid nineteenth century. This was a Romantic, Disraeli-ish concept, a belief that a once-idyllic society had been corrupted by industry. Akroyd said that he asked Scott to plan the village in 'the Domestic Gothic' style, because 'it was the original style of the parish of Halifax . . . this taste of our forefathers pleases the fancy, strengthens the house and home attachment and entwines the present with memories of the past'.

Sir Titus Salt was in many ways the antithesis of Edward Akroyd.[4] He was a Congregationalist while Akroyd was an Anglican. He did not regret the passage of an idyllic past but looked forward to a future made better by the fruits of industry. Born in Morley in 1803 he had gone to Bradford, then one of the fastest growing towns in Britain, in 1822 and had prospered, chiefly due to his pioneering of new fabrics like alpaca. He contemplated retiring to agricultural pursuits on his fiftieth birthday, but in 1850 resolved to found a new concern. He acquired a site alongside the River Aire, the Leeds and Liverpool Canal and the railway from Leeds and Bradford to Skipton, and a new mill and its accompanying town were designed for him by the local architects Lockwood and Mawson. Salt described his motives when the mill was opened in 1853:

> I looked around for a site suitable for a large manufacturing establishment, and I fixed upon this as offering every capability for a first rate manufacturing and commercial establishment. It is also, from the beauty of its situation, and the salubrity of the air, a most desirable place for the erection of dwellings. Far be it from me to do anything to pollute the air or the water of the district. . . . I hope to draw around me a population that will enjoy the beauties of this neighbourhood – a population of well-paid, contented, happy operatives. I have given instructions to my architects (who are competent to carry them out), that nothing shall be spared to render the dwellings of the operatives a pattern to the country.

The *Illustrated London News* remarked:

> Every improvement that modern art and science have brought to light has to be put in requisition in the erection of the model town of Saltaire. Healthy dwellings and gardens in wide streets and capacious squares – ample ground for recreation, a large dining hall and kitchens – baths and wash houses, schools, a mechanics' institution, a church; these are some of the characteristics of the future town of Saltaire.

Dominating the new town was the mill, built in the Italian style, 72 feet and six storeys high, 545 feet long. Its chimney 18 feet square, in the style of an Italian campanile, was 250 feet tall. The confidence of Dissent in relation to the Establishment, of the provinces in relation to London, was expressed in the oft-repeated assertions that the mill was as long as St Paul's Cathedral and the chimney 50 feet higher than the Monument in the City of London. Saltaire took two decades to complete. By the mid 1870s there were some eight hundred cottages of various grades, the houses of the senior workmen being very grand three-storey buildings. The simple grid pattern of the streets is everywhere relieved by careful detailing. Saltaire has a profusion of communal buildings, a Congregational Church built in 1859, a school, almshouses and a hospital of 1868, an institute and a park provided in

1871. The school and institute are set back from the main road through the town and guarded on the street frontage by four lions, *War*, *Peace*, *Vigilance* and *Determination*. Salt found that 'in passing along the streets of Saltaire his eye was sometimes offended by the lines of clothes which on washing days were hung out of doors. In visiting the dwellings he had ocular proof of the inconvenience connected with domestic laundry.' Accordingly a wash house with six washing machines powered by three steam engines, together with a centrifugal dryer, a hot air drying room, and mangling and folding rooms was built in 1863, which enabled washing to be completed within an hour.

Saltaire displayed the confidence of Victorian manufacturers as much as the Crystal Palace. It was not a simulated village but a small industrial town, in which not just Salt but many of his contemporaries took great pride. The Mayor of Bradford observed at the opening ceremony that:

> within the memory of persons present . . . the whole process of the stuff trade was carried on by hand labour and in the cottages of the poor. Then the cheerful hum of the spinning wheel was heard in the cottage of the humble worker; and the good old English wool was the only raw material of which they knew. . . . The man was still living . . . who carried the first gross of machine-spun yarn to Bradford market. What had been the result – what had been the progress? Instead of the manufacture being confined to the cottages they had built palaces of industry equal to the palaces of the Caesars; instead of hand labour they had, to the utmost, availed themselves of the almost miraculous resources of mechanical science; instead of a master manufacturer carrying a week's production upon his own back, he harnessed the iron horse to the railway train, and daily conveyed away their goods by the ton; instead of being content with old English wool only, they now ransacked the whole globe for materials to work up.

The Great Exhibition reflected very different tendencies in manufacturing. There were multitudes of individual small exhibits, many of them highly eccentric, the work of hatters, saddlers or cabinet makers in provincial market towns, demonstrating that the great majority of the goods which people actually used were still made in shops and workrooms rather than in factories. They also reveal the incentive to seek national markets which was stimulated by the competitive but frustratingly inhibiting economic and social climate of the average market town, where society was deeply split along political and religious lines. They show too how industrialization, the production of goods for national and international markets in relatively large manufacturing units, was coming to affect almost every town of substance in Britain. Products which had previously been made on a small scale for local consumption were increasingly being taken by rail not only to customers in Britain but in all parts of the world.

'The most remarkable feature in the agricultural operations of the present day', said one commentator on the British agricultural machinery section of the Great Exhibition, 'is undoubtedly the rapid introduction and use of small or portable steam engines for agricultural purposes.' The spread of such engines, and of the machines they powered, had an importance in the economic history of Britain far beyond its effects on agricultural practices. Ironmongers and millwrights made iron castings in many market towns in the early nineteenth century. As the railways made coke and pig iron more easily available, some such concerns grew rapidly, producing agricultural implements for the national market, exporting their goods and diversifying into other kinds of mechanical engineering. Market town foundries were rarely spectacular in appearance. They were usually centred round two or three cupola furnaces, with their attendant pattern makers' and moulders' shops. There would be one or two forges for fabricating wrought iron parts for machines, a sawmill and carpenters' shops for making wooden parts and a larger building for the final assembly of machines. The assembly shop at Leiston, Norfolk, where Garretts' traction engines were built, was so large that it was called the 'Cathedral'. Power for turning lathes and grindstones, for working the sawmill and blowing air into the cupolas, would probably be derived from one or more steam engines. A foundry, like a Victorian pottery, often presented a formal facade to the outside world with offices and sometimes, as at the Plowright foundry at Swaffham, showrooms on the street frontage, through which there was frequently a large arch giving access to a yard behind. Many foundries were built near navigable water or in the vicinity of a railway, from which the piles of coke, pig iron, and bars and sheets of wrought iron would be drawn, invariable features of the landscape of such works. In East Anglia foundry buildings are characterized by cast iron window frames with vertical glazing bars. Often the name of the foundry would be recorded in iron on the building. At Whittlesford, Cambridgeshire, the foundry of John Maynard is identified by wrought iron letters on the wall. The name of Thomas Smithdale is

209

cast on the girders of his foundry buildings at Panxworth, Norfolk. Thomas Corbett of the Perseverance Ironworks, Shrewsbury, discreetly cast his name on the bases of the iron columns of the windows on the street frontage of his premises. The origins of the foundry industry are symbolized in some towns by cast iron tracery in front of the windows of ironmongers' shop, examples of which can be seen in Beaminster, Leominster, Witney and Whitchurch, Shropshire.

The evolution of the casting shops of market town ironmongers into engineering works began long before 1850, but it reached its peak in the second half of the ninteenth century. A recent study of East Anglia[5] has shown that there were foundries at Bassingbourn, Chatteris, St Ives, St Neots and Whittlesford in Cambridgeshire; Brentwood, Burnham on Crouch, Chelmsford, Colchester, Colne Earls, Euping, Halstead, Heybridge, Maldon, Manningtree, Saffron Walden and Walton on the Naze in Essex; Acle, Brancaster, Burnham Market, Carbrooke, East Dereham, Kenninghall, King's Lynn, Marsham, North Walsham, Northrepps, Norwich, Panxworth, Swaffham, Thetford, Thornage, Thurton, Great Walsingham, Watton and Great Yarmouth in Norfolk; and Bury St Edmunds, Eye, Haverhill, Ipswich, Leiston, Lowestoft, Peasenhall, Stowmarket and Wickham Market in Suffolk. While the majority of these concerns began by making agricultural implements or castings for millwrights, by the end of the nineteenth century they were manufacturing such diverse products as traction engines, milling machinery, bridges, equipment for gold and diamond mines, cast iron piano frames, electrical apparatus, deck winches for ships, parts for malt kilns, lawnmowers, street furniture and tortoise stoves.

John Howard of Bedford was one of the most substantial makers of agricultural implements. One of his bill headings of 1838 shows the two components of his business—a three-storey shop fronted by an elegant small-paned window, with an entrance on either side and an inscription with scrolls on the parapet, and the Britannia Foundry, two ranges of two-storey buildings at right angles to each other, with a large doorway for machines and chimneys from five furnaces or hearths protruding from the roof. Howard described his business as 'Ironmonger, iron and brass founder, locksmith, bellhanger and brazier, iron, zinc and tinplate worker, brick, tile and lime burner, garden pot manufacturer'. His products included patent ploughs, stoves, kitchen ranges, fenders, fire irons, iron chests and book cases, park fencing and gates, iron hurdles, verandahs, balconies and all sorts of agricultural implements.

Another large foundry was Burnhard Samuelson's Britannia Ironworks at Banbury in the South Midlands, which originated as a workshop manufacturing the Banbury Turnip Cutter, invented by James Gardner early in the nineteenth century. Samuelson acquired the works in 1849 and, after exhibiting at the Crystal Palace, obtained the right to manufacture the American McCormick reaper in England. The works employed over three hundred people within a decade, and its reapers and mowing machines were exported to Australasia, Russia and all parts of Western Europe. Thomas Corbett's Perseverance Ironworks in Shrewsbury, built on the edge of a canal wharf within easy reach of the railway, expanded steadily in the 1870s, a growth recorded by date stones on the various extensions to the buildings. The inscription 'Speed the Plough' can still be deciphered over the great arched entrance.

An engineering industry grew up in the Medway Valley in the 1850s, largely to provide plant for the brick and cement industries.[6] Some firms originated as the foundry departments of ironmongery businesses. Outstanding among them was Aveling and Porter, begun in Rochester in 1850 when Thomas Aveling, a farmer, began to repair agricultural machines. In 1858 he started to make self-propelled portable steam engines, or traction engines, initially for agricultural use. A large new factory was built in 1861, and by 1872 it gave employment to four hundred men and specialized in the manufacture of steam rollers.

The firm of Stothert and Pitt originated in an ironmonger's shop in Bath in 1779, where George Stothert was superintendent of an assortment of braziers, smiths and tinmen.[7] He later worked on his own account, as an agent for the Coalbrookdale Company and a manufacturer of carpenters' planes. His son established a foundry in Bath in 1815, whose early products included pumps and iron bridges. The firm displayed a dockside crane at the Great Exhibition, and subsequently became one of the world's principal suppliers of such machines. A picture of the works on the Lower Bristol Road, Bath, in 1885, shows a long and elegant street frontage with a gateway at one end giving access to a yard, around which are grouped chimneys and several scaffolds.

There were implement factories of considerable size in Gainsborough, where Messrs Marshall, established in 1856, employed 500 people by 1872 and 5000 by 1913, and in Lincoln, where Clayton and Shuttleworth had 1400 workers in 1885 and 2300 in 1907, and

Rustons, established in 1857, employed 5000 in 1911. In 1865 a government commissioner noted that the crowded condition of Basingstoke was due in part to the foundries there.[8]

Exhibits at the Crystal Palace included numerous preparations of artificial manures, and the makers of such compounds came to flourish in many market towns during the second half of the century. The world's first superphosphate factory, manufacturing its own sulphuric acid, was built by Edward Packard at Bramford in Suffolk in 1851 on a site served by the Great Eastern Railway and the Ipswich and Stowmarket Navigation. An adjacent works was operated by Joseph Fison, who subsequently became Packard's partner. The usual process was to treat ground bones with sulphuric acid to make superphosphates. In East Anglia, in parts of Suffolk and on the edges of the Cambridgeshire Fens, round phosphatic nodules of coprolite were extracted by shallow open-cast workings and used to make superphosphates. At Duxford in Cambridgeshire William Thurnall set up a water-powered bone mill in 1836, using in it bones from a mound thirty feet high. During the 1850s he established a new steam-powered mill and called his concern the Cambridge Manure Company. In Shropshire James Austin established a factory making superphosphates from bones on a site at Allscot, alongside the Shrewsbury-Wellington railway, during the 1850s. He employed sixteen men in 1861, when he was known as a manure manufacturer, and twenty-four ten years later when he called himself an agricultural chemist. His concern was subsequently known as the Wrekin Chemical Company, and he became involved with the manufacture of naptha from twigs. Works of this kind were to be found in and around market towns in most parts of Britain. Like the small foundries they were rarely of imposing appearance. They usually contained lead-lined chambers for the manufacture and storage of acid, and brick-lined containers called 'dens' in which the acid was mixed with the bones. Storage areas were often built of timber rather than iron, for it was less damaged by fumes from the acid and fertilizer. Just as the foundries brought the techniques and discipline of the Industrial Revolution to country towns, and formed the foundations of the engineering industry, so the factories producing artificial manures introduced similar work disciplines, and in some cases provided the nuclei for substantial and varied chemical manufactures.

Shoemakers were almost ubiquitous in the mid nineteenth century. Large numbers were to be found in every town, and there were some in most rural parishes. The industry was essentially a domestic one, catering largely for local needs, but in certain areas, like Northamptonshire, there was some concentration of the trade for the purpose of supplying the London market. Changes followed the introduction in about 1860 of sewing machines for stitching together the various parts of shoes.[9] In Northampton, Wellingborough, Rushden and other shoemaking towns in the county, the main features of the areas built in the late nineteenth century were terraced houses with workshops at the ends of the gardens, where skilled men cut out the leather for shoes, and small factories where the parts were sewn together. A surviving factory from this period in the village of Brigstock is built in stone, of thirteen bays and four storeys, with round-headed windows and a pediment in the centre in which is a bell in a kind of niche. Shoemaking factories were also built in Staffordshire. Stone was described by a government commissioner in 1865 as 'a shoemakers' town', and by 1900 it had four small factories as well as several tanneries. In Stafford the trade was widely dispersed until the second half of the nineteenth century, when it was concentrated in several factories to the north of the town.[10] The growth of Leicester, which doubled its population between 1861 and 1891, owed much to the sudden development of the boot and shoe industry. Shoemaking also expanded in Norwich, where the large factory built about 1856 by Tillyard and Howlett included currying shops as well as areas for the manufacture of shoes. In the parishes of Sawston and Pampisford in Cambridgeshire, where there had been tanyards as early as the seventeenth century, the manufacturing of parchment began in the early nineteenth century. Steam power was introduced under the management of Thomas Sutton Evans in the 1850s, and new products like gloves and chamois leather were made, until over two hundred workers were employed by 1871, many of them being housed in company cottages.

Similar changes took place in clothing manufacture. Luton in Bedfordshire grew rapidly due to the stimulus of the straw hat trade, which moved there from London during the Napoleonic Wars.[11] Most hats were made in two-storey workshops, with large windows and one-way pitched roofs, which were attached to terraced cottages. Materials were supplied via service roads running along the backs of the terraces. This was an unheroic landscape, like that of the Northamptonshire shoemaking towns, and only one degree removed from domestic industry.

In the Nottinghamshire and Leicestershire hosiery trade there was a similar move away from purely domestic production into weaving

213

shops which held up to eight frames, and subsequently into powered factories. The first of these was constructed at Loughborough about 1840. Other garments which had previously been manufactured largely for individual customers by master tradesmen were increasingly made in factories. There were several glove factories in Worcester. At Littleport in Cambridgeshire is a three-storey factory, enlarged in 1888, for the manufacture of shirts. It has the large windows found in most textile or garment factories, and rows of chimneys on one side which were probably flues from the stoves used to heat smoothing irons. In the 1860s the manufacture of corsets was increasingly concentrated in factories. A six-bay, three-storey stay manufactory of 1864, with a waggon arch giving access to a yard at the rear, still stands in Ashbourne, Derbyshire, and in Ipswich is a large four-storey building with an octagonal chimney built by a firm of drapers and staymakers in 1881.

The presence of Colman's mustard, Reckitt's starch and Schweppe's mineral waters at the Great Exhibition indicated early trends towards the factory production of food and drink. Brewing had been the first industry in which manufacture was organized in large units, in the early nineteenth century, but the industry underwent many changes in the mid nineteenth century. Some manufacturers began to supply national markets. Local newspapers in many parts of the country reveal the arrival of Guinness stout, made in Dublin in the 1830s and 1840s, and a decade or so later Burton ales became just as widely available. In most towns substantial breweries grew up in the middle of the century, supplying public houses which had previously brewed their own beer. Maltings also grew in size. There are numerous Victorian malthouses in East Anglia, and about 1860 there were seventy maltings along the River Stort in Hertfordshire. In Shrewsbury two large maltings were built in the 1880s, and another converted from a flax mill. After displaying his mustard in the Crystal Palace, J.J. Colman of Norwich moved to the new Carrow Works in 1854, where he built ranges of red brick buildings with white-brick dressings, blind arcading, and iron-framed windows. The manufacture of vinegar, gelatine and isinglass was also concentrated in factories in the mid nineteenth century. One of the most interesting food factories was the Ellis Soda Water Works at Ruthin in North Wales, completed in 1866.[12] This concern was established in the town by Robert Ellis of London in 1825, and prospered by supplying drinks to London hotels. By the 1860s it claimed to employ half the working population of Ruthin. The new factory was designed by David Walker of Liverpool and was said to be the largest manufactory of aerated waters in the world. It included bottling shops capable of filling 10,000 bottles a day, and rooms for making hampers; the willows for these were grown on tracts of land set aside for the purpose along the railway between Ruthin and Denbigh.

Burton on Trent above all other towns was changed by the growth of a national market for drinks.[13] Burton had always been famous for its ale and its brewers had sent beer to distant customers via the Trent and Mersey Canal, but the town grew most rapidly after the development of the railway system. It came to be dominated by tall brewery chimneys, the geometrical outlines of malt kilns and the characteristic nineteenth-century brewery buildings, where water from tanks on the top found its way by gravity from floor to floor and emerged as beer in the bottle or barrel at ground level. Burton became a maze of railways. Tiny tank locomotives hauled waggons loaded with barley for the maltings, anthracite for the malt kilns, coal for pumping engines and beer in the barrel or crate around a dense network of lines, linking virtually every brewery or maltings.

The manufacture of furniture was also increasingly organized on a factory basis. At Lavenham and Long Melford in Suffolk were several horsehair works. At Boston in Lincolnshire was a 'Steam Feather Manufactory', four bays wide, nine bays deep and three storeys high. It was severely damaged by fire in 1876 soon after its erection, when it was claimed to be the largest business in the feather trade in Britain. Feathers from France, Germany and the Baltic states were imported and purified, and both feathers and down supplied to British and American furniture manufacturers.

Before 1850 many market towns had few concerns employing as many as a dozen people, but by 1870 there were frequently several companies employing hundreds. The three- or four-storey factory of ten to fifteen bays, with a steam engine and a tall chimney sprouting from its boiler house, with several smaller buildings around a yard and perhaps a railway siding or a frontage to a canal, was not in any sense the centre of an heroic landscape. It did, however, represent the spread to almost every town of consequence in England of the principles of production established in the mid eighteenth century in the cotton and iron industries.

Some parts of England and Wales which were largely rural in 1850 were completely transformed by the growth of industry in the following decades. One of the most dramatic changes in the landscape took place on the banks of the River Tees in Cleveland. The town of Middlesbrough was founded by the 'Middlesbrough Owners', a group of Quakers associated with the Stockton and Darlington Railway, who bought an estate in 1829 and sought to develop it as a coal-shipping port.[14] A church, chapels and a market, schools and a mechanics' institute were built with a town laid out on a grid-iron pattern. The population grew from less than 200 in 1831 to more than 5000 in 1841, but growth was much less rapid during the 1840s, since the development of the national railway network reduced the proportion of coal entrusted to coastal shipping.

In 1850 exploitation of the Cleveland iron ores began, and development commenced on an altogether different scale. Before 1850 Middlesbrough was a modest enterprise, about the size of Goole or Ellesmere Port. By 1862 it had a population of 20,000, and Mr Gladstone called it an 'infant Hercules'. The first blast furnace was blown in in the year of the Great Exhibition, and within ten years there were more than forty furnaces in the area. By 1901 the population exceeded 90,000. The breathless, uncontrolled nature of the town's growth was well described by Lady Bell, wife of one of the principal ironmasters:

> It is obvious what a field for labour is suddenly opened by the discovery of iron in any such part of the country. The genesis of an ironmaking town which follows such a discovery is breathless and tumultuous, and the onslaught of industry which attends the discovery of mineral wealth, whether ironstone or coal mines, has certain characteristics unlike any other form of commercial enterprise. The unexpectedness of it, the change in the condition of the district, which suddenly becomes swamped under a great rush from all parts of the country of people, often of the roughest kind, who are going to swell the ranks of unskilled labour; the need for housing these people; all this means that there springs and too rapidly, into existence, a community of a pre-ordained inevitable kind, the members of which must live near their work. They must therefore have houses built as quickly as possible; the houses must be cheap, must be as big as the workman wants, and no bigger; and as they are built, there arise, hastily erected, instantly occupied, the rows and rows of little brown streets of the aspect that in some place or other is familiar to all of us. A town arising in this way cannot wait to consider anything else than time and space, and none of either must be wasted on what is merely agreeable

to the eye, or even on what is merely sanitary. There can be no question under these conditions of building model cottages, or of laying out a district into ideal settlements. As one owner after another starts ironworks in the growing place, there is a fresh inrush of workmen, and day by day the little houses spring hurriedly into existence, until at last we find ourselves in the middle of a town.

Middlesbrough gained a reputation for unhealthiness and overcrowding. The new parts of the town were mostly in the possession of the 'Middlesbrough Owners'; they laid out new streets to a symmetrical grid-iron plan and then sold housing plots to speculators. When the Prince of Wales opened the town hall in 1887 the mayor referred with pride to the town's smoke, as an indication of plenty of work, prosperous times and freedom from want. The new town of the 1830s was isolated, cut off from later developments by the railway tracks. Middlesbrough was a raw, inelegant town, whose landscape was sensitively described by Lady Bell:

> The fact of this swift gigantic growth has given to the town a romance and dignity . . . the dignity of power, of being able to stand erect by its sheer strength on no historic foundation, unsupported by the pedestals of time. And although it may not have the charm and beauty of antiquity, no manufacturing town on the banks of a great river can fail to have an interest and picturesqueness all its own. On either shore rise tall chimneys, great uncouth shapes of kilns and furnaces that appear through the smoke on a winter afternoon, like turrets and pinnacles . . . at Middlesbrough we have left verdure far behind. The great river has here put on its grimy working clothes, and the banks on either side are clad in black and grey. Their aspect from the deck of the ferry-boat is stern, mysterious, forbidding: hoardings, poles, chimneys, scaffoldings, cranes, dredging-machines, sheds. The north shore, the Durham side, is even more desolate than the other, since it has left the town behind, and the furnaces and chimneys of the works are interspersed with great black wastes, black roads, gaunt wooden palings, blocks of cottages, railway lines crossing the roads. . . . A dusty, wild, wide space on which the road abuts, flanked by the row of the great furnaces, a space in which engines are going to and fro, more lines to cross, more dangers to avoid; a wind-swept expanse, near to which lie a few straggling rows of cottages.

The growth of Barrow in Furness ran parallel to that of Middlesbrough.[15] In 1840 it was merely a ramshackle quay to which carters brought iron ore from mines further inland, for shipment to Stafford-shire and South Wales. In 1846 the Furness Railway was opened, conveying slate from Kirkby Ireleth and iron ore from Landal Moor to Barrow and Piel. It was extended to Ulverston to meet the Ulverston and Lancaster Railway which, with its long, embanked crossings of the Kent and Leven estuaries, linked Furness with the national railway system at Carnforth. The Ulverston and Lancaster was opened in 1857 and taken over by the Furness Railway in 1862.

Barrow was entirely the creation of the Furness Railway company, and in particular of James Ramsden, who was the company's engineering director and, from 1857, its general manager. Before the railway was built the inhabitants of Barrow only numbered about 250. The company began to build cottages for its workers in 1849 when a terrace, ruggedly constructed from local sandstone, was built at Salthouse. Vast reserves of iron ore were discovered, and in 1854 the Furness Railway purchased seven thousand acres of land for industrial development. The smelting of iron began in 1859, and by 1872 the Barrow Haematite Iron Company had sixteen furnaces in blast and two building, eighteen Bessemer converters for making steel and seven rolling mills. The Furness Railway combined with other companies to build the South Durham and Lancashire Union Railway across the Pennines, to enable Furness ore to be taken to the furnaces of Co. Durham and, ultimately, to allow Durham coke to be conveyed to Barrow.

The plan drawn up for the development of Barrow in 1856 showed large areas on either side of the Barrow channel set aside for industrial development, with rail connections laid in. Most of the streets were sixty feet wide, and the main approach road to the town was no less than eighty feet. A large area was set aside for a market and three sites for a 'square, church, chapel or public building'. Behind the main streets the residential areas present an unspectacular if sanitary appearance. The brick houses are no better and no worse than those in other Victorian industrial cities, but the streets themselves are wider than most and even the back alleyways, following the same rigid byelaw pattern which can be seen in Manchester or the Potteries, are wide enough to allow the passage of cars. The Barrow Building Society, formed by Ramsden in 1848, played a large part in the building of the town and many idiosyncrasies typical of areas con-structed by small speculators can be observed in Barrow. In Rawlin-son Street there is a pair of three-storey red brick houses, identical except for yellow brick lintels and string courses on one of them. Perhaps a small investor used his savings to build them, intending one for his own residence—which he decorated with the yellow bricks— and the other as a source of income. Barrow's public buildings reflect its origins. There is a vast town hall of 1878, a technical college of red brick with terracotta reliefs and a bath house, built in 1872, inscribed 'Presented to the town by James Ramsden, Esq., First Mayor'. The railway company fostered the growth of other industries. Three docks with a total area of over 130 acres were constructed, and shipping links encouraged with the Baltic, India, the United States and Ireland. Jute mills and a shipyard were built, and Scottish-style tenements provided to house those who came to work in them. Corn mills were constructed to grind imported American grain. The development of Barrow nevertheless faltered in the 1880s and 1890s, but revived with the takeover of the shipyard by Vickers, Son and Maxim in 1897.

Barrow's growth in the 1860s and 1870s had been prodigious. The population grew from 250 in 1841 to nearly 50,000 in 1881. A writer in 1872 commented:

> In 1854 we observed only a few straggling houses at Barrow: now we found a large town with sixty or seventy thousand inhabitants, oil mills, a well-conducted newspaper . . . imposing shops, hotels; thousands of well-built houses; wide streets, running, as they ought, at right angles, the style of the whole being in accordance with modern architectural principles; elegant churches and chapels of all denominations abounding.

The grid-plan, the little-altered Victorian terraces, the imposing public buildings and the channel, with its distant view to the Lake District and the ruins of vast ironworks, give Barrow one of the most evocative of industrial landscapes.

The demands of the iron industry began to transform the landscape of the Jurassic limestone belt from Wiltshire to Lincolnshire at this period. By the early 1870s a million tons of ironstone a year were being quarried or mined in Northamptonshire. Most of it was sent by rail and canal to the Black Country, but some was smelted in Northamptonshire's twelve blast furnaces, three of which were situated alongside the London and Birmingham Railway at Heyford near Weedon. Four furnaces at Frodingham and Lincolnshire were to form the nucleus of the Scunthorpe iron industry, and there were furnaces in Wiltshire at Westbury and Seend. The generally low quality ores of the Jurassic limestone belt could not, except in the vicinity of good supplies of coal, be smelted with great profit, and except at Corby and Scunthorpe such ironworks remained relatively small concerns in predominantly rural counties. 'We are aware', remarked a Northampton newspaper in 1853, 'that an array of tall chimneys and blazing furnaces will not add to the beauty of the picturesque scenery of Northamptonshire.'

Coal had been one of the bases of British prosperity in the early stages of the Industrial Revolution and the mining industry continued to expand rapidly in the second half of the nineteenth century. Production rose from 64,700,000 tons in 1854 to 181,600,000 tons in 1890 and 225,200,000 tons in 1900. In many areas coal mining remained an industry of the countryside, with pits at no great distance from fields or open moorlands. Mining along the banks of the Tyne and Wear contracted as seams were exhausted, and the early coal-dependent industries—glassworks, soap factories and potteries—declined, to be replaced by shipbuilding and engineering. New pits were opened in the North-East to the north of the Tyne and along the coast, many of them in areas where there was no previous mining activity. These pits were deep, capital-intensive and productive, and the owners attracted new labour by creating pit villages, of which Ashington is the archetype. Ashington's earliest houses are of stone, as in many North-Eastern mining villages, but it is dominated by a huge rectangular grid of brick terraces facing inwards on to greens, with rear service roads, and gardens dotted with outside privies. Along one side of the grid run the sidings of one of the Ashington pits; beyond them are the headstocks, and then the vast pyramidal heaps of colliery waste. The dated buildings of Ashington, the chapels and co-operative stores, were mostly built in the 1890s and 1900s. No other pit village in the North-East was as large as Ashington, but it is an extreme example which illustrates a general trend.

The most dramatic changes in the landscape of the colliery districts came in South Wales, where production rose from 8,500,000 tons in 1854 to 28,100,000 tons in 1890 and 39,300,000 tons in 1900. The labour force grew from 29,100 to 109,900 to 147,600 in the same period. The mining activity in the late eighteenth century had been concentrated along the heads of the valleys, where the iron ore seams outcropped and there were ample sources of limestone, but the great expansion of the 1860s, 1870s and 1880s was lower down the valleys, where it was possible to gain access to the rich seams of steam coal. The settlements which grew up during the great steam coal boom are thus nearer the coast than those associated with the Industrial Revolution in the iron industry.

The archetypal settlement of this period is the Rhondda Valley. Large-scale mining in the area began in the 1840s, following the opening of the Taff Vale Railway and the Bute West Dock in Cardiff. In 1864 David Davies of Llandinam became active in the valley, and two years later his miners struck the famous Two Foot Nine seam of steam coal which was to provide the basis for his great fortune. After 1887 his firm was called the Ocean Coal Company, and by the 1890s it was producing two-and-a-quarter million tons of coal a year. A journey up the Rhondda Fawr remains an impressive experience. Pontypridd, where the valley is joined by that of the Taff, was the centre from which radiated a dense network of branch railway lines whose passenger trains met under the vast overall roof of the station. All up the valley, through Porth, where it is joined by the Rhondda Fawr, Tonypandy, Treorchy and Treherbert, curving stone terraces with brick dressings face inwards across the valley, looking down on the river, the road from Cardiff and the railway, along which can be seen the engine houses and yards of numerous pits sunk during the steam coal boom but now abandoned. The cottages are punctuated with various communal buildings, particularly pedimented chapels, while at the bases of the hills are the grim and threatening heaps of colliery waste. Beyond Treherbert the modern road climbs across Mynydd Ystradffernal towards Brecon, providing a dramatic view of the reservoir at the head of the valley, the settlement of Blaen y Cwm and the last traces of coal working in the Rhondda, before it reaches open moorland.

There was fierce competition among the railway companies in South Wales for the profitable coal traffic, and several of the valleys were served by more than one company. The docks at Newport and Cardiff were much expanded to deal with coal exports, and new ones were built at Penarth by the Taff Vale Railway and at Barry by the Barry Railway, a company especially created to take advantage of the steam coal boom. While the characteristic features of the landscape of the North-East's coal ports were staithes and coal drops, both catering for hopper waggons, the coal ports of South Wales were notable for their tall hoists, which lifted waggons and tipped their contents into the holds of waiting ships. The distinction between the two arrangements can be traced back to the two separate kinds of railway which evolved in the seventeenth century. In the North-East it was traditional

221

to use hopper waggons, with doors in the bottoms; in Shropshire, from which South Wales derived its railway practices, it was not.

The coal industry also grew rapidly in the East Midlands. A typical example was the Shireoaks estate in Nottinghamshire, purchased in 1810 by the Duke of Newcastle, who demolished most of its mansion and felled most of its trees. During the 1850s the estate was leased to a mining company, which began to work a 1545-foot shaft in June 1859. The Duke erected sixty new cottages for workmen and 'neat villas for the use of the officers' in the village. The sense of change in the landscape on passing into the coalfield was sensitively conveyed by Elihu Burrit, in an account of a journey made in 1864:

> When about half-way from Mansfield to Chesterfield, a remarkable change came over the face of the landscape. The mosaic work of the hillsides and valleys showed more green squares than before. Three-fourths of the fields were meadow or pasture, or in mangel or turnips. There was but one here and there in wheat or other grain. The road beneath and the sky above began to blacken, and the chimneys of coal pits to thicken. Sooty-faced men, horses and donkeys passed with loaded carts; and all the premonitory aspects of the 'black country' multiplied as I proceeded. I do not recollect ever seeing a landscape change so suddenly in England.

The coal industry of South Lancashire was stimulated by the expansion of exports to Ireland, the demands of steamships calling at Liverpool and the needs of expanding coal-using industries like glass-making, alkali manufacture and soap boiling. The town of St Helens emerged in the centre of the coalfield during the mid nineteenth century, growing up around a town hall and market place erected in 1838. The waste from the chemical industries of St Helens, Widnes and Wigan has created perhaps the most barren of all industrial landscapes in Britain.[16]

The mid nineteenth century was the last period of prosperity in many of the upland metal mining districts in the North and West. In Devon and Cornwall the copper industry languished, but the 1860s and early 1870s were years of great prosperity in tin mining. Many mines, particularly in the Redruth area, went over from copper to tin, and the view from Carn Brea hill remained dramatic. Walter White described it in 1855 as:

> a hungry landscape, everywhere deformed by small mountains of many-coloured refuse; traversed in all directions by narrow

paths and winding roads, by streams of foul water, by scream-
ing locomotives with hurrying trains; while wheels and whims,
and miles of pumping rods, whirling and vibrating, and the
forest of tall beams, make up an astonishing maze of machinery
and motion. Giant arms of steam engines swing up and down;
and the stamping mills appear to try which can thunder loud-
est, proclaiming afar the progress made in disembowelling the
bountiful old earth.

A much-visited scene of industrial activity in the West of England
was Morwellham Quay on the River Tamar.[17] Its importance had
grown gradually in the early nineteenth century, as a shipping point
for the rich metals mined in the area between Calstock and Tavistock.
Ores were ground in mills powered by waterwheels, and banks of lime
kilns were fired by coal imported up the river. In 1817 the Tavistock
Canal was opened, linking the port with mines in the Tavey Valley to
the east; it approached the quays by an inclined plane worked by a
waterwheel. What increased Morwellham's importance was the discovery of rich copper deposits at Blanchdown in 1844. Soon afterwards a mineral railway was constructed to take ores from what came
to be known as the Devon Great Consols Mines to the quay at
Morwellham, which was approached by a one in three inclined plane.
The surface workings of the mine occupied 140 acres by 1865; and the
export of ores grew so great that a dock, 290 by 60 feet, was built there
in 1859. Huge baulks of timber were brought up river to prop the
roofs of the irregular workings in Devon Great Consols and other
mines.

The Morwellham quays were on the estates of the Dukes of Bedford;
semi-detached cottages were provided, of the same high quality for
which the estate was celebrated elsewhere. Steamers from Plymouth
took visitors to picnic on the rocks at Morwellham, and to dance in
front of an inn, where a room 36 by 18 feet was added in 1858 to cater
for the needs of excursionists. The copper ores of Devon Great Consols became exhausted in the late 1860s, like other West of England
mines, and it went over to the production of arsenic. Calcining kilns
and flues were constructed to refine the ores, before they were dispatched in casks made in cooperages at Morwellham. There were at
least eight arsenic works in the West Country, each with a range of
kilns and a complex maze of flues which were usually insufficient to
prevent the poisoning of all vegetation downwind from the outlets.
Morwellham began to decline when a competing railway was opened

223

in 1859, and by the 1880s it was serving only the decreasingly profitable Devon Great Consols mines, which ceased working in 1901. However, the port remains 'one of the most evocative places in Devon'.

Another extractive industry which grew steadily in the West of England in the mid nineteenth century was the quarrying of china clay. Originally exploited for the potteries, the range of its uses expanded and it was being employed in papermaking as early as 1807. In 1800 about 2000 tons a year were being produced in Cornwall; this had expanded to 10,000 tons by 1830 and to 65,000 tons by 1858. Most workings were on a small scale. In 1858 there were eighty-five pits owned by forty-two different companies. The earliest pits had been worked by stripping off the overburden from the kaolinized granite, and digging the china clay out with picks, but by the middle of the century it was usual to wash it out in the form of slurry. Sometimes this was done by stripping a hillside site and diverting a stream across it, but the more usual method was to sink a shaft below the level of the clay, drive a level beneath it and then insert a button-hole launder—a pipe with holes in it—in another vertical shaft, ascending into the clay. Water was run over the clay from the surface and the resulting slurry pumped by a steam engine or waterwheel through the underground workings to the surface. The slurry was then passed through a series of settling tanks and drags to separate out the waste mica and quartz, which make up the characteristic white spoil heaps of the St Austell area, and then allowed to settle in pits. It was more thoroughly dried in a pan kiln, then stored in a building called a linhay before being taken away, usually in casks made by local coopers. Modern workings have eclipsed in scale those of the nineteenth century, but much remains of the earlier period's industrial landscape—huge spoil tips, the more modern ones inert, the older examples just succumbing to the enclosing march of vegetation, the remnants of wrecked railways, the granite chimneys of derelict pan kilns, empty water courses, solid stone cottages and Methodist chapels make up the landscape of the area to the north of St Austell. It was vividly described by Walter White in 1855:

> repeatedly while at breakfast, you will see carts pass the window laden with what appear to be cubes of chalk, each as big as a peck loaf . . . after a pleasant uphill walk of about two miles between trees and hedges, and across the wild down, you see, upon the shaggy slope, large white patches rising one above another, pumps working, wheels revolving, white torrent

flowing, and gangs of men, women and boys variously employed. . . . The refuse having been removed from a large patch, a stream of water, led from the higher part of the slope is made to fall on the bed of slime. Hither and thither stride the men, treading the clammy surface, stirring it with their implements, washing the clay in fact, and presently their excavation resembles a pool of whitewash. As the liquid accumulates, it flows off at the lower side of the bed into a series of six or seven broad, shallow trays, called 'launders', in which the grosser particles, mostly mica and quartz, are deposited.

The mid nineteenth century was the last prosperous period of the Welsh lead mines. While some were for a time very productive and profitable, the majority were small and unspectacular in appearance.[18] The Welsh equivalent of Devon Great Consols was the Van lead mine near Llanidloes in Montgomeryshire. It was first prospected in 1850, although it was not until the discovery of its most productive lode in 1856 that it became of any consequence. A fifty-foot waterwheel was erected to operate the crushing plant, and several more were added subsequently. A steam engine was installed to work pumps and winding gear, and a complex arrangement of dressing floors was established on several levels. Two reservoirs were constructed to supply the waterwheels and a branch railway was built to take away the ore. The mine was profitable only until the early 1880s, after which it was worked by a succession of new companies until its closure in 1901. In many ways its history typifies that of the upland metal mines. There was a sharp fall in the prices of non-ferrous metals in the late 1870s, and British mines proved less and less able to compete with imported tin, copper and lead. The output of lead ore in Britain fell from a peak of 102,000 tons in 1856 to 32,000 tons in 1900. The production of copper ore fell by eighty-six per cent between 1885 and 1913, and that of tin by forty-five per cent in the same period. After the prosperity of the 1850s and 1860s, when steam engines, dressing floors, waterwheels and flimsy timber structures of great complexity were to be seen at mines all over upland Britain, scenes of the kind which the *Mining Journal* described in 1897 became commonplace:

The hillsides are furrowed with miles of water courses, terminating in the gaunt arms and wrecks of waterwheels and machinery, while the large and frequent heaps of debris from the abandoned mines testify also to the activity which prevailed in the past.

225

The Welsh slate industry also prospered in the second half of the nineteenth century, but it showed no serious signs of decline before 1900.[19] In 1873 a peak total of 3500 men were employed at the Penrhyn quarries, and 3000 were working at Dinorwic in 1900. The Ffestiniog Railway conveyed over half a million tons of slate in every five-year period between 1868 and 1908, reaching a peak in 1893–7 when 636,849 tons were carried. The number of quarrymen in Caernarvonshire and Merioneth rose from 7679 in 1861 to 12,673 in 1881. While the most spectacular changes in the landscape occurred in and around the largest quarries—Penrhyn, Dinorwic and Blaenau Ffestiniog—there were many other smaller workings which prospered in this period; their deserted faces and waste tips can be seen all over North Wales. Many of the railways of North Wales, both standard and narrow gauge, were built to serve the quarries. The largest quarries were worked in terraces, whose names often recall the dates when they were begun. At Dinorwic they include the California, Abyssinia and Jubilee terraces. Inclined planes usually brought the slate down the mountains to points where it could be loaded on to tramways or railways, which were often the locations of dressing shops and engineering works serving the quarries. The most monumental slate quarry buildings are the Gilfach Dhu workshops of the Dinorwic quarries, built in 1870, and now the North Wales Quarrying Museum. Arranged around a courtyard, with pointed towers at the two front corners and built of blocks of granite dressed with slate, they have the appearance of buildings constructed for an industry thoroughly confident in its own future. Behind the workshops on Elidir Fawr extend the vast terraces of the quarry, with giddily steep inclines which brought the slate down to the railway for conveyance to the coast at Port Dinorwic. In the Llanberis district around the Dinorwic quarry, the Assheton Smith family made available numerous plots on which the quarrymen were allowed to build houses and cultivate crops or keep animals. This has created a totally different landscape from that of the more town-like quarrymens' settlements of Bethesda and Blaenau Ffestiniog. Throughout Snowdonia the landscape is scattered with the remains of quarrying—overwhelming piles of slate waste sloping down to grass made lush by the constant rainfall, inclined planes high on the hillsides, long ridge-roofed dressing sheds, two-doored chapels and place-names like Salem, Cesarea and Carmel.

Between the opening of the Great Exhibition on 1 May 1851 and its close on 15 October over six million visits were recorded. People travelled on excursion trains from all parts of Britain to see it, providing for many their first experience of railway travel. On one day alone, 16 June 1851, twenty special excursion trains arrived in Euston. The exhibition set a pattern for excursion traffic which was to transform many peoples' experience of their own country, and to stimulate the growth of numerous resorts. The Exhibition abounded in railway exhibits, outstanding among them being Sir Daniel Gooch's broad gauge Great Western locomotive *Lord of the Isles*, and the hydraulic press which lifted into place the 1144-ton iron tubes of the Britannia Bridge over the Menai Straits.

During the four decades which followed the Great Exhibition railways affected more and more of the landscape of Britain. In 1850 there were just over 6000 miles of main line railway in Great Britain. By 1860 the total exceeded 9000, and there were 13,500 miles in 1870, 15,500 in 1880 and over 17,000 by 1890. Railway mileage thus almost trebled in forty years, and there were few broad vistas of landscape which were not crossed at some time each day by the rising plumes of smoke and steam from a locomotive. Many towns which had one railway station in 1850 had another by 1890, constructed in a different style, with a different kind of signal box, and locomotives and rolling stock in different liveries. Towns in the West of England with two competing lines included Barnstaple, Bridgwater, Launceston, Tavistock, Yeovil, Radstock and Shepton Mallet, and except in areas like East Anglia and the North-East, where particular companies held near-monopolies, almost every market town of consequence had two railways rather than one.

The second generation of main line railways were built in the knowledge that the steam locomotive could achieve more than had been thought possible in the 1830s. Ruling gradients were accepted which were rather steeper than those of the early lines. New bridges continued during the 1850s to display the versatility of railway engineers. In 1852 Brunel's ingenious suspension and beam bridge over the Wye at Chepstow was completed. Rather more spectacular was the Royal Albert Bridge by which he carried the Cornwall Railway over the Tamar from Plymouth to Saltash. It was an unique structure—a pair of wrought iron trusses combining the principles of the arch and the suspension bridge—and was Brunel's last major contribution to the landscape. When it was opened by the Prince Consort in 1859 he was too ill to do more than travel over it on a couch placed on a flat truck. A bridge of considerable significance was the

227

Crumlin Viaduct, completed in 1857, by which T.W. Kennard carried the Newport, Abergavenny and Hereford Railway's Taff Vale extension over the Ebbw Vale. It was a lattice beam viaduct on which girders made up of wrought iron sections carried the tracks between piers constructed from fourteen circular cast iron columns. The same principles were used in the Belah and Deepdale viaducts built in the Pennines for the South Durham and Lancashire Union Railway, designed by Thomas Bouch and completed in 1859. Bouch believed that much of the engineering work of the mid nineteenth century was uneconomical in its use of materials and needlessly conservative. The Hownes Gill Viaduct near Consett, built of fire brick and opened in 1858, is a superb example of his work, but his reputation was lost when his first Tay Bridge collapsed in 1879, causing the loss of a train and all its passengers. In consequence, the railway engineering of the late nineteenth century was above all safe, although it could still, as in John Fowler and Benjamin Baker's Forth Bridge, completed in 1890, produce striking structures.

The greatest impact of railways in the decades after 1850 was on the landscapes of the great cities.[20] Around urban junctions and beyond the throats of the great terminal stations grew up complexes of goods sheds, coalyards, locomotive depots, cattle docks, sorting sidings, carriage sheds, permanent way depots and engineering shops. Areas like Holbeck in Leeds, Saltley in Birmingham, Battersea and New Cross in South London, Willesden in North London, Edgehill in Liverpool and Ardwick in Manchester were totally dominated by railways. Engineering factories producing rolling stock for export, whether owned by railway companies or by private firms, were often located in such vicinities. At Gorton in Manchester were the works of the Manchester, Sheffield and Lincoln Railway, and those of Messrs Beyer Peacock. The works of the Great Eastern Railway were situated amid a confused maze of tracks, sidings and depots at Stratford in East London.

The effects of main line railways on cities were usually detrimental. A railway terminal of any kind, whether a passenger station, a goods warehouse or a cattle dock, attracted road traffic in great quantities and added to urban congestion. Railways cut off lines of communication between districts. In many cities railway companies owned between eight and ten per cent of the land in central areas, and influenced the character of up to twenty per cent. Most large cities were intersected by lines built on arches. In London the outstanding example

54 Charles Lane, Milnrow, a range of three weavers' cottages with seven-light windows on the second floors. On the first floors the seven-light windows have been reduced to five by infilling. The two houses on the right are part of a much later Victorian terrace

55 Pitt Street, Macclesfield, which retains much of its nineteenth-century atmosphere, with weavers' houses with loomshops mixed with two-storey cottages and a stone-flagged surface

56 A haphazardly built group of houses of the early nineteenth century in the textile district of Yorkshire. This fold stands at the junction of Hollingwood Lane and the Bradford–Halifax road at Great Horton. The sundial on the extreme left is dated 1814

57 The great Macclesfield Sunday School building of 1813

58 The former school of the Chartist Land Company settlement at Snigs End, Gloucestershire, which became the Prince of Wales inn after the settlement was sold up in the early 1850s, depriving the village of educational facilities. Similar buildings survive at Lowbands and Charterville

59 Akroyden: the Cross, designed by George Gilbert Scott, and the Green

60 Salisbury Place, Akroyden. Houses in the Gothic style, with the initials of the first occupants carved over the doors

61 The Mill at Saltaire, viewed across the Leeds and Liverpool Canal, from Sir Titus Salt's park

62 George Street, Saltaire, with the Congregational Church completing the vista. Saltaire's situation in the Aire Valley is clearly evident

HELEN
STREET. 18

63 Helen Street, Saltaire, showing the careful architectural detailing typical of the model town

64 An ironmonger's shop at Beaminster, Dorset, with cast iron trace around the windows, in a style which can be seen in several market towns. It is a reminder of the origins of many foundries in the small casting shops attached to such establishments

65 A detail of one of the most elegant of late nineteenth-century railway bridges, built by the Great Northern Railway across Friargate, Derby, in 1878

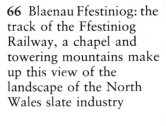

66 Blaenau Ffestiniog: the track of the Ffestiniog Railway, a chapel and towering mountains make up this view of the landscape of the North Wales slate industry

67 A theatre and a gasworks are among buildings demolished for the Great Eastern Railway's expensive extension to its new terminus at Liverpool Street in 1871

68 A temple of public health: details of the interior of Abbey Mills pumping station in East London, 1868

69 A past industrial landscape overshadowed by new technology. On the right the North Mill of 1804 at Belper, one of the earliest iron-framed cotton mills. On the left is the vastly larger East Mill of 1912, a typical building of its period, which completely overshadows the older building

70 Port Sunlight: the factory is on one side of the village, faced by these timber-framed houses and broad verges

71 Houses in the Gothic style built in 1889 by Clarks, the shoemakers, at Street, Somerset, and named after one of the great heroes of Victorian Liberalism

was the viaduct on which the London and Greenwich Railway, later the South-Eastern, approached London Bridge. In Leeds the line to York, in Manchester the link between London Road (now Piccadilly) and Oxford Road stations were other examples. Arches attracted the scavenging populations of large cities. A writer in 1866 observed:

> I travel something from 25,000 to 28,000 miles per annum by railway and have done so for the last twenty-five years. I have my eyes pretty well open generally, and I know no railway passing through a town on arches . . . without it being to my mind a very serious detriment to the town property through which it passes.

The erection of new termini, however, produced the railways' most devastating effects on cities. The lines of the first generation often terminated on the fringes of cities, but company rivalries often led them to attempt to penetrate closer to city centres. In Birmingham the London and Birmingham terminus at Curzon Street and that of the companies which formed the Midland Railway at Lawley Street were replaced in 1854 by a through-station in New Street. The mile of track from Curzon Street cost £35,000 and involved the demolition of a considerable amount of property, including several 'very objectionable houses'. It was in the summer of 1854 that George Borrow travelled from Peterborough to Chester, to begin his tour of Wales:

> At Birmingham station I became a modern Englishman, enthusiastically proud of modern England's science and energy; that station alone is enough to make one proud of being a modern Englishman. Oh, what an idea does that station, with its thousand trains dashing off in all directions, or arriving from all quarters, give of Modern English science and energy.

When the Great Western built its Birmingham station at Snow Hill (although it was not known by that name until 1858), negotiations for the first mile of approach across a viaduct and through tunnels had to be conducted with the owners of 1800 properties. The extensions of the Great Eastern to its terminus at Liverpool Street, completed in 1874, of the South-Eastern from London Bridge to Charing Cross opened in 1864, and of the North London from Kingsland to Broad Street opened in 1865, involved massive disruption of housing patterns and commercial premises, the latter alone displacing some 5000 people. When the Midland Railway approached London in the 1860s

229

the line into its terminus ran through Somers Town and Agar Town, on estates belonging to the Skinners' and Brewers' Companies.[21] Seven streets with all their houses and a church had to be demolished to clear the site for the station. These extensions usually affected working class districts, where opposition was likely to be ill-organized; and they were often the property of a single estate, which reduced the complexity of negotiations with landowners.

While the design of most railway buildings declined in quality after 1850, as companies grew more cost-conscious, that of terminal stations became more monumental. Kings Cross, designed by Lewis and Joseph Cubitt and completed in 1852, was a plain but elegant exercise in functional building, in contrast to nearby Euston. It had a double train shed, with roofs of laminated timber and divided into arrival and departure sides, a covered entrance for carriages at the front and a turret with a clock; the Great Northern Hotel was added on the western side in 1854. At Paddington the Great Western employed cast iron and glass for its three-sectioned train sheds, and for the first time in London placed a hotel transversely across the line of the tracks, facing on to the street. Charing Cross, opened in 1864, and Cannon Street, completed in the same year, both had hotels similarly placed, but in each case the tracks were covered by train sheds roofed with bold single spans, of 164 and 190 feet respectively. The grandest of all London stations, St Pancras, followed the same basic plan. It was the terminus of an extension of the Midland Railway from Bedford. Previously Midland trains had travelled through Hitchin to Kings Cross but growing congestion had made the arrangement intolerable, particularly since the Midland and the Great Northern were in competition for traffic from such towns as Leeds, Nottingham and Sheffield. The station itself, with its vast pointed arch 240 feet in span, was designed by W.H. Barlow. Since the tracks had to be elevated to clear the Regents Canal, not far north of the terminus, it was possible to construct a lower floor with direct access to the street, where beer from Burton was stored. The first train left the new station on 1 October 1868, four years after work commenced. The previous year work had begun on George Gilbert Scott's astonishing hotel, which was to stand between the ends of the platforms and the Euston Road; this opened for business in May 1873.

Some of the most significant additions to the industrial landscapes of the 1850s and subsequent decades were among the least heroic, the creation of the engineers and surveyors of the local Boards of Health,

230

set up as a result of the Public Health Act of 1848. The mean average death rate fell steadily during the second half of the century because of their work. There remained great areas of housing where standards of health and hygiene were appallingly low, but the threat of disease which had seemed so powerful about 1840 was contained and reversed. New sewers were dug, although many practical problems in the treatment of sewage remained. In most towns pumping engines and settling beds for sewage appeared in the 1850s or 1860s. Some were highly ornate, as if their builders were conscious of the improvements in public health which they were helping to bring about. None was more spectacular than the Abbey Mills pumping station in East London, completed in 1868. It stands near to the great embankment of the Northern Outfall Sewer, itself one of the dominant features of the landscape of the East End. The engine house is cruciform in plan, in an Italian Gothic style, topped by a central lantern. Each of the four bays housed a pair of steam pumping engines. The rails around the engine pits might almost be altar rails. On either side of the building was a tapering octagonal chimney set on a plinth, with a Gothic construction, rather like a butter cross, on the top. The richly ornamented interior, with heavily decorated columns and florid cast iron work in the roof, resembles a cathedral from Southern Europe rather than a public health establishment in the capital of a Protestant nation.

Boards of Health were also concerned, directly or indirectly, with water supplies. The waterworks, usually with a steam engine, became a common feature of the urban landscape. At Whitacre in Warwickshire is a water pumping engine house in the Gothic style, set among reservoirs and wide expanses of lawn. At Ryhope near Sunderland an engine house was built in 1868 containing two 100 hp double acting rotative beam engines.[22] Like the Whitacre engine house it is set among flower beds, grass, woods and water, in a landscape as contrived as that of a Georgian country house. The Papplewick water pumping engines north of Hucknall in Nottinghamshire, built in 1884, are similarly spectacular, the interior of the house being lined with ceramic tiles with gilded relief decorations, elaborate capitals on the columns and stained glass in the windows. Not all water pumping engines are so spectacular, but the most ornate examples are appropriate memorials to those who, in the words of Dr Kitson Clark:

> provided the people with water pure enough for them to drink, abundant enough for them to wash their clothes and clean their

231

bodies, to free them from disease-carrying vermin, and readily available to scour their streets, and flush their drains, and incidentally, who had provided them with drains to flush.

Another feature of the landscape brought into being by the Boards of Health was the public cemetery. Churchyard burial grounds in thickly populated town centres were regarded as serious health hazards in the 1850s, and most local Boards of Health gave high priority to the creation of cemeteries on the edges of towns. Sometimes separate cemeteries were laid out for Anglicans and Dissenters, sometimes there were separate sections within a single cemetery.

The edges of towns displayed many other characteristic features in the mid nineteenth century. Gas works increased substantially in size, and were sometimes moved from canalside sites to places where it was possible to construct railway sidings. In Ludlow the original gas works is now an agricultural engineer's yard, having ceased to serve its original purpose in the 1850s. Workhouses built by the Poor Law Unions, created by the act of 1834, generally date from the late 1830s although some were not constructed until the 1850s and 1860s. They were often designed on the panopticon principle, so that several wings projected from a single point like the spokes of a wheel, in order that one person at the hub could supervise a whole floor. The first public park was laid out at Birkenhead in the 1840s, and during the second half of the nineteenth century the provision of such parks became a popular act of benevolence. In many towns they were given by prosperous industrialists or by dominant companies, like the LNWR in Crewe or the Great Western in Swindon.

The same passion for order and regulation which had tamed wild, uncultivated landscapes around 1800 was applied in the mid nineteenth century to the centres of towns. Many new town halls were built in the 1850s and 1860s, partly as expressions of civic pride, partly because of the growing numbers of public meetings of various kinds—lectures, concerts, exhibitions of 'dissolving views' and expressions of protest—which needed accommodation. Whatever the utilitarian functions of a town hall might be—it would probably include offices, a lock-up and accommodation for a fire engine—it would almost certainly contain rooms for sizeable public gatherings. The regulation of trade was also considered desirable in the nineteenth century. The Manchester Exchange, built in 1809 and enlarged in 1838, was the nerve centre of the textile industry, but exchanges were constructed in many lesser towns after 1850, most commonly for the corn trade. These buildings were usually designed, like town halls, to be used for lectures, concerts and dances as well as for trade. In many towns reformers were as anxious to bring traders in meat, haber-dashery and greengrocery off the streets as they were to move dealers in corn from the pubs into exchanges. Such attempts at regulation were not always successful. At Bridgnorth an Italianate market hall was constructed in 1860 but, despite many efforts at compulsion, the street traders refused to move into it, and the Saturday market remains in the town's wide medieval high street. In larger towns the wholesale markets, like the Smithfield meat market completed in the late 1860s, competely transformed large parts of the landscape. The same reasons which made railway companies plan extensions through working class districts often led to the placing of markets or town halls in similar situations, which had the effect of removing the housing problems of the working class from town centres. Sometimes new roads were planned as a means of achieving the same end. Corpora-tion Street in Birmingham, conceived as 'a great street, as broad as a Parisian boulevard from New Street to the Aston Road' was begun in 1878 and involved the demolition of some of the worst property in the city.

The working class housing erected under the byelaws laid down by the local Boards of Health is rarely beautiful or spacious, yet it is significantly different from that of earlier decades. In most towns these houses have regimented back yards, approached from back alleys. They were drained, had access to privies and there was storage space for fuel. Houses were numbered and streets were officially named, with painted signs or plaques in cast iron or blue enamel. The Boards of Health did not extinguish local idiosyncrasies. In Leeds the con-struction of back-to-backs continued well into the twentieth century. In Newcastle upon Tyne the building of the characteristic Tyneside two-storey flats was unaffected by legislation. Often local Boards of Health imposed particular features on a whole town. Many houses in Northampton have front doors set back to create porches, the provi-sion of boot scrapers seems almost universal in mid nineteenth-century houses in the Potteries, while in the West Riding coal holes with cast iron doors sliding up and down in vertical grooves are very common. Houses built under the byelaws had no protruding bay windows, no porches encroaching on the public way and no boot scrapers set at right angles to the frontage. They were usually con-structed along straight building lines. Often housing developments

233

simply filled in fields, as earlier buildings had done. They were shaped by a multitude of factors—by the ornamental grounds of small suburban mansions, which might inhibit development for a long period and then suddenly give way to it, by gravel or brick pits which, once exhausted, might be built over, or by the curiously shaped properties created when railways cut across fields. Many nineteenth-century towns were surrounded by large areas of gardens, which might come on to the housing market gradually, so that houses would front on to the tracks servicing the plots; these tracks might ultimately become suburban roads. Dwelling houses could originate as summer houses, which many holders of such gardens built for recreational purposes on their plots.

Freehold Land Societies were active in most towns which grew rapidly in the 1850s.[23] Originally conceived in Birmingham as a means of creating Liberal votes in county constituencies, by developing estates of small freehold properties on the edges of towns, the idea was widely propagated by the movement's founder, John Taylor. A Freehold Land Society would invite subscriptions from the public, limiting the number of shares which any individual could take out. A plot of land would be acquired, road and other basic services would be installed and it would then be divided into plots for distribution to members, often by ballot. In practice such societies frequently aided the small-scale speculator rather than the owner-occupier. The appearance of Freehold Land Society estates is quite distinctive. They generally follow a grid pattern, often laid out behind a 'Front Row', the most prestigious part of the development, alongside a main road. Estates were often built up slowly, the empty plots frequently serving as gardens until the owners could afford to build upon them. They consist typically of short terraces of up to six houses, mixed with smaller groups and even individual houses of widely different dates. Sometimes the owner of two adjacent plots would leave one as garden ground; this may survive as garden, or it may be the site of a twentieth-century bungalow. Often the existence of such an estate is revealed by such names as 'Freehold Street', 'Freetown', or 'Union Street'.

The suburb was one of the most characteristic features of the mid nineteenth-century industrial landscape. R.K. Philp wrote in 1859:

> Every populous town and city is gradually becoming surrounded with mansions and villas, detached and semi-detached, where, with more or less of garden ground and

234

conservatory, the retired merchant or the busy tradesman reaps the rewards of years of toil, or throws off at intervals the cares of life, and gathers fresh health and energy to pursue its struggles.

Many market towns which had scarcely changed in area since the Middle Ages gained small groups of houses on their edges, either villas for traders no longer content to live above their shops, and for senior clerks and the retired, or terraces for railwaymen or the employees of newly established factories. The outward movement of the industrial cities of the North and Midlands continued unabated, while the suburbs of London grew in profusion. The haphazard character of early nineteenth-century suburbs was summarized in 1836:

> The place . . . wants completeness and unity. You see houses whose sides betray that they were intended to have others stuck upon them – all yawning, ghastly, unskinned and irregular; you see infant shrubberies struggling in awkward parcels amidst lots of yet-to be-occupied ground, and clumps of fine places and squares looking down upon clumps of old half-ruined villages, which the spreading town has taken by surprise, and which had not yet had time to get out of the way. Here and there, flanking the genteel streets, are dull, plebeian, bricky rows, full of poor grocers, and taverns which seem to have sprung up only for the annoyance of the gentlefolk.

The growth of suburbs was often described in military terms, and close examination of the expansion of almost any town shows the aptness of such language. The *Westminster Review* commented in 1864:

> The main army is preceded by an advance of villas . . . seizing a few picked positions . . . then come the more solid ranks of the semi-detached . . . along the high roads and in the neighbourhood of railway stations.

In many towns it is still possible to identify the classical and Gothic villas 'for the habitation of people in genteel circumstances' which marked the first extensions of building into the fields. In Shrewsbury a pair of classical villas bearing the date 1855 stand alongside the road to Montgomery, about a mile and a half from the town centre. They are flanked by the army barracks, built about 1880, and by large, mostly Gothic dwellings, whose names commemorate the death of Charles George Gordon at Khartoum in 1885. There were few towns which expanded steadily from the centre outwards. Most developed in

235

fits and starts along the main roads, and many years elapsed before some of the gaps were filled in.

The suburb represented many trends and assumptions in Victorian society.[24] It was a solution, for the individual, to the problems of bad sanitation and disreputable neighbours in the town centres. The suburban villa was also a mark of social status. Just as the successful cotton master or dealer in railway shares acquired a country estate, so the confidential clerk or the grocer who had prospered sought a villa from which he could travel daily to work. The suburb also provided opportunities for entrepreneurs, shopkeepers, publicans and ultimately for manufacturers. The tailor serving local demands could become a garment manufacturer, the grocer might become a maker of mineral waters, and in time the suburb became not just a dormitory but a manufacturing area in its own right.

The disjointed, unconscious way in which suburbs grew reflected the generally low returns to be gained from investment in housing. The boom periods in house building tended to be times when general economic activity was at a low ebb. When it was more profitable to invest in railways, mines or government stocks, only small investors for whom security was of overriding importance put their money into housing. Some London builders, like Edward Yates of Camberwell, worked on a large scale, assembling huge quantities of materials on sites and maintaining rigorous standards of inspection, but each boom brought into operation numerous small builders quite incapable of working in such a way. The relatively low cost of land encouraged the building of the cheapest units, small, separate family dwellings rather than the tenements to be found in many European cities. The many trivial differences in the design of very similar houses—polychrome string courses, tiled steps and porches, stained glass windows, finials and ridge tiles—characterize the restless nature of suburban building.

In the large cities improved transport facilities made possible the development of more distant suburbs. The first omnibus services in London were introduced by George Shillibeer in 1829. A writer in 1836 commented:

> A merchant whose place of business is in the neighbourhood of the Bank lives, we shall say, with his family, at Paddington, Clapham, Brixton, Wandsworth or any other pleasant part of the environs at a distance varying from three to six miles from the City; yet by the omnibusses, he is put down at almost the very door of his shop or counting house, at an hour as early as

he could have calculated upon if he had lived only in the next street. As it is only by living out of town that the health of a family can be properly preserved, a mode is thus devised of securing at small expense the advantages of both a town and country residence.

The *Railway Times*, in words ironically similar, asked in 1850:

Who would prefer living at Paddington, Islington, Kingsland or Walworth, if, he could for the same cost, reside at Kingstead, Banstead Downs, Stanmore Common, Bushey Heath, North-fleet, Slough, Epsom, Hainault Forest, Barnet or Reigate?

The development of suburban transport was considerably more complex than the quotations suggest. By the 1860s the cost of a daily journey by omnibus was within the reach of the better-paid clerks, but many who lived in the suburbs still walked to work. It was calculated in 1854–5 that 200,000 workers walked to their jobs in the City of London every day. Pedestrian commuting left its mark on the landscape in the numerous short-cuts called 'halfpenny hatches' in suburbs like Camberwell, which allowed walkers to take direct routes towards the Thames bridges rather than being forced along the circuitous routes which the development of private estates had created.

The first street tramways were established in Birkenhead in 1860 by the American, G.F. Train, who repeated the venture in London, Darlington and the Potteries. None of his projects was wholly successful, but the Tramways Act of 1870 allowed local authorities to build lines, and in the 1870s and 1880s street tramways powered by cables, steam or horses spread rapidly. In due course earlier methods of propulsion were replaced by electric traction. By 1900 tramways were being operated by sixty-one local authorities and eighty-nine private companies.

Few railway companies in the 1840s and 1850s were seriously interested in carrying passengers on their daily journey to work, preferring more profitable traffic over longer distances.[25] In London the specialist underground urban railway came into being with the completion of the Metropolitan Line from Paddington to Farringdon Street in 1863. At the same time the main line companies were forced to pay more attention to the needs of those who travelled daily to work by provisions in new acts of parliament compelling them to run trains at cheap fares for workmen, often imposed to compensate for the disruption caused by building new lines. The policies of the different

237

railway companies greatly affected the character of the suburbs of London and some provincial cities. At least before 1900 companies like the Great Western and the London and North-Western tended to scorn the carriage of working class commuters. The Great Eastern, by contrast, was almost bankrupt following its extension to Liverpool Street, and had an obligation to operate workmens' trains, so that the Walthamstow and Edmonton areas grew rapidly under its influence. It was severely embarrassed, in its attempts to build up a middle class clientele, by the working class suburbs which grew up around some of its stations. One of its managers remarked in 1884:

> I imagine that no one living in Noel Park could desire to possess the same class of neighbours as the residents of Stamford Hill have in the neighbourhood of St Anne's Road. The reports current in the district of the men residing there are of a character that would deter anyone from wishing for neighbours of that kind in any part.

South of the Thames the South London Line carried a very heavy local traffic from Victoria through Peckham to London Bridge, but beyond it there were few truly suburban services. Many of the lines which eventually served the suburbs were built by the South-Eastern and London, Chatham and Dover Railways in their competition for traffic to the continent and the coast.

Some Victorian suburbs were formally planned in the same way that Georgian residential squares had been planned. Victoria Park, home of many prominent Mancunians in the mid nineteenth century, was begun by a private company in 1836, received an Act of Parliament the following year, and in 1845 the Victoria Park Trust was formed to protect the amenities of the area.[26] Building was rigorously restricted by setting minimum values on the types of houses which could be built. In 1885, when the area was incorporated in Manchester, the park's residents retained the responsibility for maintaining their roads. The opening of the Styal loop railway in 1880 stimulated suburban growth around the park, and the rise of property values dissolved the effectiveness of the restrictions on the values of houses which could be built. Smaller houses began to appear in the 1880s, and in 1899 the building ties were finally broken: 650 two- and three-storey cottages were built on a grid-iron plan on the edge of the park.

In London planned developments of a very different kind were built by the Artisans', Labourers' and General Dwellings Company, a charitable concern with which Lord Shaftesbury was connected. The first, Shaftesbury Park near Clapham Junction station, was begun in 1872. Shaftesbury remarked that it symbolized:

> a new era in the progress of working men. It was a town on all the modern principles of sanitary arrangements, with recreation grounds, clubs, schools, libraries, baths and no public houses.

He considered that the co-operative nature of the scheme was the last hope for improving the living conditions of the working class. There are 1135 cottages, a block of flats and thirty shops in Shaftesbury Park. The entrance is between two cottages with corner turrets, which gives it something of the exclusive character of more pretentious middle class suburbs. The company afterwards laid out similar estates at Queen's Park, Kilburn and Noel Park, Wood Green.

Charitable societies were deeply concerned with the housing of London's working class.[27] Two societies were established in the 1840s. The Metropolitan Association for Improving the Dwellings of the Industrial Classes was formed in 1841, and built one block of dwellings in the Old St Pancras Road and another in Spicer Street, Spitalfields. The Society for Improving the Condition of the Labouring Classes was formed in 1844, and its first buildings were completed in Lower Road, Pentonville, in 1846. In 1849 Henry Roberts designed for the society a U shaped block of tenements of five storeys, approached by wrought iron balconies, in Streatham Street near the British Museum, which set the pattern for many other charitable housing schemes in London. For the Great Exhibition Roberts designed a pair of model cottages on a module which could be extended vertically or horizontally to form tenement blocks or terraces. Each house had three bedrooms, the first time that the principle of separate accommodation for parents and children had been accepted in towns. The cottages survive near the Oval cricket ground, where they were removed after the end of the Great Exhibition.

Streatham Street posed the dilemma which was to affect the provision of housing by philanthropic bodies for the rest of the century. The rents were between four and seven shillings a week, so the accommodation was only accessible to the skilled artisan class, and was far too expensive for the poor whom the society was trying to help. Roberts went abroad in 1853, but the multi-storeyed tenement block became a common feature of the London landscape. The Metropolitan

239

Association continued to build during the 1850s, 1860s and 1870s. One of their surviving blocks, Gatcliff Buildings in Chelsea, finished in 1867, bears the name of the association's secretary. In 1874 the association built Farringdon Buildings which accommodated 260 families in five blocks, sixty-seven feet high and only twenty feet apart. They have been condemned for being 'as inhuman as only that moment in history could make them', but such densities were unavoidable if dwellings were to be provided at rents which the poor could possibly hope to pay. It was only by providing cheap transport from cottage estates in the suburbs, or by bringing in alternative sources of finance, that matters could be altered. The most active provider of tenement accommodation was the Peabody Trust, established in 1862 by George Peabody, the American banker who personally paid for the United States display at the Great Exhibition. The first block was built in Whitechapel in 1864, and by 1875 nearly 4000 people were accommodated in Peabody dwellings, although the aim of improving the condition of the poor was scarcely realized since most of the occupants were artisans. In 1875 the Metropolitan Board of Works began to clear slums. It did not build houses itself, however, letting the cleared land instead to various charitable bodies.

The urban and suburban growth of the mid nineteenth century demanded huge quantities of building materials. In many districts the majority of bricks were locally made almost until the end of the century, in small brickyards supplied with coal by railways and canals and using clay dug on the spot. In 1865 brickmaking and tilemaking around Crewe were said to find work for men and their children 'as fast as they can be got'. The ruined structures of such brickyards can still be found in country areas, while on the edges of towns many suburban gardens end at the overgrown face of a disused clay pit.

A number of areas specialized in the manufacture of bricks, tiles and cement for more than just local distribution. Some were rough open villages in rural areas like Harbury in Warwickshire or Much Wenlock in Shropshire, where there were numerous lime kilns. In Jackfield in the Ironbridge Gorge were numerous small brick and tileyards. Most operated only in the summer months, largely on a sub-contracting basis and with considerable use of child labour. The installations consisted of little more than a shallow pit, a few kilns and several hovels in which the brick- and tilemakers plied their trades.[28] There were numerous similar works in the Black Country and the East Midlands coalfields. From the Jackfield industry grew two large con-

240

cerns making high quality encaustic and glazed tiles. By the 1880s these were operating complex factories from which tiles were sent to decorate the floors and walls of numerous public buildings all over the British Empire, as well as countless suburban porches.

Few landscapes were more radically changed by industrial growth in the nineteenth century than that of the lower Medway Valley.[29] A journey by train from Strood to Maidstone passes through a landscape as industrialized as any in Britain, yet its transformation had hardly begun before 1850, and owed nothing to the manufactures traditionally associated with the Industrial Revolution. It came about principally because of the need to supply building materials to the growing suburbs of London. 'Portland' cement, which would set under water, was patented by Joseph Aspdin, a Leeds bricklayer, in 1824. The process was subsequently improved by I.C. Johnson, who set up the first Portland Cement works at Frindsbury on the Medway in 1851, on the site of an oil mill whose Boulton and Watt steam engines he continued to employ. Many other factories were established using local limestone and clay, and coal imported by barge. A works at Strood Dock was described thus:

> There were a number of conical shaped kilns in which the cement was baked; these kilns were nearest the mouth of the basin. Beyond these the ground had been dug out in the form of dripping pans, and from the works ran a number of wooden gutters, in an inclined direction towards these dripping pans. The cement, in a liquid form, ran down these troughs, looking like pure milk. When one of these squares was full, the fluid was diverted to another. This was left for several days until it began to harden; its colour used to change, with dust and soot, until it became a kind of ashen grey. As it dried, cracks and fissures were observable on the surface. Then, men with puddlers' spades dug out these pans and loaded into wheelbarrows, which were wheeled on planks into the kilns. Fires were lighted, and the cement baked until the fires dried out; it was then taken to the grinding mills and ground into fine powder.

Quarries, chimneys and kilns accordingly came to dominate the Medway Valley. All the works had their own wharves on the river where coal was unloaded and cement dispatched. Increased competition from about 1870 led to the concentration of the industry in larger works, mostly with rotary kilns. By 1898 15,000 tons of cement a week were being manufactured in the area.

Bricks were also made in the Medway Valley. Many were used locally, in cement factories and cement workers' houses, but a large proportion of the output was sent to London by barge. Some works, like that of Thomas Cubitt at Burham, established in 1852, were very large, but many bricks were made in small yards as primitive as those of Jackfield. By the 1890s Medway bricks were encountering severe price competition in London and the industry was in decline.

The Medway towns grew rapidly to accommodate those employed in cement- and brickmaking, and the numerous trades which served the two basic industries. Many boatyards were set up to build and repair barges employed in the brick and cement trades. The local engineering industry was prosperous, partly because it was a supplier of brick- and cement-making machinery, and numerous secondary trades grew up in the region.

Another area transformed by the demands of the London brick-layers was around Peterborough, where Oxford clay was discovered in the parish of Fletton in 1881.[30] This clay contained between five and ten per cent carbon, and so provided much of the fuel needed in firing. The new works of the period were large establishments with continuous Hoffman kilns, vastly more efficient than the intermittent kilns employed in traditional brickworks. Brick presses were powered by steam engines, most works had direct access to railways and the clay pits were excavated to much greater depths than previously. The population of the parish of Fletton rose from 189 in 1831 to 1841 in 1881. A similar development took place in the Stewartby area on the railway from Bletchley to Bedford. In areas like Ruabon and Accrington in the 1880s brickworks began to make the high quality hard red bricks which became so popular for the frontages of middle class villas. These, together with the cheaper Fletton bricks from Peterborough, began to force from the market the products of small, local brickyards. Cement-making also grew in scale in the closing decades of the century, around Thurrock and Purfleet in Essex, and around Rugby.

As the manufacture of building materials became concentrated in large units, so two of the most widespread industrial activities, the small brickyard and the lime kiln, gradually began to close down. Bricks and mortar had, until the 1880s, been essentially local products, like shoes and clothes; and like tailors and shoemakers, their makers were slowly forced out of business. This brought about far-reaching changes in the landscape. By 1900 the typical upper working or lower middle class house might be faced with red bricks from Accrington, with its side and rear walls made of Flettons; it could have tiles from Jackfield or from Minton of Stoke on Trent in its porch and around its fireplaces; and cement from Rugby, Thurrock or Strood could have been used in its construction.

Between 1850 and 1890 the industrial landscape reflected the preoccupations and ambiguities of a society prosperous enough to regard itself as the 'workshop of the world', which still contained substantial pockets of poverty and squalor. New structures could reflect the optimism of the times, like the Crystal Palace or the mill at Saltaire, or they could reflect hankerings after a lost medieval innocence, like the cross at Akroyden. This was a period when some of the characteristic structures of the Industrial Revolution—the factory, the foundry, the railway station—spread to the majority of towns. While some regional traditions remained strong, like the building of back-to-backs in Leeds or of two-storey flats in Newcastle, in many ways it was a time of increasing uniformity. The growth of the great brick-and tile-making concerns epitomized the changes which were taking place.

References

1 Owen Ashmore, *The Industrial Archaeology of Lancashire* (1969).
2 J.D. Marshall, 'Colonization as a Factor in the Planting of Towns in North-West England' in H.J. Dyos, ed., *The Study of Urban History* (1968).
3 Vanessa Parker, *The English House in the Nineteenth Century* (1970).
4 Roger Suddards, ed., *Titus of Salts* (1976). R. Balgarnie, *Sir Titus Salt: His Life and its Lessons* (1877). *Illustrated London News*, 1 October 1853.
5 David Alderton and John Booker, *The Batsford Guide to the Industrial Archaeology of East Anglia* (1980).
6 J.M. Preston, *Industrial Medway: an historical survey* (1977).
7 Hugh Torrens, *The Evolution of a Family Firm: Stothert and Pitt of Bath* (1978).
8 S.B. Saul, 'The Market and the Development of the Mechanical Engineering Industries in Britain, 1860–1914', *Economic History Review*, 2nd Series, XX, 1 (1967).
9 *Report of the Childrens' Employment Commission*, British Parliamentary Papers, 1864, XXII.

10   Robert Sherlock, *The Industrial Archaeology of Staffordshire* (1976).
11   Peter Bigmore, *The Bedfordshire and Huntingdonshire Landscape* (1979).
12   *Eddowes Salopian Journal*, 8 August 1866.
13   The Arkwright Society, *Burton on Trent* (1978).
14   Asa Briggs, *Victorian Cities* (1963).
15   J.D. Marshall, *An Economic History of Furness, 1711–1900, and the Town of Barrow, 1757–1897, with an Epilogue* (1958).
     S. Pollard and J.D. Marshall, 'The Furness Railway and the Growth of Barrow', *Journal of Transport History*, I, 2 (1953).
16   T.C. Barker and J.R. Harris, *A Merseyside Town in the Industrial Revolution: St Helens 1750–1900* (1959).
17   Frank Booker, *The Industrial Archaeology of the Tamar Valley* (1967).
     Frank Booker, *The Story of Morwellham* (1970).
     Walter Minchinton, *Industrial Archaeology in Devon* (n.d.).
18   W.J. Lewis, *Lead Mining in Wales* (1967).
19   Jean Lindsey, *The History of the North Wales Slate Industry* (1974).
20   J.G. Kellett, *The Impact of Railways on Victorian Cities* (1969).
21   Jack Simmons, *St Pancras Station* (1968).
22   S.M. Linsley, *Ryhope Pumping Station* (1973).
23   S.D. Chapman and J.N. Bartlett, 'The Contribution of Building Clubs and Freehold Land Societies to Working Class Housing in Birmingham' in S.D. Chapman, ed., *The History of Working Class Housing* (1971).
24   H.J. Dyos, *Victorian Suburb: a study of the growth of Camberwell* (1973).
25   J.G. Kellett, *The Impact of Railways on Victorian Cities* (1969).
26   Maurice Spiers, *Victoria Park, Manchester, a nineteenth-century suburb in its social and administrative context* (1976).
27   Nikolaus Pevsner, *Studies in Art, Architecture and Design* (1968).
     J.N. Tarn, *Working Class Housing in nineteenth-century Britain* (1971).
28   *Fifth Report of the Childrens' Employment Commission (1862)*, British Parliamentary Papers, 1866, XXIV.
29   J.M. Preston, *Industrial Medway: an historical survey* (1977).
30   Peter Bigmore, *The Bedfordshire and Huntingdonshire Landscape* (1979).

Rusticity and Uncertainty

The landscape of industry began to change in many respects after 1890. Some of the characteristic features of the Industrial Revolution began to disappear, although staple industries like coal and cotton continued to expand. Gigantic new cotton mills in Accrington brick displaced many of the older structures which derived their pedigree from Arkwright and Bage. At Belper the North Mill of 1804, one of the first generation of iron-framed buildings, was totally dwarfed by the vast East Mill of 1912. The iron trade changed rapidly, with many furnaces closing in inland areas like the Black Country, Shropshire and the heads of the South Wales valleys, but a growing concentration on coastal sites well-located for the import of foreign ores. The blast furnace was less and less a simple masonry structure with a steam engine alongside it. With its top closed and hot blast stoves around it, it was becoming a complex piece of chemical apparatus. The mining of non-ferrous metals contracted rapidly, and on many hillsides only waste tips and the shells of engine houses remained as remnants of once-flourishing concerns. This was part of a severe decline in the economy of upland Britain, as marginal agriculture, like mining, was exposed to foreign competition. The Industrial Revolution had stimulated growth in the upland regions until about 1870, but the subsequent growth of industry brought decline to such areas.

The railway system continued to expand. There were 17,328 route miles in 1890, 18,680 in 1900 and just over 20,000 in 1912. The Great Central London Extension, completed in 1899 from Annesley north of Nottingham to a junction with the Metropolitan Railway near Aylesbury, was 'the last main line'. It served no town of consequence which did not already have trains to London and the confident style of its buildings—its deep, gently sloping cuttings, its stations on island platforms and its blue brick bridges and viaducts—was never matched in peacetime by the density of its traffic. The Great Western Railway built several 'cut-off' lines, shortening its routes to Plymouth and

245

Birmingham, while the Severn Tunnel, opened in 1886, shortened the route from London to Cardiff and made possible a new range of services between the North-West and the South-Western peninsula. The Hull and Barnsley and the Barry Railways were built to challenge other companies for profitable export traffic in coal. Many of the new lines were 'light railways', built under the terms of the Light Railways Act of 1896, which enabled travellers to journey on iron rails to such towns as Tollesbury (Essex), Lynton and Llanfair Caereinion, but through level crossing gates opened by train crews and at no great speed.

The turnpike road system came to an end in this period. The last road on which tolls were collected was, ironically, the Anglesey portion of the Holyhead Road, where the gates were removed in 1894. The canals of the Industrial Revolution remained, without being significantly improved. The Manchester Ship Canal, completed in 1894, and the hydraulic lift at Anderton, linking the Weaver Navigation with the Trent and Mersey Canal, opened in 1875, were quite exceptional examples of enterprise. Some canals, like the Oxford and the Grand Junction, still carried appreciable quantities of long-distance traffic. Others, like the Birmingham and and the Bridgewater, were busy with short hauls. Many, particularly in the South of England, silted up under railway ownership and ceased to carry commercial traffic. The atmosphere of the decaying waterways was beautifully captured by Temple Thurston as he made one of the last journeys up the Thames and Severn Canal from Brimscombe to Sapperton about 1910:

> For more than three miles the canal divides the wooded hills, a band of silver drawn through the valley of gold. Lock by lock it mounts the gentle incline until it reaches the pound to Sapperton tunnel, and at the summit spreads into a wide basin before it passes into the last lock, some few hundred yards before the tunnel's mouth. The whole way from Stroud upwards is almost deserted now. We only met one barge in the whole journey. An old lady with capacious barge bonnet was standing humming quietly to herself at the tiller. That was the only boat we found on those waters . . . the draught of water is bad; in some places we just floated and no more. . . . It was golden to the last. Even in the water itself the weeds grew more luxuriantly than I have seen in any river. In and out of the forests of trailing weed, the fish moved mysteriously like mermaids in a fairy-tale. It was all a fairy-tale beneath that water. There were dense growths and

then clear spaces on to which the sunshine fell in brilliant patches.

There were many new features of the industrial landscape: electric power stations, electric trams and railways, concrete bridges and buildings, oil refineries and chemical plants. Yet the most significant changes were those which were, in effect, repudiations of industry. There was widespread agreement that it was industry which had created slums and other sources of social unease, arising in part from an increasing preoccupation with what Henry George defined as 'the persistence of poverty amid increasing wealth'. London, with the ostentation of its wealth-consuming West End in startling contrast to the abject poverty of the East End, was the centre of concern. Edward Pearse, historian of the Fabian Society which was founded in 1886, attributed the new anxiety about social problems to a new generation who had absorbed the teachings of Charles Darwin, Herbert Spencer and T.H. Huxley. He saw the influence of Henry George, who visited England in 1881, as particularly important. George had summed up a common belief about the English poor:

> It is my deliberate opinion that if, standing on the threshold of being, one were given the choice of entering life as a Tierra del Fuegan, a black fellow of Australia, an Esquimaux in the Arctic Circle, or among the lowest classes in such a highly civilized country as Great Britain, he would make infinitely the better choice in selecting the lot of the savage.

Such opinions became commonplace and many writers, profound or otherwise, attributed the lot of the poor to the effects of industry. Temple Thurston, author of *The Flower of Gloucester*, wrote:

> You have only to go into the Black Country to know what can be done with a wonderful world when God delivers it into the hand of man. I know very well that there is the pulse of England's greatness, that out of Bradford, Halifax, Huddersfield, Rochdale and Burnley, the stream of molten metal flows through the veins and arteries of a great nation. . . . But what a price to pay and what a coinage to pay it in . . . those belching furnaces and that poisoned land must make you marvel as you pass it by. The black sweeping hills with scrubby bushes, leafless and dead; the men and women, white-faced and dirty with the everlasting falling of the sooty air; the thousand factories and the countless furnaces; the utter lifelessness in all this seething mass of life.

247

The plight of the London poor was examined in numerous publications in the 1880s. Andrew Mearns's *Bitter Cry of Outcast London* raised much interest in 1883. Charles Booth began his survey of *The Life and Labour of the People in London* in 1886 and published his first report three years later. His wife subsequently wrote: 'People's minds were very full of the various problems connected with the position of the poor, and opinions the most diverse were expressed, remedies of the most contradictory nature were proposed.' Much attention was paid to the religious observances of the poor. The recognized denominations experimented with city missions, among 'people of all trades and no trade, reeking in sin and misery, whose social and spiritual condition is at once a menace, a sorrow and a shame'. William Booth, who founded the Salvation Army in 1878 and published *In Darkest England and the Way Out* in 1890, attracted much attention. His book described 'the darkness', comparing England with Africa, and examined the 'submerged tenth', the homeless, the unemployed, the criminals, the orphans. He proposed a series of remedies, outlining the role which the Salvation Army might play in implementing them. Among his suggestions was the establishment of suburban villages twelve miles from London, with terraced cottages, gardens, co-operative stores and no public houses, from which railway companies, 'in consideration of the inconvenience and suffering they have inflicted on the poor', would offer cheap travel to London. The pictorial chart illustrating the Salvation Army Social Campaign is full of images of urban despair being transformed into rural hope.

The most considerable critic of the landscape of industrial capitalism was William Morris. He wrote in *News from Nowhere* in 1890:

> England was once a country of clearings amongst the woods and wastes, with a few towns interspersed, which were fortresses for the feudal army, markets for the folk, gathering places for the craftsmen. It then became a country of huge and foul workshops and fouler gambling dens, surrounded by an ill-kept, poverty-stricken farm, pillaged by the masters of the workshops.

In 1885 in *Useful Work versus Useless Toil* he observed:

> For all our crowded towns and bewildering factories are simply the outcome of the profit system. Capitalistic manufacture, capitalistic landowning and capitalistic exchange force men into big cities in order to manipulate them in the interests of capital; the same tyranny contracts the due space of the factory

so much that (for instance) the interior of a great weaving-shed is almost as ridiculous a spectacle as it is a horrible one.

Morris insisted that there were alternatives to such squalor:

> People engaged in all such labour need by no means be compelled to pig together in close city quarters. There is no reason why they should not follow their occupations in quiet country homes, in industrial colleges, in small towns, or, in short, where they find it happiest for them to live. . . . The factories might be centres of intellectual activity . . . and work in them might well be varied very much; the tending of the necessary machinery might to each individual be but a short part of the day's work. . . . Beginning by making their factories, buildings and sheds decent and convenient like their homes, they would infallibly go on to make them not merely negatively good, inoffensive merely, but even beautiful.

He saw the possible future landscape as 'a garden, where nothing is wasted and nothing is spoilt, with the necessary dwellings, sheds and workshops scattered up and down the country, all trim and neat and pretty'.

It was not surprising that the new industries of the 1890s and 1900s sought to be as little like those of the Industrial Revolution as possible. Some of the entrepreneurs of the period tried to atone for the collective guilt of those who were blamed for creating the slums by providing drinks and meals in factories, granting and organizing holidays, encouraging workers by adopting factory mottoes. Above all they built factories and workers' housing in completely new styles. James Templeton and Co. built a carpet factory overlooking Glasgow Green in brightly coloured brick, modelling it on the Doge's Palace at Venice. 'There is no need to label such a building with the name of its owners', wrote one admirer, 'few of those who admire it will fail to ascertain that for themselves and be grateful.'[1] The Footshape shoe factory at Northampton, built in 1913, copied the style of Castle Ashby, the ancestral home of the Marquesses of Northampton. It was in polychrome brick and an openwork inscription on the parapet proclaiming the name of the factory was modelled on the seventeenth-century inscription at Castle Ashby.

Richard and George Cadbury moved their cocoa business from central Birmingham to a site four miles south-west of the city in 1897, and built some not especially distinguished houses for numbers of their workpeople. Some fourteen years later George Cadbury purchased a hundred and twenty acres of land in the vicinity and, with W. Alexander Harvey as his architect, began to develop a model, socially balanced community, membership of which was not confined to his workpeople. By 1900 some 313 houses had been constructed, and the development was vested in the Bournville Village Trust, whose object was defined as:

> the amelioration of the condition of the working class and labouring population in and around Birmingham and elsewhere in Britain, by the provision of improved dwellings with gardens and open spaces to be enjoyed therewith.

Harvey wrote, in terms similar to those of William Morris:

> Bournville stands as an example of what the village of the future might be, a village of healthy homes amid pleasant surroundings, where fresh air is abundant and beauty present, and where are secured to its people by an administration co-operative in its nature, numerous benefits, which under present conditions are denied them elsewhere.

If Bournville now appears commonplace and unexciting it is because the ideas which it incorporates have become so widely accepted. Compared with the straggling late Victorian and Edwardian terraces which join it to the rest of Birmingham, it appears a revolutionary landscape. The houses are of local brick, mostly with tiled roofs. While there is no ostentation, the houses have a rural appearance, some with overhanging eaves and hipped roofs. All are set in substantial gardens, some with open fronts along tree-lined roads, with large curving grass verges. The older parts of the factory have a rustic appearance and the No. 1 Lodge is a half-timbered building set amid trees and lawns. Communal buildings abound: a Quaker meeting house, a church, schools, colleges, a public hall and half-timbered shops, most of them grouped around a central green with an octagonal 'rest-house' in the centre. The most significant buildings in Bournville are Selly Manor and Minton Greaves, fourteenth-century timber-framed houses moved there to create a more authentic village atmosphere. Bournville arose from the assumption that industry was the cause of slums and poverty. Its landscape proclaims that the ideal society is a rural one, with trees, grass and half-timbered buildings, and that there was an ideal pre-industrial past, represented by Minton Greaves and Selly Manor. The very names of the roads—Elm Road, Laburnum Road, Sycamore Road, Acacia Road and Linden Road—

reflect the builders' preoccupation with rural ideals. No one would ever visit Bournville and describe the partly hidden, partly disguised chocolate factory in the terms that eighteenth-century tourists used of the mills at Cromford or the furnaces at Coalbrookdale.

Port Sunlight, the creation of the soap manufacturer William Hesketh Lever (later Lord Leverhulme), is superficially a very different settlement from Bournville. In 1888 Lever purchased a site near the Mersey for his expanding business, with the intention of creating a model village alongside the new factory, and by 1900 four hundred houses had been completed. The planning objectives at Port Sunlight changed several times during its history, but the overwhelming impressions created by its landscape are of open spaces, high standards of craftsmanship and of an attempt to recreate antiquity. 'It's all very old' was the reaction of an eight-year-old seeing it for the first time. Lever employed many architects, some of them of national standing. The factory is self-effacing, entirely to one side of the village and presenting only one front towards it. The houses reflect an astonishing range of architectural styles—timber-framing, sometimes carefully copied from ancient originals, sometimes brilliantly imaginative, roughcast plasterwork and Tudor chimneys in Ruabon brick executed with great precision. One terrace has terracotta dormers in a fifteenth-century French Gothic style. There are numerous halls and institutes, schools, a Congregational church, an art gallery, bowling greens and an inn modelled on an Elizabethan original. A bandstand, an open air theatre and a replica of Shakespeare's birthplace have been demolished. Port Sunlight was an advertisement for soap, magnificent in its style and superb in its craftsmanship. But, unlike Bournville which was intended to present realistic standards which might be applied elsewhere, it was too expensive to be copied. It is nevertheless a reflection of contemporary attitudes to the industrial landscape. The factory is relegated to the sidelines, the houses and the communal buildings are all-important and, in an idyllic setting, they are of what a sympathetic writer in 1905 called 'a chaste antique design, the better ones half-timbered, two to seven of them in a block and no two blocks alike'.

There were many similar but smaller developments, some built by entrepreneurs. The Quaker Clark family, shoemakers, built Gothic terraces for their workpeople at Street in Somerset, providing a Gothic community centre named after the patron saint of shoemakers and an unlicensed public house. Sir William Hartley built several streets named after the fruits he used in his jams around his factory at Aintree,

Liverpool. Vickerstown at Barrow in Furness and the garden village built by Reckitts in Hull were further examples. Some garden settlements were co-operative ventures. One of the most interesting was Burnace in the suburbs of Manchester, founded by clerks from the Co-operative Wholesale Society who had been inspired by a lecture from Ebenezer Howard, prophet of the Garden City movement, in 1908. There were similar developments at Liverpool, Oldham, Wolverhampton, the Potteries and elsewhere. The majority had a quasi-rural appearance created by the use of roughcast plaster, hanging tiles and elements of timber framing, and most had curving streets, large gardens and extensive verges. The most influential of the new settlements founded after 1900 was New Earswick built by Joseph Rowntree, the Quaker chocolate manufacturer, on the northern edge of York. Even more than at Bournville the intention was to set a pattern which others might realistically be expected to follow. The purpose, defined when a trust was established in 1904, was 'an attempt to provide houses which shall be artistic in appearance, sanitary, and thoroughly well-built, yet within the means of working men earning about 25s. a week'.[2] Terraces were built at various angles, spaced so that the main rooms would catch the sun. Many of the road names had the same rustic qualities as those at Bournville—Chestnut Grove, Poplar Grove and Sycamore Avenue—and the social centre was named the Folk Hall. New Earswick was very influential, and its architects, Raymond Unwin and Barry Parker, later worked at Letchworth Garden City and Hampstead Garden Suburb.

The other great change affecting the industrial landscape in the period after 1890 was the increasingly direct influence of both central and local government. The powers enjoyed by local authorities to clear slums and build lodging houses were gradually extended during the 1890s until, in 1900, they were given the authority to build on any land, not just that cleared of slums. The Housing and Town Planning Act of 1909 gave the Local Government Board powers to prompt local authorities to take action over housing, so that by 1914 the council house was becoming a familiar part of the industrial landscape. Government was also becoming concerned with the location of industry. In areas affected by the decline of particular industries local councils, like those in Luton and Medway, began deliberately to attract new factories. This was something which earlier generations would have regarded as being entirely outside the scope of government. These tendencies, together with the pace of technological development, were intensified during and after the First World War to such an extent that the history of the industrial landscape during the greater part of the twentieth century demands a separate study.

Landscapes are the most fragile remains of past industry. Machines can be preserved and placed in museums. Buildings can be conserved and adapted for new purposes. But the features of one period are almost inevitably overlain by those of subsequent generations, whether a site has continued in industrial use or not. Yet an understanding of industrial history demands a sensitivity to landscape as well as an awareness of how machines and processes worked and an unpatronizing sympathy for past generations of workers. Such characteristic landscapes of the Industrial Revolution as remain need to be cherished as much as its most famous structures if our children are to gain an adequate understanding of one of the critical periods of our history.

Some historically important landscapes are lost for ever. The east end of Leeds, Little Ireland and the Liverpool cellars have long since been destroyed, and none can regret that such living conditions have been eradicated. On Parys Mountain there are still some precipitation pools and a few crumbling stone walls, but the most terrifying legacy of its industrial past is the utter aridity of the mountain top, with its many coloured rocks utterly scoured of vegetation by chemical action. Other landscapes are more readily recognizable. Cromford, the scene of momentous innovations and still a bewitching melange of stately mills, dignified terraces in millstone grit and tumbling waters, is devotedly conserved and much visited. Some little-known industrial landscapes are historical sources of enormous value. Squatting on commons was a vitally important factor in the growth of the industrial West Midlands, but only in the Clee Hills in South Shropshire does there survive a landscape remotely like that of an eighteenth-century industrial squatting community. Ironworking ceased about 1840, coal mining declined and no town sprawled on to the hills. In consequence it is still possible to wander along packhorse tracks and among gorse and bracken on open commons, to pick over the spoil around bell pits and slag heaps and to see cottages in their hedged enclosures round the edges of the commons and on islands in the middle. Similarly, along the road from Bradford through Great Horton and Queensbury to Halifax is a whole history of textile housing—solidly built Pennine houses which were standing in the time of Defoe, folds filled with varieties of small stone cottages, terraces illustrating the

253

evolution of the West Riding back-to-back terrace, and rows of mid nineteenth-century housing attached to sizeable mills.

In other areas it is still possible to sense something of past industrial landscapes from a few surviving structures and patterns. After his visit to Middleton in 1849 A.B. Reach caught an omnibus from outside an inn to the centre of Manchester. To follow the same route is to pass through the relics of more than four generations of industrial activity. Few weavers' cottages now remain in Middleton, but a mill once powered by water is still recognizable, as well as a Congregationalist chapel and several public houses which must have been standing in Reach's time. The great Warwick mill, with its tower like that of a town hall and its detached chimney, recalls the prosperity of late Victorian Lancashire. Past an Arndale shopping centre, Alkington Park Garden Village, shrunken marshalling yards and an aircraft factory are vast expanses of grass recently cleared of housing, with three-decker board schools and the occasional public house standing up like pebbles in eroded sandstone. Central Manchester is full of ironies. Monumental buildings like those of the Co-operative Wholesale Society, Victoria Station and the markets survive like whales marooned on a beach, mocked by the tawdry warehouses brimming with cheap clothing, oriental radios and plastic toys, which were once the houses of prosperous citizens.

East of Rochdale's memorials to Victorian civic grandeur it is possible to sense the growing numbers of 'long light' weavers' cottages amid the late Victorian urban sprawl through Smallbridge. At Littleborough such cottages dominate the main street, and the main road crosses the Rochdale Canal and the Lancashire and Yorkshire Railway. Beyond Littleborough the limit of urban sprawl is passed, and the occasional weavers' cottage stands isolated on the moors as the road climbs Blackstone Edge, as it must have done in the time of Defoe.

The early morning London train from Wolverhampton similarly stimulates a dialogue between past and present industrial landscapes. A plume of smoke rising vertically from a high metal stack and silhouetted against the rising sun is but a fragment of the smoke of 1850. The gaunt, dead, rusty ruins of Elisabeth, the Black Country's last blast furnace, flash by the carriage window. A once-handsome polychrome brick foundry building is shrouded with soot and apparently unused, but the occasional flame-topped cupola testifies that molten iron is still poured into moulds in the district. Swifts flash across water which has accumulated in cavernous depressions caused by mining subsidence, while the crumbling skeleton of an engine house, a memorial to a late Victorian attempt to save the mines from flooding, is almost engulfed by the tipping of twentieth-century garbage. A twisting, crumbling embankment, which once carried trains from Euston to Wolverhampton via the Oxford avoiding line and Worcester, serves as a monument to the gauge war of the 1840s. Power lines lead towards distant cooling towers whose erupting steam is dramatized by the eastern light. The yards of steel stockholders and perforators, oil tank farms and an old foundry turned into an industrial estate are evidence of persistent vitality. The housing is predominantly that of the 1920s and 1930s, Bournville made mean by borough treasurers, but here and there huddle groups of cottages which were standing when the Black Country was one of the world's great iron-producing regions. A West Indian, his midday meal in a plastic box, trudges from a smoke-blackened Victorian terrace along the broad towpath of Telford's improved Birmingham Canal towards a bus stop. Above the rim of the Smethwick cutting Adam's Old Monk Port is still advertised in much-faded paint on the wall of a house awaiting demolition, at 4s 6d a bottle. The landscape reveals countless subtleties and ironies, and poses innumerable questions about two centuries and more of English history.

Impressions of industrial landscapes are altered by circumstances. Morwellham full of summer tourists is a thorough delight, but there is no longer smoke from the lime kilns and the fumes from the arsenic refineries have ceased to exercise their poisonous influence. The drizzle-bearing westerly which rasps along the 1200-foot contour at Blaenavon asks questions, which would not occur in different circumstances, about the quality of shelter afforded to the families of early nineteenth-century ironworkers by the back-to-back cottages of the now-vanished Bunkers Row.

Like any other features of the landscape, the relics of industry are best understood in areas with which we are well acquainted. The fifteen-mile road from Shrewsbury to Ironbridge is not one which, except in its last mile, has been affected more than most by manufacturing and mining activities, but it does demonstrate how varied the influence of industry has been upon the landscape. In The Square, in the heart of Shrewsbury, is Walter Hancock's Market Hall of 1596, for two centuries the scene of bargaining between weavers from the Welsh hills and the Shrewsbury drapers. The High Street leading out of the Square was vigorously cleared of encroachments by the local Improvement Commission in the 1820s. At the head of the slope towards the English Bridge stands the Lion Hotel, from which Robert Lawrence operated his coaches to Holyhead, London and Bristol. John Gwynne's English Bridge of 1768–74 has been much altered, but it retains its stone scallops and dolphins. From the steps by the bridge it was possible, on Monday mornings in the eighteenth century, to catch the 6 am passenger wherry to Worcester. Beyond the bridge the road passes into what was the medieval borough of Abbey Foregate. Modern buildings cover the site of the Abbey Mills, a source of contention for centuries between abbot and townspeople, and the viaduct of the Shrewsbury and Hereford Railway strides over the course of the millstream. The road alongside the Abbey Church was built in 1836 and isolates the church from the refectory pulpit and some medieval stone walls which today form part of a builder's yard. The old road is now a loop used mainly for parking, rather like an oxbow lake. At the end of the planned medieval borough the road passes mileposts of both the road to Wellington and that to Bridgnorth, which separate about a mile from the Square. The Wellington road runs downhill to join the bypass built in the 1930s, through a cutting excavated under Telford's direction in the 1820s. A little more than a mile further on a narrow lane branches off to the south, towards Dorrington. It was once turnpiked, the only possible reason for which must have been to prevent its use by toll evaders. At Atcham the road crosses the Severn again, on a concrete bridge opened in 1929 by Herbert Morrison, Minister of Transport, alongside which survives John Gwynne's bridge of 1769–71, unaltered, narrow and steep. On the upstream side are the unmistakable earthworks of a fish weir and bypass channel. The wall to the north hides for a time George Steuart's Attingham Park, a late eighteenth-century mansion alongside the site of an ironworks of 1710 powered by the River Tern, which the road crosses on a widened version of William Hayward's bridge of 1774. On the downstream side, at the confluence with the Severn, are the remains of an eighteenth-century lock which allowed small barges into the Tern. Beyond the bridge the traveller to Ironbridge turns on to a turnpike road built while the Iron Bridge was under construction.

Within the boundaries of the Roman city of Wroxeter a cottage at a crossroads was probably a turnpike tollhouse on a branch road which still used the Roman crossing point over the Severn in the early nineteenth century. A mile or so beyond, the road dips into a valley at

Lower Long Wood, where small heaps of spoil, now much overgrown, and a few cottages bear witness to the existence of a colliery. In the late 1790s Thomas Telford and others launched a series of speculations, mining coal at this spot and quarrying limestone on Wenlock Edge, and carrying both products in both directions across Telford's bridge at Cressage, which was the third speculation in the series. The road passes the turning to the bridge, which was replaced in 1914. The branch road to it is an early example of Telford's work. In another valley is the village of Leighton where the main tollhouse on the road was situated. Beneath the village inn, whose present form dates from the mid nineteenth century, are the remnants of a water corn mill and below them the tuyère arch of a seventeenth-century blast furnace. The fields beyond it are strewn with slag, and the remains of a string of pools can be traced up the valley. On the hill beyond the village are clear signs of an older road, which the turnpike trust replaced with the present route around the shoulder of the hill; this gives a magnificent view of the meanders on the River Severn, themselves reminders of the failure in the eighteenth century to improve the river. The road passes through the shrunken medieval hamlet of Adney and the village of Buildwas, where the steel truss bridge of 1905 over the Severn still displays some castings from Telford's iron bridge of 1795–6. On the far bank of the river are two power stations, one of the early 1930s and one of the mid 1960s; the latter occupies the site of Buildwas Junction station, once the hub of local branch line passenger services, and of the Stone Port, where limestone brought by wooden railway to the river was loaded on to barges. On the northern bank, to which the road clings, are undulations marking the site of a landslip in 1774 at which the great Evangelical John Fletcher preached a most powerful sermon. Beyond them is Strethill Farm, near to a wharf which was the terminus of a wooden railway built in 1729. This portion of road belonged to the Madeley Turnpike Trust, whose tollhouse stands at the approach to Coalbrookdale, at a point where it is possible to glimpse the iron Albert Edward Bridge, built in 1862 and still carrying coal trains to the power station.

As the road enters the Ironbridge Gorge it becomes part of a landscape totally dominated by industry. To the north are the ironworks of Coalbrookdale, alongside the river is an assortment of warehouses and on the opposite bank are lime kilns, the viaduct of the Severn Valley Railway and a boatbuilding hamlet. On the slopes of the Gorge are layers of industrial history. Adits, mostly blocked up, are

257

relics of early mining activities, and many of the maze of footpaths and flights of steps mark the routes of wooden railways. The occasional roughly built cottages, which ignore modern roads and building lines, were the homes of seventeenth- and eighteenth-century miners. The present road system dates from the late eighteenth century, as does the formally designed market square at the north end of the Iron Bridge. The villas covering the hillside were mostly built in the nineteenth century, in a landscape grossly disfigured by earlier coal and iron ore workings. The Iron Bridge itself is once more, as it was in the late eighteenth century, a spectacle to be visited and observed, but it is only one feature of an industrial landscape of great complexity and subtlety.

The landscapes of the Industrial Revolution are in many respects as elusive as those of open field agriculture. We can still see bridges, engine houses and textile mills, as we can see castles, cathedrals and city walls, but they are only remnants of past landscapes. We can, and should, interpret them as part of the whole impact of man's activities upon the English landscape, together with prehistoric burial mounds and Georgian follies. They can also be seen as pieces of evidence which help us in imagination to recreate the landscapes of a particular period, one of the most critical in the whole of our past. By attempting such re-creations we can come nearer to an understanding of our ancestors' experiences of the Industrial Revolution.

References

1 Budget Meakin, *Model Factories and Villages: ideal conditions of labour and housing* (1905).
2 *One Man's Vision*: the story of the Joseph Rowntree Village Trust (1954).

Further Reading

General

Two books more than any others have shaped our understanding of the history of the English landscape during the last quarter of a century. W.G. Hoskins, *The Making of the English Landscape* (1957 and subsequent editions), and Maurice Beresford, *History on the Ground* (1957/1971) are essential first reading in any study of the subject, even if Hoskins is rather unsympathetic to the landscape of industry, and if, in this particular book, Beresford does not deal with strictly industrial subjects. In another sphere, that of art history, Francis D. Klingender, *Art and the Industrial Revolution* (1947 and subsequent editions) has been equally influential. Stuart Smith, *A View from the Iron Bridge* (1979) is a thorough survey of artists' impressions of the Ironbridge Gorge, which supplements Klingender in many respects. Alisdair Clayre, *Nature and Industrialization* (1977) is a useful selection of documents on the subject, largely from literary sources. E.J.T. Collins, *The Economy of Upland Britain: 1750–1950: an illustrated review* (1978) is a stimulating and penetrating study of the period from an unusual viewpoint.

There are numerous general surveys of industrial archaeology in Britain, of which by far the best is Neil Cossons, *The BP Book of Industrial Archaeology* (1975) which is a model of clarity, and which does not, like most of its rivals, painfully argue about the meaning of the subject, and offer patronizing advice to would-be practitioners. Brian Bracegirdle, *The Archaeology of the Industrial Revolution* (1973) is the best of the growing number of pictorial surveys.

Several series publications provide material for the student of the industrial landscape. There are important studies of many locations in the various volumes of the *Victoria County History*. Most volumes in 'The Making of the English Landscape' series, originally edited by W.G. Hoskins, include chapters on industry. Of particular merit are

259

those in Lionel Munby, *The Hertfordshire Landscape* (1977), Christopher Taylor, *The Cambridgeshire Landscape* (1973), Peter Bigmore, *The Bedfordshire and Huntingdonshire Landscape* (1979), Arthur Raistrick, *The West Riding of Yorkshire Landscape* (1970), Trevor Rowley, *The Shropshire Landscape* (1972), K.J. Allison, *The East Riding of Yorkshire Landscape* (1976) and D.M. Palliser, *The Staffordshire Landscape* (1976). The county and regional volumes in the David and Charles series 'The Industrial Archaeology of the British Isles' vary in quality, but Owen Ashmore, *The Industrial Archaeology of Lancashire* (1967), Morgan Rees, *The Industrial Archaeology of South Wales* (1975), and Robert Sherlock, *The Industrial Archaeology of Staffordshire* (1976) can be particularly commended. The quality of the new Batsford series 'Industrial Archaeology of the British Isles' is similarly uneven, but David Alderton and John Booker, *The Batsford Guide to the Industrial Archaeology of East Anglia* (1980) is a model of what this sort of survey should be. Walter Minchinton, *Industrial Archaeology in Devon* (n.d.) is a short but excellent survey, which is not part of a series. The Eyre Methuen series 'Regions of Britain' has much to interest the student of industrial landscape in Roy Milward and Adrian Robinson, *The West Midlands* (1971), *The Welsh Marches* (1971) and *Landscapes of North Wales* (1978), and J.T. White, *The Scottish Border and Northumberland* (1973) among other volumes.

Several of the standard regional economic histories are of value in the study of industrial landscapes, among them, A.H. John, *The Industrial Development of South Wales* (1950), A.H. Dodd, *The Industrial Revolution in North Wales* (1951), T.C. Barker and J.R. Harris, *A Merseyside Town in the Industrial Revolution: St Helens 1750–1900* (1959), J.M. Preston, *Industrial Medway* (1977), J.D. Marshall, *An Economic History of Furness, 1711–1900, and the Town of Barrow, 1757–1897, with an Epilogue* (1958), Barrie Trinder, *The Industrial Revolution in Shropshire* (1973), and Trevor Raybould, *The Economic Emergence of the Black Country* (1973).

Individual Topics

A.R. Griffin, *Coalmining* (1971) is the best guide to the remains of the coal industry, and Frank Atkinson, *The Great Northern Coalfield*

1700–1900 (1966/1968) is a lively and perceptive regional survey. I.J. Brown, *The Mines of Shropshire* (1976) and W.G. Thomas, *Welsh Coal Mines* (1977) are collections of pictures with unusually informative commentaries. D. Bradford Barton, *A History of Tin Mining in Cornwall* (1967) and *A History of Copper Mining in Cornwall and Devon* (1961) deal with the principal mines of the South-West. J.R. Harris, *The Copper King* (1964) is a study of Thomas Williams, which is essential to an understanding of Parys Mountain. The copper works, together with the textile mills and other industries of the Holywell area, are described in K. Davies and C.J. Williams, *The Greenfield Valley* (1977). W.J. Lewis, *Lead Mining in Wales* (1967) and Jean Lindsey, *The History of the North Wales Slate Industry* (1974) are the standard works on two of the principal industries of Wales. There are numerous books on the lead mines of the Pennines, among them Arthur Raistrick, *Lead Mining in the Mid Pennines* (1973) and *The Lead Industry of Wensleydale and Swaledale* (1975). F. Brook and M. Allbutt, *The Shropshire Lead Mines* (1973) is a short but perceptive account of mining and its impact on the landscape.

L.T.C. Rolt and J.S. Allen, *The Steam Engine of Thomas Newcomen* (1977) is now the standard account of the early history of steam power. George Watkins, *The Stationary Steam Engine* (1968) is an informative pictorial account of its many later varieties.

Jennifer Tann, *The Development of the Factory* (1970) must be the beginning of any study of textile mills and of factories in general. Stanley D. Chapman, *The Early Factory Masters* (1967) is the standard study of the transition from the domestic to the factory system in the Midlands textile industry, and the same author's *The Cotton Industry in the Industrial Revolution* (1972) is an excellent summary of the economic history of the industry and essential to an understanding of its landscape. Richard Hills, *Richard Arkwright and Cotton Spinning* (1973) is a useful introduction, and C. Charlton, D. Hool and P. Strange, *Arkwright and the Mills at Cromford* (1971) is a detailed study of the first water-powered cotton mill and its surroundings. The various trail guides produced by the Arkwright Society describe the landscapes of some of the other Derbyshire textile colonies.

Most modern work affecting the history of the landscape of the iron industry is contained in the various regional studies mentioned above, but E. Straker, *Wealden Iron* (1931/1967) is a remarkably thorough survey of the industry in the South-East which contains much of interest to the landscape historian. W.K.V. Gale, *Iron and Steel* (1969) is the best survey of the technology of the industry. Marie Rowlands, *Masters and Men in the West Midlands Metalware trades before the Industrial Revolution* (1975) and David Hey, *The Rural Metal-workers of the Sheffield Region* (1972) are scholarly works about ironworking communities which give good accounts of the landscapes of the regions they describe. The Ironbridge Gorge Museum issues several detailed guides to the landscape of the Gorge. Neil Cossons and Barrie Trinder, *The Iron Bridge* (1979) is a full account of one of Britain's principal industrial monuments, which also deals with sub-sequent generations of iron bridges.

For a study of the history of waterways the series 'Canals of the British Isles', edited, and to a large extent written by Charles Hadfield is indispensable. The landscape of the canals is beautifully portrayed in three books by the late L.T.C. Rolt, *Narrow Boat* (1944 and subsequent editions), *The Inland Waterways of England* (1950 and subsequent editions) and *Landscape with Canals: an Autobiography* (1977). J.D. Porteous, *Canal Ports: the Urban Achievement of the Canal Age* (1977) is a stimulating study of great merit. John Pudney, *London's Docks* (1975) deals thoroughly with a neglected subject.

Few modern books on road transport, whatever their merits in other respects, contain much to interest the historian of landscape, who will probably find that Sir Henry Parnell, *A Treatise on Roads* (1835) is still the best guide to what roads looked like during the Industrial Revolution.

On railways, the starting point must be Jack Simmons, *The Railway in England and Wales 1830–1914* (1978). Michael Robbins, *The Railway Age* (1962) is a slim volume containing some profound observations. J.G. Kellett, *The Impact of Railways on Victorian Cities* (1969) is a study of great importance. Jack Simmons, *St Pancras Station* (1968) deals in masterly fashion with its subject, and also discusses city termini in general. G. Biddle and J. Spence, *The British Railway Station* (1977) is less profound, but admirably broad in its vision. The series 'Regional History of the Railways of Great Britain' varies in quality. Vol. 1 on *The West Country* (1960/1973) by David St John Thomas is particularly good. By far the best study of a railway town is W.H. Chaloner, *The Social and Economic Development of Crewe* (1950). M.J.T. Lewis, *Early Wooden Railways* (1970) is an excellent account of railway prehistory.

For the study of towns the two standard general works are C.W.

Chalklin, *The Provincial Towns of Georgian England* (1974), and Asa Briggs, *Victorian Cities* (1963 and subsequent editions). H.J. Dyos, *Victorian Suburb: a study of the growth of Camberwell* (1973) is far and away the best book on the growth of suburbs. Maurice Spiers, *Victoria Park, Manchester* (1976) is a thorough but less ambitious study of a very different kind of suburb. H.J. Dyos, ed., *The Study of Urban History* (1968) and S.D. Chapman, ed., *The History of Working Class Housing* (1971), both contain essays of importance to the student of the industrial landscape. Enid Gauldie, *Cruel Habitations* (1974) is the best general study of working class housing. Colin and Rose Bell, *City Fathers* (1969) and Gillian Darley, *Villages of Vision* (1975/1978) both survey planned and model settlements, the breadth of coverage of the latter making it particularly useful. Vanessa Parker, *The English House in the Nineteenth Century* (1970) sets industrial housing in its wider architectural context. Two recently published detailed studies of working class housing are of especial merit. J.G. Timmins, *Handloom Weavers' Cottages in Central Lancashire* (1977) uses field evidence in a masterly fashion to examine a series of problems in economic and social history, while J.B. Lowe, *Welsh Industrial Workers' Housing 1775–1875* (1977) is a superb study of dwellings of many kinds.

Articles and monographs on particular topics are listed in the footnotes which follow each chapter.

Contemporary Accounts

One of the best ways in which to approach the history of the industrial landscape is through the writings of those who observed it in the past. The following is a selection of the more accessible works:

J. Aikin, *A Description of the country from 30 to 40 miles round Manchester* (1975).
Richard Ayton, *A Voyage round Great Britain undertaken in the summer of 1813* (1814).
R. Balgarnie, *Sir Titus Salt: his life and its lessons* (1877).
Samuel Bamford, *Early Days* (1844).
Lady Bell, *At the Works: a study of a manufacturing town* (1907).

263

W. Bingley, *Excursions in North Wales* (1839).

W. Bingley, *North Wales Delineated* (1804).

David Blair, *A Mother's Question Book* (1834).

Abbé le Blanc, *Letters on the English and French Nations* (1747).

Charles Booth, *Life and Labour of the People in London* (1889 *et seq.*).

William Booth, *In Darkest England and the Way Out* (1890).

George Borrow, *Wild Wales* (Everyman ed., 1958).

William Bray, *Tour through some of the Midland Counties into Derbyshire and Yorkshire* (1777/1783/1809).

Elihu Burritt, *A Walk from London to John O'Groats* (1864).

John Campbell, *A Political Survey of Britain* (1774).

Thomas Carlyle, *Chartism* (1839).

C.G. Carus, *The King of Saxony's Journey through England and Scotland in the year 1844* (1845).

Edwin Chadwick, *Report on the Sanitary Condition of the Labouring Population of Great Britain* (1842/1965).

Chamber's Edinburgh Journal (1832–6).

William Cobbett, *Rural Rides* (Everyman ed., 1957).

Daniel Defoe, *A Tour Through the Whole Island of Great Britain* (Everyman Univ. Library, 1975).

Charles Dibdin, *Observations on a Tour through almost the whole of England and a considerable part of Scotland* (1801–2).

Charles Dupin, *The Commercial Power of Great Britain* (1825).

Charles Dupin, *Voyages dans la Grande Bretagne depuis 1816* (Paris, 1824).

Joseph Farington, *The Farington Diary*, ed. James Greig (1922).

Leon Faucher, *Etudes sur l'Angleterre* (Paris, 1845).

William Felkins, *History of the Machine Wrought Hosiery and Lace Manufactures* (1867/1967).

Richard Fenton, *Tours in Wales 1804–13*, ed. John Fisher (1917).

M. Ferber, *An essay on the Oryctography of Derbyshire, a province of England* (n.d., *c.* 1778).

Celia Fiennes, *The Journeys of Celia Fiennes*, ed. Christopher Morris (1947).

Henry George, *Progress and Poverty* (Everyman ed., 1911).

Don Manuel Gonzales, *The Tour of Don Manuel Gonzales of Lisbon* (1730).

J. Hassel, *Tour of the Grand Junction Canal* (1819).

Charles Hatchett, *The Hatchett Diary*, ed. Arthur Raistrick (1967).

Baron D'Haussez, *Great Britain in 1833* (1833).

F.B. Head, *Stokers and Pokers* (1849/1968).

Sir George Head, *A Home Tour through the Manufacturing Districts of England in the summer of 1835*, ed. W.H. Chaloner (1968).

John Holt, *A General View of the Agriculture of Lancashire* (1795).

W. Hutchinson, *An Excursion to the Lakes with a Tour through Part of the North of England 1773–4* (ed. 1809).

Illustrated London News.

Per Kalm, *Per Kalm's Account of his visit to England on his way to America in 1748*, trans. Joseph Lucas (1892).

Peter Keating, ed., *Into Unknown England 1866–1913* (1976).

Count Friedrich von Kielmansegg, *Diary of a Journey to England in the year 1761–2* (1902).

J.G. Kohl, *Ireland, Scotland and England* (1844).

Karl Marx and Friedrich Engels, *On Britain* (Moscow, 1962).

William Mavor, *A Tour in Wales and through Several Counties of England performed in the summer of 1805* (1806).

Budget Meakin, *Model Factories and Villages: ideal conditions of labour and housing* (1905).

Memoirs of a Working Man (1845).

Carl Philipp Moritz, *The Travels of Carl Philipp Moritz in England in 1782*, ed. P.E. Matheson (1924).

William Morris, *Selected Writings and Designs*, ed. Asa Briggs (1962).

A.J. Munby, *Munby: Man of Two Worlds*, ed. Derek Hudson (1972).

Thomas Newte, *A Tour of England and Scotland in 1785 by an English Gentleman* (1788).

Thomas Pennant, *A Journey from London to Chester* (1780).

Thomas Pennant, *Tours in Wales 1778–1800*, ed. John Rhys (1883).

R.K. Philp, *The History of Progress in Great Britain* (1859).

Joseph Plymley, *A General View of the Agriculture of Shropshire* (1803).

Richard Pococke, *Travels through England of the Revd Dr Richard Pococke*, ed. J.J. Cartwright (1888–9).

Joseph Priestley, *Priestley's Navigable Rivers and Canals*, ed. Charles Hadfield (1969).

Friedrich von Raumer, *England in 1835* (1836/1971).

P.E. Razzell and R.W. Wainwright, *The Victorian Working Class: a selection from letters to the 'Morning Chronicle'* (1973).

David Rubinstein, *Victorian Homes* (1974).

'Lord' George Sanger, *Seventy Years a Showman* (1910).

Stebbing Shaw, *A Tour of the West of England in 1788* (1789).

Samuel Sidney, *Rides on Railways*, ed. Barrie Trinder (1973).

L. Simond, *Journal of a Tour and Residence in Great Britain during the years 1810 and 1811 by a French Traveller* (1815).

Henry Skrine, *Two successive tours through the whole of Wales and several of the English counties* (1798).

Alexander Somerville, *The Autobiography of a Working Man* (1848).

Robert Southey, *Letters from England by Don Manuel Alvares Espriella*, ed. Jack Simmons (1951).

E.I. Spence, *Summer Excursions through parts of Oxfordshire, Gloucestershire, etc.* (1809).

Harriet Beecher Stowe, *Sunny Memories of Foreign Lands* (1854).

Erik T. Svedenstierna, *Svedenstierna's Tour of Great Britain 1802–3*, ed. M.W. Flinn (1973).

Hippolyte Taine, *Notes on England*, ed. Edward Hyams (1957).

William Cooke Taylor, *Notes of a Tour in the Manufacturing Districts of Lancashire* (1842).

E. Temple Thurston, *The Flower of Gloster* (1911/1968).

Alexis de Tocqueville, *Journeys to England and Ireland*, ed. J.P. Mayer (1958).

The Torrington Diaries, ed. C.B. Andrews (1934–8).

Barrie Trinder, ed., *The Most Extraordinary District in the World: Ironbridge and Coalbrookdale* (1977).

Andrew Ure, *The Philosophy of Manufactures* (1835).

Charles Vallancey, *A Treatise on Inland Navigation* (1763).

Charles Vancouver, *A General View of the Agriculture of the County of Devon* (1808).

Revd Richard Warner, *A Second Walk through Wales in August and September 1798* (ed. 1813).

Revd Richard Warner, *A Tour through Cornwall in the autumn of 1808* (1809).

Revd Richard Warner, *A Tour through the Northern Counties of England* (1802).

Revd Richard Warner, *A Walk through some of the Western Counties of England* (1800).

Freidrich August Wenderborn, *A View of England towards the end of the eighteenth century* (ed. 1791).

John Wesley, *Journals of the Revd John Wesley*, ed. N. Curnock (1938).

Walter White, *A Londoner's Walk to Lands End* (1855).

William Wordsworth, *A Guide to the Lakes*, ed. Ernest de Selincourt (1977).

Arthur Young, *A General View of the Agriculture of Essex* (1807).

Arthur Young, *A General View of the Agriculture of Lincolnshire* (1794).

Arthur Young, *A General View of the Agriculture of Oxfordshire* (1813).

Arthur Young, *Tours in England and Wales* (ed. 1932).

Index